FAITH and PRACTICE

2009

First edition

Cover photograph by Kathi Sutton

Intermountain Yearly Meeting
of the Religious Society of Friends

www.imym.org

FAITH and PRACTICE

Intermountain Yearly Meeting
of the
Religious Society of Friends

Contents

Introduction

The need for a book describing Intermountain Yearly Meeting rose out of the same impulse toward order as was recognized during the early years of the Religious Society of Friends. What early Friends called a "book of discipline" evolved from minutes describing guidelines that Friends found enabled them to carry out actions consistent with their faith. It described the basic framework of monthly, quarterly (or regional), and yearly meetings set up by the founder, George Fox. Not long after its founding, the Society realized that, in order to assess the health and progress of Friends, certain information was needed. Focused questions, now called *queries*, were formulated to gather this information. In 1791, the first *advices* were adopted. Together, the advices and queries reminded Friends (and still do) of the basic faith and principles held to be essential to the life and witness of the Religious Society of Friends. This collection of materials, with periodic revisions, served as both record and guide, never as rule or creed, and was open to change as times and society changed. A Quaker book of discipline, also called a *faith and practice*, sets forth our current understanding of how we are organized, what we believe, and how our lives bear witness to what we believe.

Intermountain Yearly Meeting began in the 1960s as a fellowship of Friends. In 1974, it became a yearly meeting. Unlike other yearly meetings, ours did not evolve as an outgrowth of a pre-existing yearly meeting. Because it developed independently, it had no *Faith and Practice* to guide its constituent monthly meetings. Between 1976 and 1979, Friends created the *Guide to Clerks and Monthly Meetings*, which later became *The Guide to the Procedures of Intermountain Yearly Meeting*. In 1993, Intermountain Yearly Meeting created a committee charged with developing a *Faith and Practice*. In 1998, we adopted the 2nd edition of North Pacific Meeting's *Faith and Practice* (1993), pending development of our own.

This present version, in response to the changes that have occurred over time, attempts to describe Intermountain Yearly Meeting and the Society of Friends both as we were and as we are now. Advices and queries help us see if we are living our faith in Truth and ask us to be honest with ourselves. At the same time, our *Faith and Practice* reminds us of what joins us in the Spirit despite the great variety of ways Friends experience and express that Spirit moving in, through, and among us in the world. Such differences are valuable for the breadth and richness they bring to our Society.

A word about the words we use: early Friends used words that described their experience—*seed* and *light* come to mind. This allowed both an openness and a precision that could easily have been lost if they had prescribed or limited the words available to them. To strengthen the understanding of our own experience, we look to the experience and understanding of others. We listen as others describe their experiences in their words, and work to describe our own experiences as best we can using our own words. Language is precise when it opens doors and illuminates broad vistas. Please feel free to interpret the language of this work in ways that open up the world for you beyond the limits of your material senses.

This book explores the current practices and ways of living of Intermountain Yearly Meeting Friends. It reminds us of what Quakers believe and how they are to behave. It is not a book of prayer or liturgy. Our *Faith and Practice*

- reflects not our individuality but the spirit of our corporate body;
- shows us how to live and act as Friends in our meetings;
- guides and advises us as we seek our way through the confusions of our world;
- reminds us that we are Friends and that we continue to be led by the inward Spirit;
- directs our actions as Friends in our communities;
- shows our commonality despite the breadth and variety of our beliefs;
- helps each of us, new to or familiar with Friends, to learn more about who we are and how we do things;
- helps us maintain order in practicing our faith;
- reminds us of who we are and what it is that joins us in God's spirit;
- declares that we care about who we are and what we believe and consider it worth sharing.

I. Friends' Faith

A History
of the Religious Society of Friends

This chapter offers an overview of the origins and development of the Religious Society of Friends. There are a number of good, readable histories of the Society available for more extensive study, including John Punshon's *Portrait in Grey: A Short History of the Quakers*, Howard Brinton's *Friends for 300 Years* (now with an historical update and notes by Margaret Hope Bacon as *Friends for 350 Years*), and *The Quakers* by Hugh Barbour and J. William Frost. *A Western Quaker Reader*, edited by Anthony Manousos, is a good resource for first-hand information about the development of the three independent western yearly meetings, of which Intermountain Yearly Meeting is one.

Planting Seeds

The Religious Society of Friends was born in seventeenth-century England. Historians date the birth to 1652, when George Fox, a young man in his late 20s, brought a message of hope—the promise of the immediate presence of God—to a community waiting in silence. Francis Howgill, who was there, later wrote

> . . . *and God, out of his great love and great mercy, sent one unto us, a man of God, one of ten thousand, to instruct us in the way of God more perfectly; which testimony reached unto all our consciences and entered into the inmost part of our hearts, which drove us to a narrow search, and to a diligent inquisition concerning our state, through the Light of Christ Jesus. The Lord of Heaven and earth we found to be near at hand and, as we waited upon him in pure silence, our minds out of all things, his heavenly presence appeared in our assemblies, when there was not language,*

tongue nor speech from any creature. The Kingdom of Heaven did gather us and catch us all, as in a net, and his heavenly power at one time drew many hundreds to land.[1]

While England was engaged in civil wars in the 1640s — wars in which the rights of kings did battle with the rights of citizens and in which the armies were driven by religious fervor — Fox, the "one of ten thousand," was traveling around England for nine years. He left his family at the age of nineteen, searching . . . for something. Today we would say he wanted a guru, but in his years of wandering, he found many who had ideas about God, but no one who seemed to answer his searching questions. Remembering this time years later, he said that he had struggled with "a strong temptation to despair,"[2] but the Spirit was continually teaching him. He learned that education, institutions, books, pretty words, and experts were not sufficient. In fact, he learned that *he* was not sufficient. He described his turning point as follows:

As I had forsaken all the priests, so I left the separate preachers also, and those called the most experienced people. For I saw there was none among them all that could speak to my condition. And when all my hopes in them and in all men were gone, so that I had nothing outwardly to help me, nor could tell what to do, then, O then, I heard a voice which said, "There is one, even Christ Jesus, that can speak to thy condition," and when I heard it my heart did leap for joy. Then the Lord did let me see why there was none upon the earth that could speak to my condition, namely that I might give him all the glory. For all are concluded under sin, and shut up in unbelief, as I had been, that Jesus Christ might have the pre-eminence, who enlightens, and gives grace and faith and power. Thus when God doth work, who shall let [prevent] it? And this I knew experimentally.

My desires after the Lord grew stronger, and zeal in the pure knowledge of God and of Christ alone, without the help of any man, book, or writing. For though I read the Scriptures that spoke of Christ and of God, yet I knew him not but by revelation, as he who hath the key did open, and as the Father of life drew me to his Son by his spirit.[3]

Fox continued to roam the country, debating, convincing, offending, growing. In the churches of the time, a period was often provided after the sermon for comment from the congregation. Fox was not discreet. Blunt in his expression, he was often thrown out of the building and beaten by some members of the congregation even while his message reached others. He met many who became leaders in what became the Religious Society of Friends, among them Elizabeth Hooton, James Nayler, William Dewsbury, and Richard Farnsworth. He was called a Quaker for the first time, and he called the "tender" people he met "Friends."[4]

Still, it was not until 1652 and his meeting with the Seekers in the north of England that the society as we know it began to take shape. There were other groups rejecting the authority of the church, but some, such as the Ranters, were more anarchic. With the Seekers, Fox's message was heard and taken to heart by an entire community, which already practiced worship in silence, with the freedom to speak given to all whom the Spirit moved. It was there that a message of individual authority — "you have an inward teacher" — found a context and practice in which the Inward Teacher spoke to all and deepened all. Thus some seeds of Quakerism can be found in the English Reformation with its revolt against the strict authority of the established Church, but there is also a strain of mysticism in the inward experience of the divine.

From their base in the north of England, convinced Friends fanned out, first across England and then to the rest of the Western world, leading to explosive growth on the part of the Society and suspicion on the part of others. It is impossible to have a feel for this time in our history without having some understanding of early Quakers' inner fire and the consequences they bore. A great many Quakers were severely persecuted, imprisoned, and even killed because of their faith.

In addition to problems that arose from opposing the established churches, much suffering occurred as a result of Friends' refusal to take oaths even in court, in part because taking an oath suggested that truth would not be spoken or expected without the oath. When the crown gained the ability to confiscate property from anyone refusing to swear an oath of loyalty, Friends (including Margaret Fell and George Fox) were hauled into court, and then to jail, on various pretexts so that they could be put in the position of having to take the oath.

These are just some examples of the sufferings Quakers endured for carrying out their testimonies in their lives. Nevertheless, by 1690 there were some 60,000 Friends in Britain.

Margaret Fell, mistress of Swarthmore Hall and at first somewhat protected by her position as the wife of a judge, became a key supporter and center of communication for the Society. She maintained correspondence with many of the far-flung missionaries, managed the Kendal Fund which helped to support Friends' evangelical work, spent some years in prison, and wrote various epistles. Some years after the death of Judge Fell, Margaret married George Fox. The Valiant Sixty, itinerant preachers traveling in pairs, met occasionally with others to plan missions and spread the word. Over time, however, this personal network became insufficient for dealing with the issues — some religious and some political — that arose as the result of the exploding population of enthusiasts. This led to the development of a system of local and regional meetings for business and discipline (see the Organization of the Society chapter for more details).

In the growth of the first fifty years, one can see the seeds of our modern religious society planted — with all its diversity of thought, conflict over the source of authority, and strong social testimonies. Women were in evidence as strong leaders. Driven by a self-proclamation of honesty and a discipline of simplicity, Friends initiated use of plain speech and plain dress.

The denial of wars that became our peace testimony began when George Fox refused to accept a commission in the army as a way out of jail, and developed through the end of the century as the Society defended itself against charges of fomenting violent rebellion. Individual Friends discovered themselves unable to plan bombardments and felt compelled to quit their duties in the military.[5] (See the section on "War" later in this chapter.)

The first general advices were written at Balby in 1656, along with an admonition to pay attention to the Spirit behind the advices and not just the letter of them.[6] Controversies over leadings by the Spirit were resolved in favor of discernment within the community. Such discernment addressed the challenge of leaving all Friends open to the Spirit's possibility and at the same time checked rampant, egoistic individualism. An important publication from these early years is Robert Barclay's *Apology for the True Christian Divinity,* which offers a theological justification of early Quaker belief and practice.

What the world knows today as civil disobedience, Friends practiced by holding open meetings for worship in contradiction of the law, hence suffering the severe consequences. Such actions eventually led to the Act of Toleration in England and acceptance of the idea that people within a nation could differ over spiritual matters and remain good neighbors and loyal citizens.

Lying Fallow

With the death of George Fox in 1691, leadership passed to Steven Crisp and George Whitehead. Steven Crisp also died in 1691, however, leaving George Whitehead alone to lead the Society into a new century. The Act of Toleration gave Quakers freedom to worship, yet the Society[7] had to learn to live together without the charismatic leaders it had known, many of whom had died in prison.

> *Friends now clearly stood for a distinct emphasis within Christianity which asserted that all people were possessed of the light of Christ within, which was sufficient to save them if they obeyed it and drew upon its power; that God's saving grace is universal and not confined to nominal, or outward Christians; that human beings are under an obligation to seek perfection; and that God's revelation of himself is not limited to nature or the printed word, but continues directly down the centuries, informing both individuals and the Church.*[8]

Quakers traveled to the New World as early as the 1650s, some of them outspoken ministers. These felt so strongly their calling to preach and hold meetings in communities that they continued to do so in defiance of the Puritan laws that led even to the execution of four Quaker ministers

In what became the United States, Friends grew in political power. William Penn was central to the creation of a new commonwealth, now known as Pennsylvania, which attempted to conduct its affairs with Quaker principles. This became known as the Holy Experiment. Friends became wealthy through industry, frugality, and creativity, and then became uncomfortable with their wealth and the involvement with the world that it brought. Skirmishes with the Indians and the wars with the British in America led the Friends to withdraw for the sake of conscience.

In their spiritual lives, Friends increasingly embraced a kind of quietism. This meant waiting for a strong, sure leading before engaging in spiritual activity. In order to hold more strongly to inward, individual revelation of Truth, the Society turned away from corporate teaching and tradition. Paradoxically, the lack of a statement of formal *belief* led them to develop many statements of *behavior*. This became a period of self-containment in which Friends removed themselves from active involvement in the world around them even as they became successful merchants and manufacturers. Acceptable styles of dress became more and more restricted. Plain speech was mandated, with advices reminding Friends to use it at all times and not to speak one way at home and another way in the world. Marrying outside the meeting became a cause for disownment. Meetings became more and more silent as Friends worked to ensure that no vocal ministry was given but by direct inspiration of the Spirit.

It is common to look at the Quietist Period (roughly the eighteenth century) as a time when the Society became rigid and required greater and greater conformity to those outward behaviors that made Friends a "peculiar people," but there were benefits to intense introspection as well. It was his focus on self-abnegation in the face of God's will that inspired the efforts of John Woolman, "possibly the greatest Quaker of all and an adornment of the period of quietism,"[9] to clear his conscience, and then his efforts to clear the society of slavery in the face of intense economic pressure. Woolman's life and writings continue to be an inspiration for Quakers and others. In addition to grappling with the issue of slavery, an inward focus made it possible for the Society to maintain the principle of the spiritual equality of women, producing in America a generation of strong female abolitionist and feminist leaders and supporting the social activism of women like Elizabeth Gurney Fry in Britain.

Transform the Society, transform society: On Abolition and Women's Rights

Friends can be justifiably proud of their place in the history of antislavery.

> *The honor [of pioneering the antislavery movement] belongs to the Quakers, for the Quakers were gentle people, living by the precept of the golden rule, believing in the inherent dignity of man, the freedom of the human will, and the equality of all men . . .*

> *These Quakers abhorred all violence. They never spoke in harsh language. They opposed slavery from first to last on moral and religious grounds — as sin. They made tremendous financial sacrifices to rid themselves of the contamination. They never asked anything for themselves by way of profit — political, social, or economic — from their friendship for the oppressed. Nevertheless, they were violently denounced, charged with inciting rebellion, suppressed, and finally driven out of Barbados because they sought to Christianize and educate their slaves. They were denied the poor privilege of freeing their slaves in the Southern states, and in the early congresses of the United States were accused of treason and incendiarism because they petitioned for suppression of the African slave trade.[10]*

When Friends first testified to the equality of all people, they were testifying to equality in God's possibility. The Spirit was no respecter of social position. To doff the hat was to offer to a person what should only be offered to God. To call someone "master" out of politeness was simply to lie. It was not an attack on social distinctions, per se. Quaker households had servants, but the servants joined the families for meals, went to meeting, and when led were released to follow the Spirit's guidance. At first, slavery appeared to be one calling among many, a different kind of service. George Fox, writing in 1671 to calm the fears of slave owners in Barbados, could speak of mutual obligations between owner and property, obligations that went beyond care for the body to care for what made a person human — the soul. However, as the world moved to put the power of government and custom into the institution of slavery, Friends moved in a different direction.

9

In his essay "Some Considerations on Keeping Negroes," John Woolman argued that the golden rule itself militated against slavery, because no slaveholder would ever wish to be a slave and be treated as a slave was treated. Friends began to see that slavery was not a calling, but an evil, and the Society moved to clear itself. It must be noted that the movement was slowed by self-interest and that the final minutes against slavery were written only after a generational change in the leadership of the Society. From the time of George Fox's letter to the governor of Barbados, it took American yearly meetings approximately 100 years to decide that involvement in any way with slaveholding was an occasion for disownment. This happened at about the same time as the United States declared its independence from Britain. New England's minute is dated 1773, Philadelphia's 1774, and Baltimore's 1777.[11]

Quakers actively supported free and freed African Americans in many ways, setting up schools for children and adults, providing relief for escapees, and working with the Underground Railroad. After Woolman and Anthony Benezet, a Quaker school teacher whose pamphlets were copied rather exactly by John Wesley when he wrote *Thoughts upon Slavery*,[12] male leadership in the antislavery movement quickly moved beyond the Society, especially following the Great Revival in 1825. Friends continued to be the largest single source of women in antislavery leadership, including Lucretia Mott, Abby Kelley, Angelina and Sarah Grimké (by convincement), and Susan B. Anthony.[13] Of these five, only Lucretia Mott remained an active Friend for her whole life, and it wasn't easy for her. Susan B. Anthony chafed at the Society's limited involvement with radical abolition and the women's movement and attended the Unitarian church after 1848, although she remained a lifelong member of her meeting in Rochester, NY.

Men, Friends or not, found it easy to focus on freedom for slaves alone. For the women in the movement, it quickly became obvious that their own position was remarkably similar to that of the slaves they were trying to free. The 1848 Seneca Falls Convention, with its Declaration of Women's Rights, was planned over tea at the home of Jane Hunt. Hunt was joined by Lucretia Coffin Mott and her sister Martha Coffin Wright; Mary Ann McLintock; and Elizabeth Cady Stanton, Lucretia's long-time friend, fellow antislavery activist, and the only non-Friend present. Part of the impetus for the meeting and the ensuing convention was a promise Mott and Cady Stanton had made to each other when the World's Antislavery Conference in London in 1840 refused to seat women delegates accredited by American antislavery societies. The revolutionary tea followed the 1848 Genesee Yearly Meeting, at which the Michigan Quarter had been terminated for "demanding more freedom to engage in the antislavery cause, less authority for the ministers and elders, and equal rights for women."[14]

There is a great deal of complexity to Friends' involvement in societal transformation. Looking back, we see giants of human endeavor speaking for equality and justice, leading the Society and society in general to new ethical understandings. At the same time, we see others in the Society who believed that involvement in a sinful world was probably wrong and at least wasted effort. Friends' business process is essentially conservative, because change must be validated through unity; once achieved, however, that unity has immense power. The value Friends place on individual conscience allowed them to stand against the world on ethical issues. It also accustomed them to difference, to the point where they were comfortable with *not* making an effort to influence freed slaves to be Quakers.

Finding Fault Lines / Judging the Inner Light[15]

There is a common switch in religious movements that base their appeal on an inward change that is expected to be manifested in outward behavior: the move from preaching the inward to judging the outward. The unifying and transforming experience of the Spirit is lost. For Christians, the problem is older than the letter of James: "But someone will say, 'You have faith and I have works.' Show me your faith apart from your works, and I by my works will show you my faith."[16] According to Matthew's Gospel, Jesus said, "A sound tree cannot bear evil fruit, nor can a bad tree bear good fruit."[17]

Even as Friends were clearing themselves of slavery, many among them were becoming dissatisfied with uninspiring meetings and the worldly entanglements of the wealthy and powerful in the Society. In the early nineteenth century, Elias Hicks—Long Island farmer, recorded minister, and indefatigable reformer—became a flashpoint. One of the principal sources of irritation was his attack on the wealth that many leaders in the society derived through trade in slave goods. (It was as difficult to escape slave goods then as it is today to be clear of military technology.) Today, unprogrammed Friends look at Hicks as the defender of the Inner Light against the inroads of Biblical creedalism. Hicks and other reformers believed the world was enticing the Society away from the Inner Light. They struggled for a stricter observation of the outward standards they thought had been eaten away by Revolutionary War fervor and the American ideology of freedom. Their struggle for transformation of the Society became a challenge to the power of the elders.

The institution of the elder has deep roots in the Society. Although the model of Friends' discernment gives final authority over leadings to the community, in practice the voice of authority was given to weighty Friends. This especially applied to vocal ministry. The gift of inspiration in meeting for worship was closely watched.

> *And our advice to all our ministers is, that they be frequent in reading the scriptures of the old and new testaments; and if any in the course of their ministry, shall misapply, or draw unsound inferences or wrong conclusions from the text, or shall misbehave themselves in point of conduct or conversation, let them be admonished in love and tenderness by the elders or overseers where they live, and if they prove refractory and refuse to acknowledge their faults, let them be further dealt with, in the wisdom of truth, as the case may require. — 1723[18]*

The people most likely to be irked by Hicks's preaching against worldly entanglement were the powerful, who were also the ones most likely to sit as elders. And it was the elders whose job it was to mind the orthodoxy and behavior of the preachers. In keeping with the times, and in reaction to a non-Christian deism common in society at large, this orthodoxy looked to Protestant theology extracted from an absolutely authoritative Bible. The orthodox seemed to be moving away from the Friends' tradition that said the Bible was the *words* of God, but only the Spirit of Christ was the *Word* of God.

The division, when it came, was driven by theology, politics, power, and personality. Hicks's movement was attractive to the rural majority in Philadelphia Yearly Meeting, which found itself passed over and ignored by the citified merchants who had the time and opportunity to meet and lead the Society. In 1827, the issues were decided in favor of declaring one's opponents not real Quakers. From Philadelphia, the division spread to New York in 1828, and then to the yearly meetings that had developed in Ohio, Indiana, and Baltimore. New England, Virginia, North Carolina, and London did not divide but aligned themselves with the orthodox yearly meetings. Within the Orthodox branch there were further separations as the years went by; these are beyond the scope of this chapter. In order to prevent further schism within itself, Philadelphia Yearly Meeting (Orthodox) simply stopped corresponding with other meetings. It took almost 130 years before the different branches began to recognize one another again as Quakers.

In the United States, Friends colonized different areas which quickly developed yearly meetings. As the population moved west, new yearly meetings formed: Ohio Yearly Meeting spun off from Baltimore Yearly Meeting, for example, and Indiana Yearly Meeting subsequently spun off from Ohio. The Midwestern meetings tended toward the orthodox and then evangelical vein, some eventually developing a pastoral ministry.[19]

In the 1880s, Iowa was one of these pastoral yearly meetings. Moving from there, Hannah and Joel Bean set up a meeting in San Jose, California, and established it along unprogrammed lines. Iowa Yearly Meeting eventually disowned the Beans and officially laid the meeting down. The Beans and their meeting ignored this proceeding, however, and became an "independent" meeting—one founded and overseen by no prior yearly meeting. As originally conceived, it was to be a place where Friends from anywhere could worship in the unprogrammed manner and where they would retain membership in their old meetings.[20] Their College Park Association became the nucleus of Pacific Yearly Meeting, which eventually divided into the Pacific and North Pacific Yearly Meetings.

As was the case with the Beans and the meeting they started in San Jose, other monthly meetings that were established in the West were composed of Friends from various Quaker branches. The independent yearly meetings still reflect this diversity.

The divisions between unprogrammed meetings and those following a pastoral tradition still exist, and many of the meetings around the world, for example in Africa and Central America, have adopted the pastoral pattern for their churches.

War After War After War

The Quaker movement was born in the midst of civil war. Quakers quickly moved to disavow any inclination to go to war for any cause. In their declaration to Charles II in 1660, they stated:

> *That spirit of Christ by which we are guided is not so changeable, so as once to command us from a thing as evil, and again to move unto it; and we do certainly know, and so testify to the world, that the spirit of Christ which leads us into all Truth will never move us to fight and war against any man with outward weapons, neither for the kingdom of Christ, nor for the kingdoms of this world.*[21]

Their assertion that they would not use outward weapons against anyone for any cause was to make Quakers, in the eyes of kings and presidents, something less than loyal and less understandable (even less dependable) than any traitor.

For American Quakers, wars and conflicts have presented special challenges to our testimony against war and for peace. Quakers dominated the legislature in Pennsylvania during the French and Indian Wars. The non-Quaker residents of western Pennsylvania suffered under the attacks by Indians and the crown demanded that the legislature enact a specific tax to support the war. Friends had already determined that it was acceptable to pay taxes that fed a general fund, even if some of that fund was used for military purposes. This specific tax would not be acceptable, however, and Friends would refuse to pay it. They believed that they could not in good conscience authorize the tax when they knew that they would not pay it themselves; they also knew that the legislature would lose its charter if they did not approve it. It was one thing for an individual Quaker to say that he would not fight but quite another for Quaker legislators to apply their principles to the acts of government and not defend their western citizens. Friends resigned from the government and never exercised real political power again.

The Revolutionary War represented a different trial. The peace testimony made Friends a suspect population for both revolutionaries and royalists. Philadelphia Yearly Meeting disowned more than 1,200 members for their participation in the war, and the ideology of liberty led many to depart the Society on their own. At the same time, the colonies/states confiscated property to cover unpaid war taxes.[22]

John Punshon describes succinctly a subtle problem faced with the Civil War: "The Civil War (1861–1865) was a grave challenge to the Quaker conscience, willing the end but being denied approval of the means."[23] Much is made of the dangerous and marvelous Underground Railroad; yet when comparing the number of slaves freed to the total slave population, it was no more than a flea-bite on the body of slavery. The result of the dilemma Quakers faced is interesting. Friends became skilled in refugee work. The Society did not go to war, but rather it began to work healing the effects of war.

By the time of World War II, Friends seem to have come to some kind of accommodation regarding the claims of conscience in relation to particular wars. Disownment was no longer a common response to enlistment. In *A Quaker Book of Wisdom*, Robert Smith points with some pride to his own decision to fight in that war.[24] However, beginning with Friends' work with displaced former slaves, and moving through the founding of the various service committees during and following World War I [American Friends Service Committee (1917); in Britain, the Council of International Service (1918), which joined with another group in 1928 to become the Friends' Service Council; and the Canadian Friends Service Committee (1931)], Friends were able in an organizational way to work to heal the world rather than harm it.[25]

Although there is a place in law for conscientious objection—a place where one can in theory remain a good citizen without having to actively support one's country's military ambitions—the double edge of "will not fight for x against y" still puts Friends' opinions at odds with many in government. Resistance to war takes many forms, including refusal to pay war taxes. And in 2004 the American Friends Service Committee was classified as a "criminal extremist organization" by the police department in Denver, Colorado, and people associated with it have been followed and interviewed by the FBI.[26]

By the twenty-first century, our society has seen other developments that relate to a concern for equality, among which are: the civil rights movement, the women's movement, sanctuary, gender issues, migrant and border concerns, and torture. These movements have not necessarily been Quaker in form, but many Friends have been involved in the issues.

Emphasis Shift: A Summary

The principle of science, the definition, almost, is the following: The test of all knowledge is experiment. Experiment is the sole judge of scientific "truth."[27]

Until the Reformation, a European believer found his or her faith reinforced at every turn: the Church blessed the culture along with the crops, animals, children, and couples. The Church was woven into every aspect of life, including death. After the Reformation, everything changed, and yet nothing did. Culture and the institution of the Church were no longer bound together. In order to criticize the institution, the authority of tradition as embodied in the Church was discarded and replaced with an original source—the Bible as reconstituted by Martin Luther. Yet reality still had an ultimate, single, creative source, a One Person who stood over against His creation, loving it, judging it, and calling it to a perfection that He best understood in His wisdom.

Early Friends knew the Bible backwards and forwards, but reading the Bible wasn't good enough. They, too, turned to an original source: the Spirit of the Author Himself. From there, their experience of the Spirit led them within the Bible to what was important. As we have already seen, this set up a later conflict between the clarity of a visible and culturally accepted interpretation of the written source and the invisible and individual interpretation of the inward source.

Shortly before the turn of the nineteenth century, Rufus Jones, an influential philosopher and scholar of mysticism, met John Wilhelm Rowntree of England. Out of this meeting came the "Rowntree Histories," ultimately penned by Jones and William Charles Braithwaite. Their purpose was to identify Friends, especially Friends of the first generation, as a part of the long tradition of Christian mystics. The project was a great success and sparked a liberal Quaker renaissance.[28] It also moved the foundation of Quakerism from the Spirit to human experience of the Spirit. The early Friends believed they were the rebirth of the apostolic church of the first Christian century, from which Christianity had strayed, even been apostate, for 1,200 years. Although they recognized that the Spirit had been present and could be seen in individuals in history, their experience had a different quality. Rowntree, Jones, and Braithwaite placed Friends in the mystical line, just as other historians have placed Friends among the Puritans or as a "third way" between Catholicism and Protestantism.

The base has widened even further. For early Friends, their experience was *normative*—that is, it was the proper, true way to relate to God. Even if God, in His mercy, had supported others in the past despite their erroneous ideas and practices, and even though the Spirit made itself available to all people in all times and places, there was a "best practice," and it was theirs. The next generation saw itself as *peculiar*—that is, specially called by God, a light in the wilderness. When the Rowntree historians placed Quakers in the mystical tradition, they claimed membership in an ongoing spiritual movement, but in so doing reduced our claim to originality. In the last fifty years, some branches of Friends have opened themselves even further. What was once normative has become part of a broad human possibility rather than the only path to union with the divine.

Intermountain Yearly Meeting is growing from this foundation: *The test of all spiritual knowledge is experience.* It is not the easiest basis upon which to build a community. We have more than three centuries of tradition and experience behind us as Friends, but we also have several thousand years of other human experience that we can draw on. We are open to the possibility that the Spirit leads us to inspiration, using all of human history. The tension between individual perception and community acceptance continues as it did in the first Quaker century. Finding common language is difficult because the words some find comforting can be experienced by others as bludgeons. Yet, if we rely on personal experience as a shared possibility instead of as an escape from mutual responsibility, we can move beyond words to their source and join the stream.

Conclusion

According to Jesus of Nazareth,[29] the primary principles of a properly ordered life are to love God with one's entire being and to love one's neighbor as if the neighbor and the lover were one and the same. The history of Friends is the history of a people who have held these principles to be so intertwined that one is neither more nor less than the flip side of the other. Historically, Friends began by loving God, but they never found a time when that did not lead them into concern for their neighbor—first to share the good news of God's intimate presence and then to express that caring in service to others. When their neighbors did not choose to join them, Friends cared for them anyway. Today, Friends' care for others is the more visible of these two principles, but inquirers who come into our meetings soon learn that loving our neighbors doesn't happen without the inward support and guidance of the Spirit.

The means of loving God and caring for our neighbors has not always been clear. Sometimes the love of God has seemed to require being clear of entanglements, whereas at other times love of neighbor has seemed to require every sacrifice—for some, even going to war. Friends have been active in prison reform, against slavery, for the rights of women, against war, for religious tolerance, and against social distinctions. Friends have rocked the boat, and have disowned people for being too loud. Still, and always aware of the contradictions in our past, we can say with our seventeenth century forebears that this road of ours may be difficult and demanding, but it is worth the effort of walking it.

---

[1] Francis Howgill, quoted in *Quaker Faith and Practice*, The Yearly Meeting of the Religious Society of Friends (Quakers) in Britain, 19.08.

[2] George Fox, *The Journal of George Fox*, rev. and ed. John L. Nickalls (Philadelphia: Philadelphia Yearly Meeting, 1995), p. 4.

[3] Fox, *Journal*, p. 11.

[4] To Fox, "tender" people were open to the Spirit and its possibilities. "Friends" is a reference to Jesus' statements in John 15:14: "Ye are my friends, if ye do whatsoever I command you . . ." and John 15:15: "I have called you friends, for all things that I have heard of my Father I have made known unto you." The language is from the King James Version, which Fox knew so well that even his enemies said that if the Bible were lost, he could reproduce it.

[5] Hugh Barbour, *The Quakers in Puritan England* (New Haven and London, Yale University Press, 1964), p. 121.

[6] Quoted in full in Appendix 1.

[7] The Society of Friends: " … the first recorded use of the phrase in the modern sense seems only to date from 1793." John Punshon, *Portrait in Grey: A Short History of the Quakers* (London: Quaker Home Service, 1984), p. 71.

[8] Punshon, *Portrait in Grey,* p. 103.

[9] Punshon, *Portrait in Grey,* p. 119. Punshon's succinct summary of Woolman (pp. 118—119):

> "[John Woolman] is still admired—and imitated—by Friends the world over for the way he testified to the power of his beliefs by the quality of his personal life. He could not write a bill of sale for a slave. When soldiers were billeted on him, he refused payment. Believing that the light of Christ was in all, he sought and found it among the Indians, to whom he made a special journey in the ministry. Devoted to the art of persuasion rather than debate, he sought to move Friends to free their slaves by enlisting their consent, again making special journeys in the ministry for the purpose.
>
> He avoided the temptations of wealth by avoiding wealth when it could have been his, seeking holy sufficiency rather than holy poverty. He felt what we would call the environmental damage of the dyeing industry, so he wore undyed clothes as a personal testimony."

[10] Dwight Lowell Dumond, *Anti-slavery: The Crusade for Freedom in America* (Ann Arbor: The University of Michigan Press, 1961), pp. 16–17.

[11] *The Old Discipline: Nineteenth Century Friends' Disciplines in America* (Glenside, PA: Quaker Heritage Press, 1999). In addition to those of New England, Philadelphia, and Baltimore, disciplines from the New York, North Carolina, and Virginia Yearly Meetings are included in this publication, but their final determinations on slavery are undated. All were first printed between 1800 and 1820, and all make involvement with slavery a disownable offense. North Carolina is a special case. Because manumission was illegal there, when the yearly meeting made ownership an offense all slaves were given to the yearly meeting, which then let them live in freedom.

[12] Dwight Lowell Dumond, *Anti-slavery: The Crusade for Freedom in America.*

[13] This and the following paragraph lean on *Mothers of Feminism: The Story of Quaker Women in America* by Margaret Hope Bacon (San Fran-

cisco: Harper and Row, 1986). Abby Kelley Foster's name is spelled differently in different sources—sometimes Kelley and sometimes Kelly.

[14] Bacon, *Mothers of Feminism*, p. 114.

[15] This section relies on the work of H. Larry Ingle in *Quakers in Conflict: The Hicksite Reformation* (Wallingford, PA: Pendle Hill Publications, 1998).

[16] RSV, James 2:18.

[17] RSV, Matthew 7:17.

[18] *The Old Discipline*, p. 74, from Philadelphia Yearly Meeting.

[19] This can be squared with Friends' ancient testimony against the hireling ministry by recognizing that a Quaker pastor is a released Friend—someone whose leading in the world is recognized and supported by the monthly meeting.

[20] Chuck Fager, http://www.quaker.org/liberal-history/bean.html.

[21] Britain Yearly Meeting, *Quaker Faith & Practice: The Book of Christian Discipline of the Yearly Meeting of the Religious Society of Friends (Quakers) in Britain,*1994, section 24.04.

[22] Ingle, *Quakers in Conflict: The Hicksite Reformation*, p. 4.

[23] Punshon, *Portrait in Grey*, p. 181.

[24] Robert Smith, *A Quaker Book of Wisdom*, pp. 64 ff.

[25] A short history of the AFSC and its work can be found at http://www.afsc.org/about/history.html.

[26] Jim Spencer, "Authorities Terrorize Dissenters,*" Denver Post*, May 20, 2005). Online at: http://denverpost.com/ci_2746311 (now in archives).

[27] Richard P. Feynman, Robert B. Leighton, and Matthew L. Sands, *The Feynman Lectures on Physics*: Commemorative Issue, vol. 1 (Redwood City, CA: Addison-Wesley, 1963, 1989), p. 1-1.

[28] Punshon, *Portrait in Grey,* p. 221.

[29] Matthew 22:34–40, with slightly different versions in Mark. 12:28–31 and Luke 10:25–28. Jesus was not alone in this summation. Perhaps a generation before Jesus, when challenged to teach a gentile the Torah while standing on one foot, Rabbi Hillel the Great summarized it this way: "That which is hateful to you, do not do to your neighbor. That is the whole Torah; the rest is commentary. Go and study it." Jesus's contemporary, Rabbi Akiba, said of Leviticus 19:18—"… you shall love your neighbor as yourself …"—"This is the greatest principle in the Torah."

History of Intermountain Yearly Meeting

As a young yearly meeting, we sense the adventure of the journey, sometimes unsure of our destination, but always committed to the searching steps.

Norma Adams Price, in Epistle from IMYM, June 1978

In 1974, at Ghost Ranch, New Mexico, a gathering known as Intermountain Friends' Fellowship declared itself to be Intermountain Yearly Meeting of the Religious Society of Friends. The individuals present were members and attenders of monthly meetings in Texas, New Mexico, Arizona, Utah, and Colorado. Before creating Intermountain Yearly Meeting, some of the monthly meetings had been members of Pacific Yearly Meeting, an independent yearly meeting; others had been associated with the Missouri Valley Yearly Meeting, a conservative yearly meeting; and still others were from unaffiliated monthly meetings and worship groups. Many of the monthly meetings were founded by people who moved to the area and were unable to find existing unprogrammed meetings to attend. Although some were birthright Friends, others had come to Quakerism through conscientious objection, work camps, and even independent study. Yet in creating this new thing—the yearly meeting connected only loosely with meetings that had come before—these Friends claimed the history and experience of all Quakers as part of their own spiritual story.

Although meetings in Arizona, New Mexico, and Utah had been part of Pacific Yearly Meeting and some meetings in Colorado participated in the annual gatherings of Missouri Valley Friends, the great distances prevented all but a few Friends from attending gatherings, serving on committees, or knowing and being known by the larger groups. Because western Friends recognized these drawbacks, local retreats were held in 1951, 1952, and 1953, attended by Friends from Arizona and New Mexico. Although the 1955 annual gathering of Pacific Yearly Meeting was held in Prescott, Arizona, further efforts to create a regional group faltered. In 1969, as newcomers spoke with older Friends who desired closer contact with other Quakers, the value of a retreat was reaffirmed. Sixty Friends met at the home of Clarissa and Samuel Cooper in Camp Verde, Arizona, for fellowship and worship. Discussions led to a gathering the following year at Ghost Ranch near Abiquiu, New Mexico. Friends from Utah and Colorado were also invited to attend, and over 150 Friends came together, choosing to name themselves the Intermountain Friends' Fellowship. Responsibility for the gathering, held each year at Ghost Ranch, began to be rotated among regional meetings in the area. Five years later, as members of the Fellowship recognized among themselves a desire to become a yearly meeting, the following minute was adopted:

> *Following several years of prayerful search, it is the present sense of the meeting that the Intermountain Friends' Fellowship now constitutes itself a yearly meeting to be know as the Intermountain Yearly Meeting of the Religious Society of Friends, emphasis to be on fellowship, community, and spiritual renewal. The organizational structure is to be minimal. The monthly meeting is the primary place for business and caring for members and attenders. (June 8, 1974)*

Monthly meetings and worship groups that became members of the new organization included Flagstaff, Pima, Tempe, Phoenix, (Arizona); Paradise Valley (Las Vegas, Nevada); Albuquerque, Santa Fe, El Paso, Gallup, Taos, Los Alamos, Las Cruces, (New Mexico); Lubbock, High Plains (Amarillo), (Texas); Mountain View, Boulder, Durango, Fort Collins (Colorado); and Logan (Utah).

Despite a continuing desire to minimize the formal structure of IMYM, between 1976 and 1979 Friends felt it necessary to create a *Guide to Clerks and Monthly Meetings,* which later became *The Guide to Operations of Intermountain Yearly Meeting* and in 2008 became *The Guide to Procedures.* As the yearly meeting matured, some called for development of a statement of faith and practice that would reflect the unique aspects of our understanding of Truth and serve as a descriptive guide to the practices of our members and meetings. This led to the adoption in 1998 of the *Faith and Practice of North Pacific Yearly Meeting, 1993.* The *Faith and Practice* that you are reading began as an adaptation of that volume but evolved into its own voice, one more representative of this yearly meeting.

Since its formation in 1974, Intermountain Yearly Meeting has doubled in size. Friends have been active in a number of social issues, including opposition to the deployment of the MX Missile system; antinuclear activities at the Nevada Test Site and Rocky Flats Nuclear Arsenal; aid for those fleeing oppression, concern for violence and unjust conditions in Central America, including working within the sanctuary movement; treatment of native peoples; action against the death penalty; and respectful consideration for all people regardless of sexual orientation. Members of the yearly meeting have actively opposed military action in response to worldwide terrorist threats and the wars in Iraq and Afghanistan. During the sanctuary movement, in which many IMYM Friends were involved, a Committee on Sufferings was set up to support those Friends arrested, fined, or imprisoned for acts of conscience. Because of our location near the border with Mexico, Friends in the yearly meeting have had particular concerns for the plight of refugees, originally those from El Salvador and more recently those from Mexico. An informal Committee on Migrant and Border Concerns struggles against the inequities existing for Latin Americans across our border and within the United States.

In the late 1980s, several Intermountain Yearly Meeting Friends at the annual sessions expressed deep concern about the changes in focus of the American Friends Service Committee, especially the laying down of work camps and other opportunities for Friends to participate in service projects. There was a feeling that the AFSC was losing touch with the Quaker spirit. Staff members, fewer and fewer of whom were Quakers, seemed to be unfamiliar with Friends' principles. This concern led to a dialogue that culminated in the development of the AFSC/IMYM Joint Service Project (JSP), a program that provided an increasing number of intergenerational one- to two-week service projects in Mexico, on Indian reservations, and throughout the intermountain region. The JSP became a model used in various forms by other yearly meetings, both on the West Coast and in the East. In 2009, funding for the JSP was withdrawn by AFSC. The program is being reorganized as Western Quaker Workcamps.

Intermountain Yearly Meeting, an independent yearly meeting, currently consists of 17 monthly meetings, one associated monthly meeting in Mexico City, and Wyoming Monthly Meeting newly associated in fellowship. There are more than 1,000 members spread over approximately half a million square miles. Regional meetings have been organized in Arizona, New Mexico, Colorado, and Utah. Numerous worship groups exist throughout the area. The yearly meeting has been independent of any umbrella organization such as Friends General Conference, Friends United Meeting, or Evangelical Friends International; however, at the present time, affiliation with Friends General Conference is in process. Intermountain Yearly Meeting is a member of the Friends World Committee for Consultation and is actively affiliated with the Friends Committee on National Legislation and the American Friends Service Committee. *Western Friend,* a monthly publication of Pacific, North Pacific, and IMYM Yearly Meetings, serves as a voice for the yearly meeting and its constituent monthly meetings.

Friends' Faith

What is the Quaker faith? It is not a tidy package of words which you capture at any given time and then repeat weekly at a worship service. It is an experience of discovery, which starts the discoverer on a journey, which is lifelong. The discovery in itself is not uniquely a property of Quakerism....What is unique to the Religious Society of Friends is its insistence that the discovery must be made by each of us individually. No one is allowed to get it secondhand by accepting a ready-made creed. Furthermore, the discovery points a path and demands a journey, and gives you the power to make the journey.

Elise Boulding, 1954
(Revised in a letter to Robin Powelson, 2000)

Friends have faith that the direct and unmediated experience of the Divine is available to everyone. That which Quakers call the inward Light lives in each human being. Faith is inseparable from practice. Friends are encouraged to assume personal responsibility for making their lives an active and living witness to their faith—every thought, word, and deed testifying to the transforming power of the divinity within themselves and others. Friends feel called to obey the Light and Power that leads and guides them. Each person is asked to practice the personal discipline that leads to growth of the spirit. The presence of the Spirit is often described as "that of God in everyone."

During the three and a half centuries of our history, Friends have used many names for the source of our faith—among them God, the Inner or Inward Light, the Divine Principle, the Seed, the Christ Within, the Inward Teacher, Jesus, Holy Spirit. The names we use today are appropriate to our experience. Some of us may use different names at different times, for our experiences may vary throughout our lives.

Our traditional testimonies — integrity, equality, peace, simplicity, community — are outward and visible signs of our faith. The testimonies point the way as we put our faith into action. Communal and individual concerns and actions are weighed in the light of these testimonies. The critical question remains "Is this of God?" not, "Is this right?" From the early days of the Religious Society of Friends, individuals sought truth in the seasoned discernment of the Meeting. In our experience, this process reveals the full creative possibilities of the Spirit.

Meeting for worship embodies the source and expression of many of our cherished practices. We come into meeting from our separate journeys. Our personal acts of devotion and service prepare us for our worship together. As we join together, we seek that sacred realm where our spirits unite with the Divine and with one another. We meet in expectant waiting as we become centered on the Divine Presence. "As, together, we enter the depths of a living silence . . . we find one another in 'the things that are eternal'...."[1] We listen for the Divine by endeavoring to become still within, thus opening our minds and hearts. When we succeed, that which we call "the Divine Voice" is made known to us in both silent and vocal ministry. As we wait in stillness, a message may arise out of the depth of one's soul that seems intended not simply for oneself but for the gathered meeting. It is our practice that before speaking one tests this "opening" of the Spirit, but does not fear it. When someone accepts the call to speak, fellow worshipers are called to listen with openness to the message expressed. At its best, vocal ministry is drawn from the Divine Presence, the message coming not *from* us but *through* us. We find in meeting an experience of the Divine — one eternal reality present for and directly accessible to everyone.

Friends live in the faith that the Divine Spirit exists, whether perceived or not. The Spirit has been active throughout time. Although the roots of the Religious Society of Friends lie in Christian England, today the Spirit speaks to Friends through a wide range of sources, including the religions, spiritual practices, texts, and teachers of many cultures.

For Quakers, living life is a sacrament. Knowledge of the Spirit is enhanced by the practice of spiritual disciplines — worship, study, contemplation, prayer, action. For early Friends, the *Bible* was a rich and sustaining record of inspired revelation. The Spirit they knew in their hearts spoke to them through it. They also made a profoundly important distinction: the power that inspired the *Bible* is still speaking. For this reason, Friends avoid using writings as a final or infallible authority.

The vitality of our community lies in our ability to see that the life and power of the Spirit reveals itself in diverse ways. George Fox and the early Quakers offered a radical response to lifeless religion. Friends found that the presence of the Spirit need not be mediated by rote ceremony. The absence in our worship of traditional rites grows out of our faith in the primacy of the inward experience of the Spirit. In every generation, Friends have found new paths and revitalized the ways we live our faith.

Inspiration comes from the Spirit, which reveals itself to us in many ways.

---

[1] *Quaker Faith & Practice: The book of Christian discipline of the Yearly Meting of the Religious Society of Friends (Quakers) in Britain,* London: the Yearly Meeting of the Religious Society of Friends (Quakers) in Britain, 1995: 2.01

Worship

Introduction

This chapter considers several customary forms of worship used by Friends. To focus on form is to focus on the outward, but in fact these practices were developed to make the largest space possible for the inward. They work against our habits of mind and our pleasure in external stimulation. They work to surrender initiative to the Spirit. Sitting with several people in a designated place for an hour or so will not produce a meeting for worship, but in Friends' experience, gathering together, waiting quietly, and listening for that "still small voice" is an essential part of our life together in the Light. Any form can be empty of Presence, and the Presence can fill any form it wishes. Friends in Intermountain Yearly Meeting worship without a program or ceremony to open the individual and the community to the immediate and creative possibility of the experience of God.

Friends' practices and processes rest on social and mystical[1] understandings of human nature: the individual always stands simultaneously in relation to the Spirit and to others, and it is through the Spirit that we are most intimately related to our fellow human beings. Remembered and looked for, the Spirit can gather us and lift us into creative unity.

Friends have applied the term *worship* to several practices in which Friends, singly or together, try to stand in the Presence. This chapter considers the meeting for worship, worship by individuals, worship in the home, the meeting for worship with a concern for business, and worship sharing. For many Friends, service is a form of worship as well, especially when a concern has been laid upon them. Although service is an intrinsic part of Friends' practice, nevertheless this chapter looks at those forms of worship in which we step aside from our daily lives and focus ourselves inward.

In 1676, Robert Barclay wrote, "True and acceptable worship of God stems from the inward and unmediated moving and drawing of his own Spirit. It is not limited by places, times, or persons."[2] Later, he adds,

> *We have certain times and places in which we diligently meet to-gether to wait upon God. . . . We consider it necessary for the peo-ple of God to meet together as long as they are clothed in this tab-ernacle. We concur with our persons, as well as our spirits, in be-lieving that the maintenance of a joint and visible fellowship, the bearing of an outward testimony for God, and the sight of the faces of one another are necessary. When these are accompanied by in-ward love and unity of spirit, they tend greatly to encourage and refresh the faithful.*[3]

Friends try to find a way to live in constant awareness of the "mov-ing and drawing" of the Spirit. Each form of worship considered in this chapter represents a possibility for a meeting of spirit, body, context, and purpose. Each practice has its own way of opening par-ticipants to a sense of the "inward and unmediated" Presence. Each practice helps us discern the movement of the spirit.

Among Quakers, *discernment* goes beyond insight or good judg-ment. It denotes a process used by Friends when wishing to know what Spirit is leading them to do. It is distinguished by a seeking, an inner listening to hear what the voice of God is saying. This is not an intellectual exercise in discrimination. In discernment, we are re-minded to "wait upon the Lord" and to listen for the sacred voice within. Learning discernment takes time and much practice. Instead of holding back when we feel the Spirit nudge us, we need to go for-ward, trusting that Spirit will be with us. With practice, our skill be-comes greater. It is possible that Friends with greater experience will help guide us as we learn.

Meeting for Worship: Listening and Waiting

> *Silence is the bowl in which ministry is served.*
>
> Leslie Stephens, 2005

Friends find the center of their life together in the meeting for worship.

Although Friends worship any time the Spirit moves them to, they set aside specific times and places to gather for worship as a community. Meeting for worship is a public act. "Bearing an out-ward testimony for God" has not always been legal, but Friends have never held meeting for worship in secret. All present may participate fully, as the breath of God blows where God wills. Even when Friends disowned people[4], the disowned were not excluded from worship.

Meeting for worship begins the moment someone — anyone — begins to "center down." Gradually the silence enfolds all present in communion with the Spirit and each other. In the silence, we journey into that inward stillness where even our thoughts are gone, and we wait. When successful in ridding ourselves of distracting thoughts, we become open to hearing the stirrings of a message. We need, then, to discern whether it is our ego wanting to share news or to lecture; or whether it is the divine within seeking to be known without, and whether the message is for us alone or to be shared with others. This process of discernment is solitary. Some Friends, responding to the movement of the Spirit, may be led to speak out of the silence. The meeting ends when someone, usually pre-selected, determines that the meeting has ended and greets his or her neighbors by shaking hands. In our busy times, this generally happens about one hour after the start of the meeting for worship, although those who are sensitive to the movement of the Spirit do more than simply check the clock when bringing the meeting to its official end.

In Silence ...

The earliest Friends waited because they believed that the only worship that counted was worship that God actively inspired — the inward and unmediated moving and drawing of God's own Spirit of which Barclay speaks. Although Friends today understand that there is merit in different forms of worship, our unprogrammed[5] practice teaches us to be open and vulnerable in the face of the Spirit.

> *In worship we have our neighbors to right and left, before and behind, yet the Eternal Presence is over all and beneath all. Worship does not consist in achieving a mental state of concentrated isolation from one's fellows. But in the depth of common worship it is as if we found our separate lives were all one life, within whom we live and move and have our being.*
>
> Thomas R. Kelly, 1938 [6]

31

Friends have never regarded [worship] as an individual activity. People who regard Friends Meetings as opportunities for medita-tion have failed to appreciate this corporate aspect. The waiting and listening are activities in which everybody is engaged and produce spoken ministry which helps to articulate the common guidance which the Holy Spirit is believed to give the group as a whole. So the waiting and listening is corporate also. This is why Friends emphasize the 'ministry of silence' and the importance of coming to meeting regularly and with heart and mind prepared.

John Punshon, 1987 [7]

Out of the Silence . . .

In the stillness of the meeting, the Spirit brings us messages. Sometimes these messages are for us alone; sometimes they are meant to be spoken. A spoken message may be meant for the com-munity. It may be intended to reach the heart of a single person. It may be the seed for further ministry, or it may stand alone.

People who give vocal ministry seldom know the precise pur-pose of their message—they only know they must speak. Conversa-tion among Friends about vocal ministry often turns quickly to the signs one follows in making a decision about speaking and to the inadequacy of any signs to confer certainty. In the first years, Quak-ers "trembled before the Lord," and many still tremble today. Some feel a specific kind of anxiety, a jab in the ribs. Others know it is time to speak when the message arrives with perfect calmness. For some, there is an analytical cast to their final decision, whereas others say, "If I have to ask, the message isn't for sharing." Waiting is often in-volved; if the meeting ends before the right moment comes, perhaps the message was not meant to be given. The message may come again and again with greater insistence each time. Some Friends have bottled up the urge to speak only to have someone else in the meeting give the same message.

As the message is spoken, the experience continues. One's voice may change. The body may feel different. Friends have stood up to speak having no idea what they were meant to say. Others have be-gun with a carefully worked out plan and ended with words coming from somewhere else. Sometimes the command also comes to stop. Ministers often speak of the sense of peace that descends on them when they feel their ministry has been given according to the Spirit. They also speak of the discomfort that comes when they have outrun their guide.[8] Sometimes ministers hear from others that they were touched by the words they spoke; it is well to remember then that the ministry was the Spirit's—not theirs.[9]

Vocal ministry requires practice. Recognizing the signs is a matter of discernment. According to Patricia Loring, "Discernment is the faculty we use to distinguish the true movement of the Spirit to speak in meeting for worship from the wholly human urge to share, to instruct, or to straighten people out."[10] Be ready to be flexible! Writing of his own growth as a minister, Lloyd Lee Wilson[11] recalled a time when he moved from being a rock in meeting ("Here I am, Lord, but you are going to have to blow me away before I speak today") to trusting God and his own relationship with the Spirit enough to become something like a fruit tree ("My Master has planted me in good soil, pruned me, and sent the sun and rain in order than I might bear fruit—here it is").

After someone speaks, the meeting returns to silence, waiting for further movement of the Spirit. Without the active support of prayerful silence, speech in meeting is disconnected from the Spirit and not rooted in the community.

Inappropriate ministry is another topic that comes up in conversation among Friends about vocal ministry. Each Friend seems to have his or her own example, so we remind ourselves that the Spirit does not always tell us what we want to hear, speak to us in pleasing tones, use correct grammar, or speak through people we like. As John Punshon says,

> . . . *we have to train ourselves to overcome our personal likes and dislikes and treat everything said in meeting with uniform seriousness and consideration. That is part of Friends' spiritual discipline and cannot be compromised with. It is not at all easy, but it is unavoidable. We need time and calmness to reflect on what we have heard. Only when we have taken it into ourselves shall we be in a position to decide whether or not it is from God.*[12]

Children in meeting for worship bring special joys and distractions. Within Intermountain Yearly Meeting, there are various ways of fostering their participation. The most common approach splits the children's time between attendance in meeting for worship and a children's program of religious education: some meetings start with the children present in meeting whereas others bring the children in towards the end of meeting. However it is arranged, participation in meeting for worship is just as important for children as it is for adults.

Meeting for worship can be a time for healing. It *must* be a place of safety, a place where one can grow and take chances and where everyone's life is nurtured, for the Spirit is not always a comfortable companion. The Light brings risks and challenges as well as balm for the soul. Although it is the special charge of the Committee on Ministry (variously named Ministry and Oversight, Ministry and Counsel, Worship and Ministry, and so on) to foster, support, and provide guidance for those who speak in meeting for worship, the care and responsibility for the health of the meeting belongs to the whole community. One cannot learn to walk if laughter and scorn follow any misplaced step.

Worship by Individuals: Seeking Depth and Knowledge

The history of Friends is not a history of people who waited for First Day to arrive before waiting on God. Stories of the sudden experience of the Divine fill the literature of mysticism and of Quaker lives. Stories of life-long seeking can be found there, as well.

A spiritual practice is a vital part of our lives.[13] When the only experience we have of silence comes in meeting for worship, our individual needs can so dominate our awareness that we are prevented from being part of the community as we worship. As we deepen our connection to the Spirit through individual practice of spiritual disciplines, our participation in the meeting for worship also deepens. The experience of Friends suggests that the form of the discipline is less important than the fact of it: there is no single path to follow. The movement of the Spirit has not been limited to a flow into Europe out of the Middle East; nor are our exercises limited to those found in that religious history. As in everything else, the Light guides us to a useful practice.

Worship in the Home: Nurturing Spiritual Discipline

From its inception, individuals in the Religious Society of Friends have waited for the Spirit in community and maintained that the highest experience is that of the Spirit uniting the whole community. Worship in each home, whether individually or with spiritual companions, affirms this sense, finding its wholeness in and through the Spirit. In these busy times, when even First Day mornings can seem overscheduled, worship at home provides an opportunity for quiet intimacy under the care of the Spirit.

In the past, Friends' families worshiped together in the home on a regular basis, and this practice is continued in many households today. This tends to be the most programmed of the various forms of worship covered in this chapter, in part because it provides training for children through adult example. Religious passages may be read and hymns may be sung, providing seeds for centered worship. However the worship begins, it ends with a time of silence and ministry, providing a safe place for children to experience the movement of the Spirit and to share their voices.

Meeting for Worship with a Concern for Business

Friends, keep your meetings in the power of God, and in his wisdom (by which all things were made) and in the love of God, that by that ye may order all to his glory. And when Friends have finished their business, sit down and continue awhile quietly and wait upon the Lord to feel him. And go not beyond the Power, but keep in the Power by which God Almighty may be felt among you.

George Fox, 1658 [14]

Discussions of Friends' processes often get twisted up in "nots," and the meeting for business is no exception: we do not vote, we do not debate, we do not follow parliamentary procedures, and so on. How much harder is it to speak positively! The meeting for business is a meeting for *discernment*. At the meeting for business, the community gathers under the guidance of the Spirit, attempting to make decisions in unity.[15]

All of the curiosities of Friends' practice stem from this: the community is led by the Spirit, and the Spirit works through the whole community. Imagine a knotty issue as a complicated work of three-dimensional art. What is obvious at first glance to one person is not at all evident to someone else. So gradually we walk around it, different ones of us bringing aspects of the work to the attention of the community, and as we do, we come to a fuller understanding. We undertake the walk together, we consider each aspect together, and as our understanding grows, so does our ability to work together for a solution. The Light shines from all directions. Our knowledgeable Guide whispers in our ear, pointing out new vantages. We become closer, more of a community, more able to put our guidance into action together.

The community gathers . . .

In Intermountain Yearly Meeting, while members and attenders are equally welcome to participate in business meetings, the weight of major decisions traditionally rests upon those who are members. Business is conducted by and entrusted to those who are present at the business meeting. Although it would not be wise to schedule discussion of an issue when a person known to be especially interested in the problem is out of town, objecting to a discussion based on what one thinks someone who is not present might say is problematic.

under the guidance of the Spirit . . .

Listening for the Light in each person's words and waiting for guidance makes the business meeting an act of worship. Only when Friends are aware that they are functioning in the Divine Presence does the Quaker method achieve its goals. Thus, it is important that each business meeting begin in the stillness of worship so that its character will pervade the transaction of business. As a reminder, many Friends prefer to call this meeting the "meeting for worship with a concern for business."

An agenda does not preclude guidance: what is openness in worship can be lack of focus in business. The agenda is prepared by the clerk beforehand in consultation with the various meeting committees where they exist, but issues and concerns may be raised in other ways. A committee may bring a report, with or without a recommendation for action. If there is a recommendation, it eases way if in the form of a proposed minute. Individuals may bring concerns as well. Although it is helpful to approach the clerk ahead of time and ask for an item to be included on the agenda, an issue may be brought directly to the meeting. It is always useful to be able to explain to the meeting the kind of action that is being requested and the background for it, including options that were considered and discarded. After a concern is presented, the meeting holds the concern in the Light.

> *Some people don't believe it's the truth until they hear it coming out of their own mouths.*
>
> Pat Sheldon, overheard after an especially long business meeting, circa 1995

Speaking in the meeting for business is ministry just as much as it is in meeting for worship. Among Friends, speaking begins with listening. Before speaking, we ask ourselves if the point has already been addressed. Does our point carry the meeting forward? Are we aware of any undercurrents? (One may joke about God's lack of concern for the color of the meetinghouse door, but if color is a source of dissension, then God surely is interested.) Have we been listening? When one is heard the first time one speaks, one does not feel the need to go over the same ground.

As a matter of etiquette, speakers wait to be recognized and address their remarks to the clerk or presenter. Sometimes the pauses between speakers become so short that a reminder from the clerk or a request from the floor for silence may be necessary. When silence is broken again, Friends take care as they proceed that the concerns voiced before the silence have been heard. Periods of silence throughout the meeting help assure a sense of the presence of the Spirit and aid the clerk in gathering the sense of the meeting.

making decisions in unity.

Unity is possible because the Light of Truth shines in some measure in every human heart. Friends come to a meeting for business expecting that the Spirit will lead the assembled body to unity. The commitment to search for unity depends upon mutual trust, implies a willingness to labor and to submit to the leadings of the Spirit, and grows as members become better acquainted with one another.

> *When Friends make a decision . . . they are seeking the will of God*
> *in a particular matter. They have found the most reliable guide to*
> *that will to be the sense of the meeting.*
>
> Patricia Loring, 1993[16]

The most important duty of the clerk is to judge the sense of the meeting. This may be in the form of a minute, or it may be to wait and consider the concern at another time. The clerk must remain neutral, listening to all, aware of those who are hesitant, sometimes checking the long-winded, and ready to remind Friends to speak out of the silence.

The most important duty of Friends attending meeting for business is to seek Divine guidance while exercising self-discipline and self-control. Friends are urged to be mutually forbearing and concerned for the good of the meeting as a whole, rather than to press a personal preference. Time is allowed for deliberate and prayerful consideration of the matter at hand. Everyone must want to reach a decision and be open to new understanding. When the Light finds its voice, it can be helpful to the clerk that Friends say quietly, "That Friend speaks my mind." (On the other hand, when spoken early in a discussion, the sentence may bear the character of voting.)

> *The sense of the meeting . . . can only arise out of a membership*
> *which has given itself over to seeking the will of God and has pre-*
> *pared itself spiritually for the search. It may be that some present*
> *have not yet come to that condition of seeking. It may be that some*
> *have come seeking that their own will be done – sometimes for ex-*
> *cellent reasons. It may be that they come with a leading from God*
> *which is quite true for themselves but not a leading for the meeting*
> *as a whole.*
>
> Patricia Loring, 1993[17]

The sense of the meeting is not always unanimous. It is possible for an individual to recognize that the meeting is ready to go forward with a decision even though he or she is not. At this point, Friends have a number of ways of proceeding. First, if one feels deeply that the decision is not in the Light, one has the responsibility to speak one's truth frankly and with sensitivity. The meeting may decide not to go forward in order to understand this truth more fully and to season the issue further; or it may suspend decision to prevent taking action too rapidly. On very rare occasions, meetings have proceeded even when a friend "stands in the way." In all circumstances, it is a decision *of the meeting* whether or not to proceed. Second, one may accept the meeting's conclusion in the place of one's own — often the meeting leads us beyond ourselves. In some cases, one may "stand aside" from a decision, allowing the meeting to go forward while reserving judgment. Meetings should be slow to accept this action on the part of an individual, preferring to achieve unity rather than to go forward without the whole community. This is especially true if several people choose to stand aside — then perhaps the sense of the meeting has been misread.

> *It is not the individual who has the power* [of standing in the way], *it is the Holy Spirit. It is the spiritual truth which comes through an individual which the Meeting may recognize. The important observation is that it is the truth that is recognized and not the individual. It is the truth which may keep the Meeting from going forward. Not the individual standing in the way.*
> Arthur Larrabee, Pendle Hill Workshop on Clerking, 2001

There is power in unity. Decisions made through a process leading to unity carry the conviction and commitment of the whole community. We risk losing this power if we aim simply for efficiency. When we avoid conflict, when we get along by going along, we lose the ability to work whole-heartedly together. When a meeting tries to force an issue and permits itself to get away with it, the meeting runs beyond its Guide. Friends do not make decisions according to the will of the majority, nor are Friends' decisions blocked by the will of the minority. A common practice among Friends is to seek a "third way," a way led by Spirit away from polarization. The Religious Society of Friends is led by the Spirit.

Worship Sharing:
Building Community in a Fragmented World

In today's world, where people are mobile and divided by distance and circumstance, the unconscious familiarity with one another that underlies communities that have shared lives for generations is for the most part long gone. Worship sharing takes us intentionally beyond appearances and prejudices and often leads to profound connections between participants. When we join in with open minds and hearts, worship sharing can be as gathered as any meeting for worship.

Worship sharing is a small-group exercise. Eight members is a good number. With fewer than six present, individuals may feel too exposed; with more than ten, the process can become cumbersome. The composition of worship sharing groups differs depending on their purpose. There is usually a facilitator, and often there are queries to consider. When worship sharing takes place in a larger gathering, the context and purpose of the gathering may be sufficient to provide a focus. Worship sharing is confidential—what is said within the group stays within the group and may not be repeated elsewhere without the specific permission of the original speaker. In many cases, due to the nature of the sharing, permission should be obtained from the whole group.

The facilitator reviews with the participants the characteristics of the worship sharing format and may read one or more queries. After settling into silence, participants speak.

Participants may speak as they are moved, or sometimes, depending on who is present, the participants may be asked to speak in turn. This is a good approach when the group has not met before and is unfamiliar with worship sharing, or when there is a wide mix of ages. It is helpful to the facilitator and the group if a person who wishes not to speak to a particular query "passes."

Sharing is based on personal experience, coming from the heart. Each contribution is heard and is framed in silence. Having addressed a query, one does not speak to it again until everyone has had a turn, and rarely then. This process is intended to free participants from any need to consider a response or plan a contribution while someone else speaks. When one speaks, one resists the temptation to ask follow-up questions of a previous speaker, contradict or debate a point, give advice, or practice one's diagnostic and therapeutic skills. Any of these might be illuminating, but they allow the speaker to hide from personal sharing.

Although participants are mindful not to take more than their share of time while speaking, when the worship-sharing session is on a schedule it is important that the planners allot sufficient time to it. The facilitator brings the group to a close when the appointed time has passed. Closing the session may include handshakes, hugs, and further silence.

Other Issues...

Clearness committees help us discern the Truth of a leading. Friends called to an undertaking or ministry may seek a clearness committee to help discern whether or not the calling is from God. Those who serve on a clearness committee help us find answers from within while refraining from giving advice or guidance. Obstacles or impediments to moving forward can be examined while seeking the inner guidance. When our way is clear, we may proceed with the calling or may realize that it is, indeed, the wrong step at this time.

When the meeting as a whole is included in the outcome, such as in marriage or membership, the clearness is dual. In order to go forward, both those seeking clearness and the meeting must become clear. All involved must discern the rightness of the action.

Clearness committees may be requested by anyone for many other reasons. Unless a leading may affect the meeting as a body, these *do not* require a report to the meeting for business and require clearness of only the seeker.

Confidentiality is standard practice for all clearness committees.

Eldering calls up the classic Quaker aphorism "Thee canst not elder one whom thee dost not love." It is a Spirit-led, loving action which awakens and encourages the inner wisdom in each of us. This could take the form of a gentle admonishment—discouraging and/or questioning another's inappropriate behavior or speaking. It could also encourage the timid to share their gifts with the meeting. Seeking the counsel of more experienced Friends may help when eldering another is considered. Determining the best way to approach someone requires that discernment be used in order for the Light to be seen as loving and caring. True eldering does not shame or scold another.

Threshing sessions are important meetings where all aspects of an issue can be shared and explored; where the 'wheat and chaff' can be separated without rancor. No decisions are made at a threshing session. Various formats may be used in these meetings for discussion and airing of opinions and feelings. It is not uncommon for there to be several threshing sessions when difficult or contentious issues arise. Threshing sessions can lay the *foundation* for seasoning an issue as a meeting seeks unity.

The Stillness at the Heart of Things

As we look at Friends' worship practices, we often hear characterizations akin to: "It is not a debate." We are not trying to impose our will or our ideas on the community. We work together because the Spirit works in and through all of us. In all forms of worship, we open ourselves and still ourselves so that the noise of our busyness does not overwhelm that other voice we so long to hear. The Spirit unites us. We live best when we live within that Spirit.

---

[1] One definition of mysticism: " . . . the belief in or reliance on the possibility of spiritual apprehension of knowledge inaccessible to the intellect." *The New Shorter Oxford English Dictionary* (Oxford: Clarendon Press, 1993).

[2] Robert Barclay, *Barclay's Apology in Modern English*, Dean Freiday, ed. (Newberg, Oregon: The Barclay Press, 1991), p. 239.

[3] Barclay, *Apology*, p. 243.

[4] When Friends were viewed as a suspect cult, they began to "disown" the unFriendly behavior of people who might be seen as Quakers by the outside community. Later, disownment became a tool of social control. It is rarely used today.

[5] Friends today are divided in their forms of worship. Some, including meetings in Intermountain Yearly Meeting, practice the silent meeting. Other meetings have pastors and follow a program when they worship—thus the distinction between "programmed" or pastoral meetings and "unprogrammed" ones.

[6] Thomas R. Kelly, *The Eternal Promise*, (Richmond, IN: Friends United Press, 1988), pp. 44-45, as quoted in Britain Yearly Meeting *Faith and Practice*, 2.36.

[7] John Punshon, Unpublished writing, 1987. Quoted in Britain Yearly Meeting *Faith and Practice*, 2.37.

[8] John Woolman, See p.160 of this book, in section on "Friends Speak: Meeting for Worship," 4:04. From *Journal* 1740, quoted in Pendle Hill Pamphlet #51, *Worship*, 1950.

[9] As one story tells it, a Friend approached another after a meeting for worship and said, "Thee preached a pretty sermon today," to which the other replied, "I know. The devil told me so as soon as I sat down."

[10] Patricia Loring, *Spiritual Discernment: The Context and Goal of Clearness Committees* (Wallingford, PA: Pendle Hill Pamphlet #305, 1992), p. 3.

[11] Lloyd Lee Wilson, *Essays on the Quaker Vision of Gospel Order,* (Philadelphia, PA: Quaker Press of FGC, 2002), p. 178.

[12] Punshon, *Encounter with Silence* (Richmond, IN: Friends United Press, 1987, p. 78.

[13] Sources on individual practices include *Listening Spirituality, vol. 1* by Patricia Loring and John Punshon's *Encounter with Silence.*

[14] George Fox, *Epistle 162*, 1658, as quoted by Howard Brinton in Pendle Hill Pamphlet #65, *Reaching Decisions: The Quaker Method* (Wallingford, PA, 1952), p. 12. The complete epistles can be found in *The Works of George Fox*, Vols. VII & VIII (State College, PA: New Foundation Publication, The George Fox Fund, Inc., 1990).

[15] The principles and procedures that apply to meeting for business apply to committee meetings and any other gatherings of Friends to seek a way forward.

[16] Patricia Loring, *Spiritual Responsibility in the Meeting for Business,* (Philadelphia: Quaker Press of FGC, 1993).

[17] Loring, *Spiritual Responsibility in the Meeting for Business.*

II. Friends' Practice

A Quaker social concern seems characteristically to arise in a sensitive individual or very small group—often decades before it grips the society of Friends as a whole and as much as a century or more before it appeals to the secular world. . . .

The concern arises as a revelation to an individual that there is a painful discrepancy between existing social conditions and what God wills for society and that this discrepancy is not being adequately dealt with. The next step is the determination of the individual to do something about it—not because he is particularly well fitted to tackle the problem, but simply because no one else seems to be doing it.

Dorothy H. Hutchinson

The Spiritual Basis of Quaker Social Concerns, FGC, 1961
as quoted in *New England Yearly Meeting Faith and Practice*, 1985

Living Our Faith

How does Truth prosper?[1]
Let your life speak.

Friends testify through their lives. Subscribing to no creed, recognizing as authority only the direct experience of the Divine as we have found it within, Friends show forth our truth outwardly by the way we live. Our actions, not any profession of commitment to "notions," are the mark of our understanding of the Divine. We hold ourselves accountable for what we say and what we do, our words and our deeds; no circumstance of our daily lives qualifies this essential allegiance to the truth we feel driven to seek, the truth we find in experience. We give the name *testimony* to this witness of who we are.

The testimonies that have been passed down to us embody much of what guides our practice. Quakers hold testimonies regard-

45

ing simplicity, integrity, equality, peace, and community. Truth is the ground of all of them. Yet, because our experience changes as times change, our testimonies, like our understanding of truth itself, are not fixed but fluid. As a result of what we understand as continuing revelation, the testimonies have evolved in response to changing contexts, new needs, and new perceptions of our world. As was the case among Quakers historically, these changes initially are expressed as minutes in our monthly and yearly meetings; with time they become integrated into our practice. Such contemporary changes, for example, reflect our concern for our natural environment and our awareness of the human suffering and economic injustice experienced by migrant workers and immigrants who cross the borders of our country.

> *[Our] testimonies are the fruits of [our] spiritual foundation, not the foundation itself. . . . We are Quakers because we have encountered something within that convinces us we can be and should be at peace, live simply, be loving toward all or live any other witness that may rise from this experience.*
>
> Robert Griswold, 2004
> *Creeds and Quakers: What's Belief Got to Do With It?*[2]

Integrity

> *Let what you say be simply "yes" or "no"; anything more than this comes from evil.*
>
> Matthew 5:37

> *Integrity is a condition in which a person's response to a total situation can be trusted: the opposite of a condition in which he would be moved by opportunist or self-seeking impulses breaking up his unity as a whole being. This condition of trust is different from the recognition that he will always be kind or always tell the truth. The integrity of some Dutch Friends I have met showed itself during the war in their willingness to tell lies to save their Jewish friends from the Gestapo or from starvation.*
>
> Kenneth Barnes, 1972
> *Quaker Faith and Practice of Britain Yearly Meeting,* 20:44

Friends consider integrity a way of life. In the stillness of worship we come into the Divine Presence and open ourselves to the Light; we hide nothing of who we are. In keeping with that openness of spirit, Friends express themselves with honesty in their dealings with others. Plain truth needs no decorative flourishes. We speak with simple clarity to reflect in our words the reality of our perceptions and thoughts.

Our experience tells us that things honestly said are no more or less true than words spoken under oath. Friends hold one standard of truth; therefore we eschew oaths. Friends have suffered imprisonment and loss for taking this position, but time and the law have recognized the justice of this view. In our country today we are free without prejudice to declare and affirm, in courts of law and in other situations where an oath is usually required, the plain and simple truth of what we say. Friends do not want to deceive or exploit anyone. Therefore, we arrive at what we consider a fair value for buying and selling time, food, labor, material goods, and services. We do not try to gather any profit in excess of need or worth.

Friends attempt to behave with honesty in all our relationships. In speaking truth to others, we speak the truth in love.

Peace

When we are in accord with God and centered in ourselves, the earth, and all others, we move toward peace. True peace is obtainable only through unity in the life of the Spirit. Lasting peace requires determination, watchfulness, and ongoing work on every level—as individuals and in our families, society, nation, and world.

From the earliest days of the Religious Society of Friends, its followers have testified publicly against war. In the Declaration to Charles the Second of England in 1660, Friends declared: "All bloody principles and practices, we, as to our own particulars, do utterly deny, with all outward wars and strife and fightings with outward weapons, for any end or under any pretense whatsoever. And this is our testimony to the world."[3]

In all human life there exists a Light that can lay open the spirit to what is Divine, the source of our being. Because this Light is a sacred reality, and because it exists in everyone, we have embraced an abiding witness against killing, even for the sake of peace. Our peace testimony arises out of an awareness that even though it may some-times seem hidden away, the spirit of God is alive in all of us. The source of peace is peace within.

Our testimony, which is more than simply a position of pacifism, has led us into active nonviolence, direct political actions not always acceptable to the government. We offer advice and assistance to those who for reasons of conscience refuse to register for a military draft, resist cooperation with the military, or refuse to go to war. Nevertheless, when one of us joins the armed forces, though we may disagree with the choice, we hold our Friend in love. In keeping with our belief in the sacredness of that which is divine in the human be-ing, most of us also oppose capital punishment.

Like the early Quakers, we take issue also with "the occasions" that lead to war. No one in this country can hope to avoid com-pletely any entanglement in the causes of war. Still, we seek to be conscious of how our investments might be involved in practices that we do not condone or how some products are made under con-ditions adverse to life. Many choose vocations or avocations that aim to alleviate the fear and suffering that lead to violence — either through structural change or by promoting social and economic jus-tice, both at home and abroad. Recognizing that a percentage of our federal taxes goes toward the military, some of us practice war tax resistance. We try to be aware of how our daily choices might con-tribute to such "occasions." Further, we offer spiritual and usually financial support to those who refuse to pay for war or refuse to go to war. Such actions are the fruits of our experience of the sacred re-ality of the Light within that guides us to the truth. We struggle to understand how our belief in the sanctity of life influences our view of such life-and-death issues as abortion, the artificial prolongation of life, and euthanasia.

Because we do not think of peace as merely the absence of war, we try in peacetime to remain aware of the great disparities in well-being and livelihood all over the world, these being a primary cause of violence among nations. We find it important to address and alle-viate manifest injustice wherever it occurs. We believe that peace without justice is not true peace.

Simplicity

The increase of business became my burden, for though my natural inclination was toward merchandise, yet I believed Truth required me to live more free from outward cumbers and there was now a strife in my mind between the two; and in this exercise my prayers were put up to the Lord, who graciously heard me and gave me a heart resigned to his holy will. Then I lessened my outward business, and as I had opportunity told my customers of my intentions that they might consider what shop to turn to, and so in a while wholly laid down merchandise, following my trade as a tailor, myself only, having no apprentice.

John Woolman, *Journal*[4]

John Woolman never let the demands of his business grow beyond his real needs. . . . His outward life became simplified on the basis of an inner integration. . . . He yielded to the Center and his life became simple.

Thomas R. Kelly, *A Testament of Devotion*[5]

Simplicity is making sure there is always enough in reserve to answer the call.

Elizabeth Moen-Mathiot
at the Colorado Quaker Women's Retreat, late 1980s

To Quakers, simplicity is a spiritual quality that denotes an inward centeredness, a singleness of being that is responsive to the Divine within. Simple living is a creative act that frees us from extraneous concerns and enables us to devote attention to the Divine. A simple life is often hard to achieve. It means consuming or collecting nothing in excess of what is needful for our health and well-being and understanding what that is. What is needful may differ from one person to another, but in general it means that which is not extraneous in terms of time, possessions, speech, and activities.

Simplicity is at the root of what we call *plain speaking*. In the interest of declaring readily and easily our true meaning to one another rather than hiding or obscuring it, we try to avoid judgmental, pretentious, and ornamented language.

With regard to time, simplicity means handling important matters first, allowing them an appropriate share of our time, and taking care not to overcommit ourselves. Rather than rushing from one engagement to another, simplicity leads us to be deliberate in our choices about how we spend the precious gift of time. It guides us away from rigidity regarding the demands made on the hours of our days and encourages us to arrange a right apportionment of time to our religious life, our family, our work, our friends, and ourselves. Flowing through every decision we make concerning our priorities is an awareness of how we are serving the Divine within ourselves and other human beings

Early Friends wore unadorned plain dress out of a desire to observe simplicity and be free from vanity. Although most Friends no longer wear Quaker plain dress, we do dress simply without ostentatious display. Moreover, although we may affirm the human urge for self-adornment, we do not call attention to ourselves by what we wear.

Simplicity is also expressed in our stewardship of our material resources. It implies consuming no more than we need and can afford, not spending beyond our means, providing what we require for our well-being in every sense. We understand that poverty distracts from the life of the Spirit as readily as overabundance does. The measure of deprivation or overabundance is, to some degree, different for different people.

Simplicity also implies the responsible use of what we have and avoiding poisoning our environment. When we have ordered our lives according to our reasoned understanding of what we really need, we become not confined or limited by our choices but freed by them.

In its essence, simplicity means keeping at the deep center of our lives a sense of the Divine, a daily awareness of the Light within us, so that all other matters fall into their rightful place.

Equality

> *Being then desirous to know who I was, I saw a mass of matter of a dull gloomy colour, between the south and the east, and was informed that this mass was human beings in as great misery as they could be and live, and that I was mixed in with them and henceforth might not consider myself as a distinct or separate being.*
>
> John Woolman, 1772[6]

Guided by the Light of God within us and recognizing that of God in others, we can all learn to value our differences in age, gender, physique, sexual orientation, race and culture. This enables mutual respect and self-respect to develop, and it becomes possible for everyone to love one another as God loves us. Throughout our lives, we see ourselves reflected in the facial expressions, verbal comments and body-language of others. We have a responsibility to protect each other's self-respect.

Because of their commitment to social concerns, some Quakers may find it inconceivable that they may lack understanding of issues involving racism. Jesus stressed the unique nature and worth of each individual. It is unreasonable to expect assimilation or to ignore difference, claiming to treat everyone the same. This denies the value of variety, which presents not a problem, but a creative challenge to live adventurously. Personality, gender, race, culture and experience are God's gifts. We need one another, and differences shared become enrichments, not reasons to be afraid, to dominate or condemn. The media have increased our knowledge of the world, but we need greater self-awareness if our actions are to be changed in relation to the information we receive. We need to consider our behavior carefully, heeding the command of Jesus that we should love our neighbors as we love ourselves.

Meg Maslin, 1990
in *Quaker Faith & Practice of Britain Yearly Meeting*, 23.33

Quaker history bears witness to how we have acted upon the belief in the essential equality of all humanity. From the earliest days, men and women were equally regarded and equally charged with responsibilities for the care of others and themselves. Also from the beginning, Quakers have paid the same deference and courtesies to everyone. They have also refused to use honorifics and titles or to bow or doff their hats because these actions would presume a superior/inferior relationship based on a person's secular position. Likewise, recognizing the equality of all people regardless of race, they strongly opposed the inhuman institution of slavery. In more recent times, Friends have asserted the equality of people of differing sexual orientations.

Quakers have long affirmed what the laws of our country have explicitly ruled—that none of the categories that make us distinctive as individuals shall stand in the way of our realizing our lives fully and freely. Women and men are equal. All races are equal. All people are free to choose whatever religion speaks to their needs. No one person shall be subject to another, nor in regard to spirit does any person hold rank above another. Because we believe that the Light shines in the early years of life and in the last, we value and respect youth and age equally with other stages of life.

Yet not all human beings have just and equal means and opportunity to become what their gifts could enable them to be. Friends seek to empower those who are oppressed and to find ways for more equitable distribution of the resources and wealth of the world.

Community

Our life is love, and peace, and tenderness; and bearing one with another, and forgiving one another, and not laying accusations against another; but praying one for another and helping one another up with a tender hand.

Isaac Penington, 1667[7]

It is not possible to be a human being without being part of a community. We are born into a community, even if it is only ourselves and our mother. We grow up in a community, learning language, assimilating culture, and discovering the Spirit. As Friends, we know that the Spirit comes to us not only as individuals, not only as members of a community, but as the very foundation of community, moving a meeting at times as one person. The Spirit guides us when we worship in community and when we do business in community.

Although we best know a sense of spiritual unity within our families and in our meetings, we look outwards and try in love to include others in our community—our neighbors near and far, the people we meet as we go out into the world, even the very living, breathing Earth that feeds us and clothes us and that we care for in our turn.

There is a reciprocal nature to our relationships in community, but the love of God takes us beyond exchange and contract to covenant and commitment. We care for those who need us, whether they are able to return the care or not. We care for the prisoners who have harmed us, for they also are beloved of God. We have compassion for those in power, even when we disagree with their actions, for we know they are human and carry within themselves the seed of love. We care for migrants who have left home and family to seek a new life in a strange place. We care for all we love and all we might come to love.

Community calls us sometimes to set our own interests aside when the group is led in directions we may not understand or appreciate. Community also calls our Friends to hear our own leadings and help us follow the directions of the Spirit. Each of us is precious, and when our communities are at their best, we are supported in our individuality as well as our commonality. Children are precious because they need our love and care and give us light and joy, giggles and tears. Friends in their teens and twenties are precious because they need to be upheld as they move from dependence to independence to interdependence and give us the gift of believing in our highest ideals. In the middle years, Friends are precious because they need to be connected to the Spirit when the busyness of life takes over, and they give us steadiness and long-term commitment. Elder Friends are precious because they need to be remembered even as they share with us in remembrance the very lives they have lived and the truths they have discovered.

Friends carry their sense of community beyond the reaches of the family and the meeting into their careers and their political activities. Our communities can be nurseries where concerns grow in shelter and plans are prepared for addressing those concerns. Hard choices and difficult actions can be considered within the meeting community so that Friends do not have to feel alone, even when they act beyond the scope of the meeting's leading. In many cases, a leading for one Friend becomes a leading for the whole community.

Community is shelter, a safe place to grow, an arena for action, caring, and love—powered by and united in the Light.

[1] In 1682, monthly meeting representatives answered three queries, including "How has the Truth prospered amongst you since the last yearly meeting and how are Friends in peace and unity?" (*Quaker Faith and Practice*, Britain Yearly Meeting, 1995, 1.04). "How does Truth prosper among us?" became a census question. Less certain today of our identification as a community with the Truth in its entirety, we answer a little differently: "Let your life speak."

[2] Robert Griswold, *Creeds and Quakers: What's Belief Got to Do With It?* (Wallingford, PA: Pendle Hill Pamphlet #377, 2005), p. 17

[3] The complete text of the declaration is included in Appendix 3.

[4] John Woolman, *Journal,* abridged in *Quaker Spirituality: Selected Writings,* Douglas V. Steere, ed., (Mahwah, NJ: Paulist Press, 1984), pp. 176–177

[5] Thomas R. Kelly, *A Testament of Devotion,* (New York: HarperCollins, 1992), p. 94.

[6] Woolman, *Quaker Spirituality,* p.234.

[7] Isaac Penington, *Letters,* ed. John Barclay, 1828, p 139; 3rd edition 1844, p. 138 (Letter LII, to Friends in Amsterdam, dated Aylesbury, 4 iii [May] 1667).

Organization of the Society

It is earnestly recommended that, as Friends tend to the affairs of our Society, we bear in mind always that we are about God's work. We should endeavor humbly and reverently to conduct ourselves and our meetings in the wisdom and peaceable spirit of Jesus, with dignity, forbearance, honesty, and, above all, love.

Source unknown, as quoted in
Philadelphia Yearly Meeting Faith and Practice, 1978, p. 175

Where and How Decisions Are Made

In the beginning, the Religious Society of Friends mistrusted church hierarchies, believing that the path to the Divine is inward for each individual and worshiping group. Friends have kept the power of decision in religious matters as close as possible to the primary worship group and the individual. The monthly meeting, accordingly, has a freedom of action and responsibility in matters of membership not given to the yearly or regional meetings, with some exceptions. On the other hand, there are some matters on which a degree of uniformity among neighboring monthly meetings is essential to the good order of the Society.

By virtue of membership in a monthly meeting, Friends also become members of a regional and a yearly meeting. All members have the privilege and responsibility to participate in decision making within each body. All members are welcomed and encouraged to attend their regional and yearly meetings.

Within its own area of responsibility, each body is autonomous. Friends attend regional or yearly meetings not as instructed delegates of their monthly meetings but as their representatives. They join others in worship and in decision making that responds to the movements of the Spirit at that time and place.

Reporting, Oversight, and Guidance

Monthly, regional, and yearly meetings prepare and disseminate various reports, either to one another or to Friends everywhere. In Intermountain Yearly Meeting, each monthly meeting prepares an annual state of the society report for presentation to the regional meeting and subsequently the yearly meeting. The purpose of these

55

reports is to enable monthly meetings, regional meetings, and the yearly meeting to offer support, guidance, or oversight to monthly meetings as needed.

The Monthly Meeting

I was moved to recommend the setting up of Monthly Meetings throughout the nation. And the Lord opened to me what I must do...

George Fox, *Journal*, 1667

The meeting for worship is the heart of the monthly meeting and the Society of Friends. It is in this corporate fellowship that Friends experience the most profound realities of life: birth and death, marriage and family, community of the Holy Spirit, and concern for other people. A meeting in the Quaker sense is a gathering of people whose intention is to experience God. So far as this divine/human interaction takes place, there is order, unity, and power. Should this connection break down, Friends wait and pray that "way may open" once more; the good order of Friends is based on this conception of a meeting. Meetings for worship are held at established times— usually once a week but also more often as occasion arises.

The term *monthly meeting* has two meanings. Primarily, it refers to the fundamental unit of the Society of Friends; it also reflects the practice of coming together for meeting for worship with a concern for business, which usually occurs once a month.

Organization and Responsibility

The purpose of organization is to provide orderly and effective means for handling corporate business essential to the meeting's functioning with a maximum of freedom, participation, and responsibility. A meeting for business takes place in the same expectant waiting for the Spirit's guidance as does a meeting for worship. Friends' manner of conducting business is an expression of our faith that the Light, which is in all, when heeded, draws all into unity in our common affairs. It is an expression of our commitment to follow that Light.

A monthly meeting has many functions: it receives, records, and terminates memberships; provides spiritual and material aid to those in its fellowship; oversees marriages; gives care at the time of death; and counsels with members in troubled circumstances. It collects and administers funds for its maintenance and work, and it may hold property of a fiduciary nature as well as titles to real property. Meetings witness to Friends' testimonies and relate to other Quaker organizations as well as groups who share common concerns.

Organization evolves with a meeting's needs. Early in its history, a small meeting may be able to act as a committee of the whole. As it gains strength and experience, it may be appropriate to select persons and committees to carry out specific responsibilities. As long as an organizational structure proves useful, it is not changed unless there is good reason to do so; if a structure no longer serves a vital function, it is laid down. If a meeting holds title to real property, it may be advisable for that meeting to incorporate.

Officers

The organization of monthly meetings within Intermountain Yearly Meeting can vary, sometimes in the name of an office or committee, but also in some cases by function. Ministry in word and act, responsibility for the good order and material needs of the meeting, visitation, authenticity of the testimonies—all these are the responsibilities of persons in the meeting as they are guided by the Light. For practical reasons, monthly meetings appoint individuals to serve as officers and to carry out specific functions, including presiding over meetings, keeping records of business meetings and membership, maintaining stewardship of property and funds, and nurturing the community. They are appointed for defined terms of service using the nomination process described below. The names for the offices may vary, but it is important that responsibility for all necessary functions be assumed by willing and capable individuals. Larger meetings may appoint a number of officers to share the work of their meetings. The most commonly appointed officers include a clerk, a recording clerk, a treasurer, and a clerk of the Committee on Ministry and Oversight or Ministry and Counsel.

A good officer is one who, while assuming a particular responsibility, is committed to the leading of the Spirit in discerning what needs to be done and who seeks to engage the resources of the meeting, matching people to the task.

The *clerk* (also called *presiding clerk*) presides at meetings for business, gathers the sense of the meeting, formulates the minutes of the proceedings, speaks for the meeting when so directed, and carries out the instructions of the meeting to accomplish its business. Some larger meetings also appoint an *assistant clerk* or *associate clerk* to help with these functions. Although sometimes a faithful attender, the clerk is most often a member of the meeting, one who has the confidence and respect of the membership and the capability of serving the meeting with warmth and spiritual sensitivity. An effective clerk listens receptively, comprehends readily, evaluates rightly, and states clearly and concisely the sense of the meeting regarding a business item or concern. The clerk may ask any experienced Friend to preside in his or her absence.

Most meetings appoint a *recording clerk* to make faithful, concise, and accurate records of the minutes of action, as discerned and stated by the presiding clerk. It is the recording clerk who puts the meeting's insights and minutes into written words, but it is the clerk who bears ultimate responsibility for the completeness and accuracy of the minutes. The meeting may also appoint a *recorder* to prepare the census report as required by the yearly meeting; to file in the appropriate archives the minutes and reports collected by the recording clerk; and to maintain the records of births, marriages, and deaths, and the formal records of membership. In smaller meetings, these matters may be undertaken by the recording clerk. Some meetings appoint an *assistant recording clerk, recorder/archivist, librarian/archivist, correspondence clerk, records clerk,* or *minute clerk* to handle these duties.

Maintaining and disbursing the meeting's funds and giving regular reports to the meeting are the responsibility of the *treasurer*. Some meetings choose to incorporate when they begin to hold property in order to have some of the protections provided by the state in which they are incorporated. When drawing up such a charter and by-laws, special attention needs to be paid to the relationships between the officers of the meeting and its corporation. It is convenient to designate the treasurer of the meeting also as treasurer of the corporation. It is well that the meeting's accounts be reviewed occasionally by a financial professional or by a few persons appointed by the meeting.

Committees of the Meeting

Committees constitute an effective means of facilitating the monthly meeting's business because much of the work can be done more appropriately in small groups than in the meeting for business or by individuals. Each meeting decides which committees are necessary to carry out its concerns and business. Most meetings find a *Ministry and Oversight* or *Ministry and Counsel* Committee essential. *Ministry and Oversight* is responsible for the spiritual health of the meeting and maintaining a general purview of the right ordering of the affairs of the meeting. The term *oversight* can also refer to the management of property, but here it is used in the context of pastoral care and counseling. Other commmon committees include *Nominating, Peace and Social Order* (or *Peace and Social Concerns*), *Finance, Religious Education, Property,* and *Hospitality.* Although the names of committees vary among meetings, it is important that the functions of each committee be clear to all within the meeting. *Ad hoc committees* are sometimes useful for addressing particular projects or concerns. A committee no longer serving a purpose is laid down by the meeting for business.

Committees conduct business in the same manner as the monthly meeting does, waiting on the Spirit for direction in their work and unity in their decisions. It is important that committee clerks and members of committees attend meeting for business regularly to ensure regular communication of information and smooth coordination between the committee and the meeting. A written charge to each committee clarifies what is expected of it and of its clerk as well as the limits of authority delegated to it. Such clarity and communication promotes an atmosphere of trust, allowing meetings, their officers, clerks, and committees to fulfill their respective tasks without wasteful duplication or frustration.

Committee members should be selected according to their abilities and concerns. Meetings customarily appoint an experienced and capable member of the Religious Society of Friends to clerk the Ministry and Oversight (or similar) Committee, and each meeting determines the necessary qualifications for its committee members and clerks. Because committee work enables Friends to engage in the life of the meeting, it provides familiarity with Friends' faith and business practices, especially our decision-making process. Service on a committee also offers Friends an opportunity to use their particular gifts and to deepen friendships among the members.

Committees serve the monthly meeting not only by carrying on their usual functions but also by doing background work for the monthly meeting for business—examining particular matters in depth, identifying issues, gathering useful information, and preparing seasoned recommendations. When this work is done well, the monthly meeting session is able to focus quickly on the matter at hand. It is important that committees keep minutes of their meetings and that they report regularly to the monthly meeting. In bringing a matter before the meeting for business, it is important that the committee describe concisely the work it has done in support of its recommendation and offer, where appropriate, a draft of a possible minute. Mutual trust between the meeting and a committee as well as faith in the power of Truth over all will help achieve the proper balance between the discernment of a committee and that of the monthly meeting. All actions of committees in the name of the meeting are subject to approval by the monthly meeting.

Nominating Committee

> *Now there are varieties of gifts, but the same Spirit; and there are varieties of service, but the same Lord; and there are varieties of working, but it is the same God who inspires them all in every one. To each is given the manifestation of the Spirit for the common good. To one is given through the Spirit the utterance of wisdom and to another acts of compassion; according to the same Spirit, some will receive the gift of teaching in the children's program, to others the gift of building maintenance or hospitality; the same Spirit to another gives the clerking of a committee, and yet to others, even the registration of those coming to yearly meeting....*
>
> Adapted from *I Corinthians*, 12:4–7 *RSV*

The *Nominating Committee* is representative of the meeting and familiar with its members and attenders. Usually, a small ad hoc committee (often called the *Naming Committee*) nominates individuals to serve on the Nominating Committee. Those serving need to be discerning in judgment and tactful in manner and at the same time be forward-looking in considering for service younger

Friends and newer members and encouraging those who may underestimate their own potential. The responsibility of this committee cannot be too strongly stressed.

Nominating committees are concerned with how the gifts of members and attenders may best serve the meeting's needs for clerks, committee members, and other responsible positions. The committee seeks the best-qualified persons from among the whole membership, the younger and newer as well as the older and more experienced. The Nominating Committee considers the qualities appropriate to each appointment as well as how the members of a given committee will function together. It is important that the desire to fill all vacancies not distract the committee from its task of discerning the right person for a particular job.

It is well to the extent practicable to rotate meeting responsibilities or jobs among Friends to enable individuals to practice different approaches and to offer different gifts. It is equally important to recognize when a Friend is serving beyond his or her capacity and experience. The Nominating Committee is also charged with discerning the right time to ask a particular Friend to take up or to lay down a particular task. The committee explains clearly the term and scope of each appointment to those Friends asked to accept nomination as well as the need for the nomination to be brought to the monthly meeting for approval. Sometimes a Friend may request a clearness committee to help him or her reach clearness about accepting a position. In some larger meetings, the Committee on Ministry and Oversight serves as a clearness committee for the Nominating Committee. Nominating Committees should not feel unduly concerned to fill vacancies that remain after the committee has exercised its use of spiritual discernment.

Nominating Committees do not appoint, and nominations are made by the committee, not by individual members of the committee. Generally nominations are laid over for one month to enable both nominees and members of the meeting to express to the committee any concerns they may have about the nominations while carefully recognizing that of God in each person. If after thoughtful consideration unity is not reached, the committee attempts to find another person to fill the position. With any appointment, the meeting, having been fully involved in approving the nominations, extends loving support to those who take on a position.

Sometimes, following thoughtful consultation with the Ministry and Oversight Committee (or its equivalent), a need arises for bringing an appointment to a close before the end of a term, or a Friend may request release from service. Loving tenderness is essential in considering reasons for early release and in finding another person. Nominating Committees should not hesitate to bring problems back to the monthly meeting for guidance and practical help.

The Nominating Committee may also from time to time ask the Ministry and Oversight Committee to consider whether a committee should be laid down and to forward its recommendation to the meeting for business.

Ministry and Oversight / Ministry and Worship Committee

In some meetings, the functions of the Ministry and Oversight Committee (under various names) are the charge of one committee, and in others, because of the many responsibilities, these functions are divided between two committees—Worship and Ministry focusing on the spiritual well-being of the meeting as a whole, and Oversight and Counsel focusing on the care of individual Friends. The committee ideally consists of members of varied ages, genders, and gifts who are faithful in worship and sensitive to the life of the spirit—Friends both young and old looked to as spiritual elders and as having experience, empathy, good judgment, and discretion.

Care for the Meeting for Worship. The first responsibility of the Ministry and Oversight (or, where divided into two committees, Ministry and Worship) Committee's members is to deepen their own spiritual lives and their preparation for worship. When they are grounded in the Spirit, committee members are reminded that they are but vessels of the Light among many other vessels. Then they can better trust that the power of God may work through all persons in the meeting and beyond. Committee members' concern for the meeting throughout the week, their prompt arrival at and reverence for meeting for worship, and their faithfulness to the guidance of the Spirit are ways they can deepen the quality of worship.

Committee members try to discern promising gifts among Friends as well as to guide in a loving manner those who speak unacceptably in meeting for worship (such as those who speak too often or for too long). They endeavor to open the way for those who are timid and inexperienced in vocal ministry and to encourage all Friends to listen with tenderness. In trying to be helpful, they do not assume superior wisdom but rather trust that all are sharing in the search for guidance.

Care for the Meeting for Business. The responsibilities of the Ministry and Oversight Committee (or, where divided into two committees, Ministry and Worship) include nurturing business sessions of the monthly meeting. The importance of the presence of committee members at meeting for business cannot be overemphasized. The committee considers prayerfully how to contribute to the meeting's discernment of Truth and works with the presiding clerk to develop his or her skills in fostering a worshipful and faithful business meeting.

Care for Individual Lives. Ministry and Oversight Committee (or, where divided into two committees, Oversight and Counsel) attends to the spiritual lives of those in the meeting by helping discern and develop varied gifts for ministry and service as well as encouraging vocal ministry; teaching; counseling; using aesthetic, social, and practical modes of expression; and engaging in regular spiritual disciplines. The committee may support individual spiritual growth by circulating appropriate literature in addition to arranging for study groups, retreats, and worship-sharing groups. Members are personally concerned with the spiritual and physical welfare of each member of the meeting. They encourage visitation and fellowship within the meeting and try to ensure that those who are ill, troubled, or in want receive visits, spiritual help, and practical assistance as may be needed.

This committee (or a committee designated by the monthly meeting) considers requests for initiation, transfer, or withdrawal of membership; requests from persons who wish to be married under the care of the meeting; and requests for clearness committees to address individual concerns. It offers spiritual care and practical assistance at the time of death in a family. It tries to be of help in reconciling differences among people in the meeting. It endeavors to respond to inquiries about Friends and welcomes newcomers and attenders, including making clear to them ways of participating in meeting fellowship, or joining the meeting as a member. It encourages Friends to attend regional and yearly meeting sessions and other gatherings of Friends, and provides information about possible financial assistance for this purpose. It keeps in touch with committees with related concerns and may form subcommittees charged with specific responsibilities, such as clearness for membership or marriage, or oversight of a fund for special needs.

The Ministry and Oversight Committee (or two committees) should report its activities and concerns regularly to the monthly meeting. In consultation with the meeting community, this committee oversees the preparation of an annual State of the Meeting Report to the regional and yearly meetings, for they and the clerk share oversight of other committees of the meeting, with a special concern for good order. (See Appendix 5 for a description of and advices on the State of the Meeting Report.)

Sometimes a problem facing an individual is too complex for the meeting to handle. When this arises, the Ministry and Oversight Committee may turn to regional or yearly meeting Ministry and Oversight Committees for assistance. In some cases, professional help needs to be sought. Committee members need to have knowledge of available professional resources. Even when it is clear that professional help is needed, the meeting may still offer such practical assistance as meals, childcare, or transportation. At those times, spiritual support of the individual(s) is of utmost importance.

Peace and Social Order Committee

That the *Peace and Social Order Committee* (variously named *Peace and Social Concerns, Social Action, Peace and Justice, Faith in Action,* and so on) is one of the first committees formed in many monthly meetings bears witness to the commitment of Friends to make their lives speak their faith. This committee may plan and carry out service projects as activities of the meeting, recommend particular action on issues of interest to Friends, encourage members to participate in the work for social change as part of larger groups or independently according to individual leadings, support Friends in forwarding a concern to the regional or yearly meeting, and contribute services or money to help free a member of the meeting to pursue a social action as a "released Friend." This committee also may provide valuable help in seasoning concerns of an individual or group that may lead to social action or service, testing concerns and recommending courses of action.

Finance Committee

Monthly meetings must have income to pay for rent or maintenance of space, communication, outreach, insurance, educational materials, and other expenses. The treasurer, with advice from Ministry and Oversight or a separate Finance Committee, oversees funds. The procedures for securing income are generally unobtrusive. It is not uncommon for the Finance Committee to send an annual letter to members and attenders describing the meeting's broad budgetary picture and suggesting common practice in giving to the meeting. Such a letter typically explains that contributions may be less for some and more for others, depending on personal circumstances. One of the responsibilities of membership is the financial support of the meeting and other Friends' organizations.

Other duties of the Finance Committee are to oversee the maintenance of orderly accounts and expenditure procedures, and to advise the monthly meeting on the financial aspects of its affairs. In meetings without a Finance Committee, the treasurer may carry these responsibilities. In larger meetings, it may be worthwhile to hire a professional accountant and to appoint an assistant to the treasurer.

Other Committees

As a meeting grows, it will be necessary to add other committees to do the work described above and to meet other needs that arise. Some of the other committees currently identified within Intermountain Yearly Meeting are:

Religious Education (both for children and for adults)
Building and Grounds
Board of Trustees/Corporation Board of Directors
Hospitality
Long-Range Planning

Outreach
Fellowship
Right Sharing
Library
Membership Guidance
Communications
Bereavement
Scholarship

Regional Meetings

Membership in the Religious Society of Friends by individuals is obtained through the monthly meeting. Such membership also constitutes membership in the regional meeting and the yearly meeting with which the monthly meeting is affiliated. Because Intermountain Yearly Meeting was created directly from a fellowship of monthly meetings, the role of regional meetings within this yearly meeting is still developing. Currently, there are four smaller bodies within Intermountain Yearly Meeting: Arizona Half-Yearly Meeting, Colorado Regional Meeting, New Mexico Regional Meeting, and Utah Friends Fellowship.

Traditionally among Friends, a regional meeting which met twice a year was called a "half-yearly meeting." In this yearly meeting, some regional meetings call themselves "half-yearly meetings" or "Friends fellowships." For simplicity in reference within the purpose of this document, the term *regional meeting* will be used inclusively.

A regional meeting is a cooperative association of two or more monthly meetings in a particular geographical area and is composed of all the members of its constituent monthly meetings, preparative meetings, and worship groups as well as interested persons within its area who are isolated from any established Friends group.

Purpose

The purpose of a regional meeting is to strengthen the life and fellowship of monthly meetings and other Friends groups in the area and to provide a link in transmitting business and other information to and from Intermountain Yearly Meeting. Regional meetings contribute in various ways to the growth of the spiritual life and fellowship of its constituent monthly meetings and other Friends groups, including children and young Friends. Sessions of the regional meeting provide religious fellowship, a wider variety of ministry during worship than individual meetings usually experience, and programs that address the varied interests of the Religious Society of Friends. Outside its regular sessions, the regional meeting may develop programs for its young people, arrange for retreats and other gatherings, and encourage and coordinate inter-meeting visitation.

A regional meeting also provides a forum for broader seasoning of and acting upon concerns from individuals and meetings and forwarding approved minutes to the Executive Committee or annual session of the yearly meeting. It also may provide services or address issues that pertain to all Friends but for which there may not be sufficient concern or energy in any one individual meeting. A regional meeting is concerned for the condition of its constituent groups, strengthening and supporting them. With the overseeing monthly meetings, it is responsible for the nurture of new gatherings of Friends. The regional meeting would also be the appropriate body to consider a request from the members of a monthly meeting that their meeting be laid down or united with another meeting.

Formation

Each regional meeting was separately created by, and may be laid down by, its participating monthly meetings and worship groups without application to the yearly meeting. The organization and appointments of the regional meetings generally follow those of the monthly meeting.

Currently a regional meeting may be established upon yearly meeting approval of a request from two or more monthly meetings or a request from a regional meeting that wishes to be divided into two such meetings. A regional meeting also may be set up upon the initiative of the yearly meeting. In any such instance, the yearly meeting appoints a committee to assist in the organization and receives the recommendation of that committee before recognizing the regional meeting.

Responsibilities

To carry out its responsibilities, a regional meeting meets regularly, selects necessary officers and committees, and conducts its business in the usual manner of Friends. It collects and administers funds as needed. It may appoint an Interim, Planning or Continuing Committee to help plan its sessions and to act for it between sessions, within agreed-upon limits. Specific procedures vary among regional meetings, and the manuals of procedures or handbooks of regional meetings should be consulted. Information regarding the appointment of yearly meeting positions by the regional meeting is found in the "Guide to Procedures of Intermountain Yearly Meeting."

Each regional meeting prepares an annual budget, which is presented to business sessions of the regional meeting once a year. Customarily, the budget is based on an annual assessment, contributed by each of its constituent monthly meetings, of a per-capita amount based on the number of adult members reported by the monthly meeting in its most recent census. The per capita assessment rate is considered and approved by the regional meeting in its annual sessions as part of the review of the budget. Out of these funds, the regional meeting pays for items agreed upon as necessary to its operations. The adult members include both resident and nonresident members. Members sojourning by minute to other monthly meetings are counted by their home monthly meeting. Members of other monthly meetings and attenders are not included.

The Yearly Meeting

Introduction

Intermountain Yearly Meeting emerged from Intermountain Friends' Fellowship in 1974. The regional meetings were created separately by their constituent monthly meetings. Both the yearly meeting and the regional meetings exist at the pleasure of the monthly meetings and their worship groups. Intermountain Yearly Meeting has come to be organized and administered in ways that reflect the status of the monthly meeting as the fundamental organizational unit and the source of unity in all decisions. Annual gatherings are structured to emphasize the spiritual both in fellowship among those attending and in business sessions.

Affiliations

Intermountain Yearly Meeting is a member of Friends World Committee for Consultation (FWCC) and actively affiliates with the Friends Committee on National Legislation (FCNL) and the American Friends Service Committee (AFSC). Currently, affiliation with Friends General Conference (FGC) is being explored. The yearly meeting becomes a member of or affiliated with another Friends organization only after several monthly meetings have become active in the affairs of that organization and bring to the yearly meeting a request for membership or affiliation.

Membership

Members of the yearly meeting's monthly meetings are also members of the regional meeting, the yearly meeting, those Friends organizations of which the yearly meeting is a member, and the Religious Society of Friends worldwide. Members are responsible for the decisions and actions of their yearly meeting.

Annual Meeting

The annual gathering of Intermountain Yearly Meeting is a spiritually enriching occasion as Friends seek guidance from the Light Within and share their diverse insights and concerns for service in the larger world. This gathering is held at a time and place determined by the yearly meeting on the recommendation of the Continuing Committee, which has responsibility for overseeing all details of the planning. Yearly meeting attenders consider ways in which spiritual guidance, truth, witness, and friendship have been expressed over the past year and how these expressions may be extended in greater measure to those who come to us as seekers. The annual business sessions of Intermountain Yearly Meeting are held during the annual gathering. During these plenary sessions, the work of the appointees, committees, and officers of the yearly meeting is reported. The yearly meeting clerk, with the assistance of the Continuing Committee, develops the agenda for the annual business meetings. Between annual gatherings, the Continuing Committee and the

Executive Committee carry on the work of the yearly meeting, based on guidance provided at the annual business sessions and in accordance with the "Guide to Procedures of Intermountain Yearly Meeting."

Relationships of Monthly Meetings, Preparative Meetings, and Worship Groups with the Yearly Meeting

Monthly meetings, preparative meetings, and worship groups are directly affiliated with Intermountain Yearly Meeting upon the acceptance of their written request.

A new monthly meeting, preparative meeting, or worship group may be established with the assistance and oversight usually of the nearest existing monthly meeting of Intermountain Yearly Meeting. A worship group or preparative meeting may transfer from the care of one monthly meeting to another using the same procedures as for an individual transferring membership. Should a worship group or a preparative meeting be laid down, any residual responsibilities and real or fiduciary property and records are transferred to the monthly meeting having its care or to one or more other monthly meetings, as may be agreed with the responsible monthly meeting. Similarly, should a monthly meeting be laid down, the disposition of its remaining responsibilities and any property, real or fiduciary, becomes the responsibility of the regional meeting unless it is inactive, in which case they would go to the yearly meeting.

Monthly meetings affiliated with another yearly meeting may also become associated with Intermountain Yearly Meeting upon acceptance of a written request. Meetings should clear such action with their yearly meeting before requesting such association. Mexico City Monthly Meeting of Pacific Yearly Meeting has been associated with Intermountain Yearly Meeting since Intermountain Yearly Meeting's beginnings.

The yearly meeting provides guidance and discipline in faith and practice for its monthly and regional meetings and worship groups regarding their affairs and relationships with the yearly meeting and with Friends everywhere. In all matters, such guidance is descriptive and not prescriptive. The yearly meeting endeavors to maintain inclusive practices and procedures, always knowing that the monthly meeting is the fundamental unit in the affairs of the Religious Society of Friends.

Financial Support of the Yearly Meeting

Assisted by the treasurer, Intermountain Yearly Meeting's Finance Committee prepares two budgets: one for the annual gathering, which is self-supporting through a registration fee, and the other for the general operations of the yearly meeting, which are supported by an assessment on the monthly meetings based on the number of adult members according to the latest census. These budgets are reviewed and approved by the Yearly Meeting and again, at its winter meeting, by the Continuing Committee.

The annual gathering budget provides adequate child care, an inspirational program for young and adult Friends, and a smooth but simple administration.

The general operating budget supports travel and related expenses of

- yearly meeting officers to attend meetings of the Executive and Continuing Committees
- members of the Faith and Practice Committee
- representatives appointed by the yearly meeting to FWCC, FCNL, and AFSC
- representatives attending meetings of the Friends Peace Teams Committee and meetings of the corporation board of *Western Friend*.

Travel expenses to meetings of yearly meeting committees are the responsibility of the meeting or group making the appointment, except in cases where Intermountain Yearly Meeting makes other arrangements.

Rather than including support of FWCC, FCNL, and AFSC in the yearly meeting's budget, Intermountain Yearly Meeting calls on its monthly meetings and worship groups to contribute directly to these organizations. This helps avoid the need to increase the annual assessment. Similarly, it leaves to the monthly meetings decisions about allocating from their budgets financial and nonfinancial resources to other worthy groups that might otherwise approach the yearly meeting for support.

Intermountain Yearly Meeting's annual assessment is a contribution from each of its affiliated monthly meetings of a per capita amount based on the number of adult members reported by the monthly meeting in its most recent census. The count of adult members includes both resident and nonresident members whose memberships are held by the monthly meeting. Sojourning members are included in their home meeting's count. Attenders are not included in the assessment. This method of calculating the assessment is designed to be an even-handed way of arriving at each monthly meeting's share of budget responsibility. The per-capita assessment rate, as recommended by the Finance and Continuing Committees, is considered and approved by the yearly meeting in its annual sessions as part of the review of the budget.

In addition to the assessment, payment of which is the responsibility of the monthly meetings, contributions may be made directly to the treasurer of Intermountain Yearly Meeting by meetings, groups, and individuals at any time.

Bringing Concerns before the Yearly Meeting

There are four ways a concern may come before Intermountain Yearly Meeting's business sessions for consideration: by placement on the agenda by the clerk; by minute from a monthly or regional meeting; by minute from a yearly meeting committee; or from the floor when recognized by the clerk. All formal communications to the yearly meeting regarding matters of substance are in the form of minutes adopted by meetings or groups.

The clerk and the Continuing Committee, in their planning process, develop an agenda including matters that need to be addressed at the annual business session. It is expected that other concerns that may come before the yearly meeting be considered and approved previously by a monthly or regional meeting or the committee responsible for the concern. Such concerns should be described in a written minute delivered to the yearly meeting clerk in a timely fashion. The clerk, in consultation with Continuing Committee, then places the concern on the agenda.

In considering concerns brought before them by their members, monthly meetings should exercise care that their own discernment is adequate and that, if forwarding the matter to another meeting, they are not evading their own responsibility for reaching unity. This may involve consideration at more than one sitting of monthly meeting for business. In cases where urgent action is not called for, it might also be wise for a monthly meeting to seek the counsel of its regional meeting before forwarding a concern to Continuing Committee or the yearly meeting clerk. It is also recommended that the resources, implications, and actions involved in carrying out the concern be clarified early in the consideration process.

Committees of the yearly meeting may bring minutes either to the clerk or directly to the floor of the annual business sessions. As with concerns of monthly meetings, Intermountain Yearly Meeting committees are advised that they also should exercise care that their own consideration has been adequate and that their members have reached unity before bringing the matter to yearly meeting. The clerk and the Continuing Committee may place on the agenda all such matters that reach them in a timely fashion.

The yearly meeting clerk may entertain a minute or concern from the floor of a plenary session. Before such a concern is laid before the plenary session for its consideration, the clerk usually consults with the clerk of the Continuing Committee about the impact or unintended consequences that potentially could arise from the resulting action. The concern may be acted upon or may be referred for study and consideration at another annual gathering.

The Role of the Guide to Procedures

Prior to developing a Faith and Practice, the yearly meeting created "The Guide to Operations of Intermountain Yearly Meeting" (now called "The Guide to Procedures"), which contains detailed information about the functions of yearly meeting committees, roles and responsibilities of officers, terms of service, nominating procedures, and other matters. The Guide also covers qualifications of Friends who serve the yearly meeting, detailed procedures for the nomination and appointment of officers and committee members, and how travel to committee functions is to be paid for. The Guide is considered a manual of procedures rather than a statement of faith and practice. The Guide and special applications of its topics may be found on the Web at www.imym.org.

Discernment of Clearness for Service to the Yearly Meeting

Regarding discernment of clearness to serve the yearly meeting in various capacities, Intermountain Yearly Meeting follows this process for nominations:

Members of the Nominating Committee are responsible for approaching Friends concerning possible service to the yearly meeting. They make clear the duties involved in the position and explain the nominating process. A written job description (from "The Guide to Procedures of Intermountain Yearly Meeting") is given to the prospective nominee. When two (or more) persons are to work together closely on an assignment, they should be consulted about the proposed arrangement. It is made clear that the yearly meeting as constituted in its annual sessions, not the Nominating Committee, makes appointments. The Continuing Committee can act for the yearly meeting when the latter is not in session, as described in the Guide. This makes it possible to make appointments at the Continuing Committee's mid-winter meeting when necessary.

Prior to accepting a yearly meeting nomination, nominees are strongly encouraged to engage in a clearness process within their monthly meeting, preparative meeting, or worship group to assist them in seeking the answers to the following queries:

1. How does the position relate to the nominee's spiritual leading into service? What spiritual support might the nominee need from his or her meeting?

2. Given the duties of the job and the nominee's personal attributes and abilities, is there a good match? How does it fit the nominee's gifts? Does it offer the nominee potential for personal growth?

3. What circumstances might affect the nominee's ability to serve? What are the nominee's commitments within and outside of his or her meeting? Will these commitments interfere with the nominee's ability to carry out the proposed service to the yearly meeting?

4. To perform the duties of the job, what assistance will the nominee need from his or her meeting? For example, will the nominee's meeting need to host committee gatherings? Does the

nominee have duties within his or her meeting that will need to be laid down or assumed by others? Might the nominee need help from his or her meeting to meet childcare or other domestic responsibilities if travel is involved in the committee work?

Committees of Intermountain Yearly Meeting

The functions and appointment procedures regarding the following Intermountain Yearly Meeting committees are established and described in "The Guide to Procedures of Intermountain Yearly Meeting" (see www.imym.org). However, the yearly meeting may create or lay down committees as it sees fit. As of this printing, the committees are as follows:

Executive Committee
Continuing Committee
Nominating Committee
Finance Committee
Watching Committee
Operations Committee
Ministry and Counsel Committee
Long-Range Planning Committee (inactive)
Intermountain Yearly Meeting Faith and Practice Committee
Committee for Oversight of Western Quaker Workcamps
 (formerly AFSC/IMYM Joint Service Project)
Committee to Revise the Guide
Committee on American Friends Service Committee
Committee on Friends Committee on National Legislation
Committee on Friends World Committee for Consultation
Committee on Migrant and Border Concerns (no longer a
 committee, but still meeting as an informal group)

Officers and Appointees
of Intermountain Yearly Meeting

The roles and responsibilities of the following officers and appointees of the yearly meeting are also described in "The Guide to Procedures of Intermountain Yearly Meeting." The yearly meeting may create other offices and appointments as it sees fit to enable smooth administration.

Clerk
Recording clerk
Continuing Committee clerk
Recording clerk of the Continuing Committee
Registrar
Treasurer
Clerk of the Finance Committee
Clerk of the Nominating Committee
Clerk of the Ministry and Counsel Committee
Historian-Recorder
Clerk of the Faith and Practice Committee
Convener of worship sharing
Convener of interest groups
Coordinator of children's yearly meeting
Clerk of the Watching Committee
Coordinator of Senior Young Friends program
Coordinator of Junior Young Friends program
Coordinator of operations
Book sales support coordinator
Advocate for Friends with different abilities/kitchen liaison
    (may be split into two jobs as needed)
Members (3) of the corporation board for *Western Friend.*
Representative to Friends Peace Teams Project

Membership

What we have in common is not our ideas, but our selves.

Gusten Lutter, 2003

Introduction

The Religious Society of Friends is a community of faith based on individual and mutually shared direct and unmediated experience of the Divine. Friends worship and grow in the Spirit together, open and obedient to the Power within, by which we believe all may be guided. Friends welcome all visitors, inviting them to return frequently and become regular attenders. The Society desires to include in its membership all persons who find themselves in unity with its faith and practices or are committed to aspiring toward that unity. The meeting consists of its members and faithful attenders. We share ourselves without distinction; membership acknowledges a deeper commitment to the affairs of the monthly meeting.

Persons finding themselves in or seeking unity may apply for membership in a monthly meeting of the Religious Society of Friends. Membership signals a readiness to join in the common effort of the Society to seek and follow the Inner Light. This readiness involves some experience and understanding of that Light as it is known by Friends, a reality that guides and directs, gives strength to act upon that guidance, and brings unity with the Spirit of God. Membership in a monthly meeting also involves sustained commitment.

As members have responsibility toward the meeting, so has the meeting responsibility toward its members. Members are the immediate family of the Society, and although all those associated with the meeting fall under its loving care, it is for the membership that the meeting carries primary responsibility. Historically, this responsibility included provision not only of spiritual support but also of material assistance to members experiencing economic hardship. This custom continues in many meetings. A meeting's broad responsibilities to its members include, but are not limited to: mutual support, charity, guidance, empowerment, and forgiveness.

Ever since early Friends rejected the distinction between priesthood and laity, responsibility for the full range of meeting activities has rested with the membership. Meetings are enriched by members who take an active role in corporate worship, share in the work and service of the Society, and live in harmony with its basic beliefs and practices. Friends make a spiritual vocation a responsibility of all members. Membership involves a willingness to attend meetings regularly, both those for worship and those for business; to give service through committees and otherwise as the way opens; and to share in financial responsibilities. Responsibility for the meeting and its decisions resides with and is ultimately retained by the members of the meeting.

Throughout the history of the Religious Society of Friends, the community has been led by the Light shining through individual Friends, just as the Light of the community has called individual Friends back from what George Fox called "wandering in notions." Friends' suspicion of concretely formulated creeds, confessions, and doctrines comes out of respect for this dynamically unfolding experience and charges the individual and the community to challenge and test each other. This mutual discernment does not always work to perfection—sometimes we reach premature judgment; sometimes we fall into inertia. Nevertheless, by undertaking membership we agree to open ourselves—and our understanding of the Light—to the testing of the community. Likewise, when we accept individuals into the community we publicly acknowledge that their leading and measure of Light may open us to new understanding and action. As one applicant for membership said,

> *I feel very strongly that the spiritual life absolutely requires that we should not remain isolated. It is this deep need of getting out of a prolonged and dangerous relative isolation which urges me to be admitted among the Quakers. It is more and more clear to me that it is only in the bosom of a religious family, freely but strongly constituted, that the individual can render to the world the services it sorely needs. . . .*
>
> Pierre Ceresole, 1936 in a letter of application for membership to London Yearly Meeting, as quoted in *Quaker Faith & Practice: The book of Christian discipline of the Yearly Meeting of the Religious Society of Friends (Quakers) in Britain*, 1994

Attenders and Membership

When I walked into the silence of my first meeting for worship, I knew I was home.

Sentiment expressed by many Friends

People are attracted to the Religious Society of Friends for many reasons. Some discover a community that supports their quest for a personal experience of the Divine, and others find a context within which to live out a life of discipleship. Many have had disappointing or unfulfilling experiences in other faith communities and find among Friends the freedom and support to explore their own leadings. Still others see Friends as a socially engaged and politically active community.

Meeting members are encouraged to get acquainted with attenders and to be available to them for mutual spiritual support and guidance. The meeting invites regular attenders to participate in its life. Attenders are encouraged to take part in the various activities of the meeting, to attend meeting for business, and, at the discretion of the monthly meeting, to serve on committees. Attendance at regional (quarterly or half-yearly) meetings, Intermountain Yearly Meeting, and other gatherings of Friends can provide attenders with a deeper understanding of Friends than participation in just a monthly meeting typically allows. Familiarity with Friends' way of worship, manner of conducting business, organizational structure, finances, and major spiritual and historical writings, as well as Friends' periodicals and organizations, enriches the quality of attenders' participation in and experience of the meeting.

The Religious Society of Friends values the presence and participation of all persons drawn to Friends. Attenders nourished through their involvement with the meeting, familiar with and enriched by Friends' basic beliefs and practices, and desiring to undertake some responsibilities within the meeting are encouraged to apply for membership. The meeting committee charged with membership should be aware of and responsive to attenders who appear to be approaching readiness for membership. Similarly, attenders who feel ready to consider membership may broach the topic with any member of the meeting or with someone on the committee overseeing membership.

You've been acting like a member for a long time. Don't you think it's time to make it official?

Barney Aldrich, circa 1990

Preparing and Applying for Membership

Remember that moral and spiritual achievement is not what is required in an applicant: sincerity of purpose is. Complete agreement with all our testimonies is not necessary. It is important for the life of the Society that the applicant is broadly in unity with the views and practices of Friends. Many applicants have too lofty an idea of the Society, and of the quality of the lives of its members. They should be warned of possible disappointment.

Quaker Faith & Practice: The Book of Christian Discipline of the
Yearly Meeting of the Religious Society of Friends (Quakers)
in Britain, 1994, section 11.17

Membership in the Religious Society of Friends is held within a monthly meeting. The members of the monthly meeting welcome inquiries about membership and other matters concerning the Society. Friends encourage informal conversations as one step toward applying for membership. It is important that the meeting help newcomers understand the membership process and how it differs from that of other denominations.

As a person becomes acquainted with a particular monthly meeting and with Friends' ways by participating in the life of the meeting, he or she may feel led to consider membership. Preparation for membership involves regular participation in the life of a meeting over a period of time (often more than a year), including meetings for worship, meetings for business, committee service, and other activities. Additionally, attenders interested in membership benefit from a familiarity with written materials about the history and principles of the Religious Society of Friends; particular attention is invited to readings about Friends' testimonies and to the Intermountain Yearly Meeting's book of discipline, *Faith and Practice.* These preparations are assumed to accompany a prospective member's sense of being a part of the community as well as a strong spiritual persuasion.

A sense of readiness to apply for membership can come to an attender in a variety of ways. One may discover that the faith and practice of Friends has become central to her or his life. Another may feel a spiritual leading that becomes increasingly clear and strong. A third may report a sense of having found the right place, of being "at home" after long seeking. Others may identify with and feel a responsibility toward the meeting and the Religious Society of Friends.

The application procedure for membership involves several steps:

1.   An applicant writes a letter expressing her or his desire to pursue membership in the meeting. Depending on the meeting, this letter is directed to the clerk or to the designated meeting committee charged with overseeing requests for membership. This letter need be no more than a plain request to apply for membership. Customarily, an applicant also includes an account of his or her background and how he or she reached the decision to apply for membership. The request for membership is announced at the meeting for business following its receipt, and the letter may be read. The letter is turned over to the appropriate meeting committee (and eventually is archived).

2.   The meeting for business or the meeting committee responsible for membership appoints a clearness committee to meet and talk with the applicant. Care should be taken to select discerning Friends who have a strong understanding of the meaning and implications of membership. It is helpful if the applicant knows at least one member of the committee. The applicant may request that certain Friends be appointed to the clearness committee; the choice, however, is ultimately made by the meeting for business or the responsible meeting committee. Members of the monthly meeting are invited to become better acquainted with applicants and to voice approval or concerns to the committee.

3.   The members of the clearness committee meet with the applicant to explore his or her commitment to the faith and practice of Friends and to discern together the readiness of the applicant and the meeting. All visits take place in the spirit of a common, worshipful seeking for God's will and guidance. Providing suffi-

81

cient time allows opportunities for (a) the clearness committee to become acquainted with the applicant, (b) the applicant to ask questions, and (c) the meeting and the applicant to become clear about the request for membership. (See, at the end of this chapter, a list of suggested topics to be covered during clearness committee meetings.)

4.   The clearness committee reports the results of its process to the meeting for business or responsible meeting committee. If the clearness committee feels that the applicant is not yet ready for membership, it may encourage her or him to seek wider experience with Friends' beliefs and practices through additional reading; visits to other monthly, regional, or yearly meetings; and/or attendance at workshops or other activities. Membership itself is not as important as the spiritual growth of the prospective member. If it becomes clear that more seasoning is needed, the clearness committee will arrange to continue meeting with the applicant and will keep the meeting informed.

5.   If it becomes clear to the applicant, the clearness committee, or both that membership is not advisable, the application may be withdrawn, and the meeting is informed. Regardless of the outcome, Friends endeavor to treat all applicants with gentleness and respect. Friends welcome continued attendance and participation in the life of the meeting on the part of the applicant, just as before the possibility of membership was explored.

6.   If the committee recommends membership, it presents its recommendation and report to the meeting for business for approval. A decision regarding the membership may be reached during that meeting for business, or the report may be seasoned for one month with approval being sought at the next meeting for business.

7.   Upon approval of an application for membership, the meeting minutes its acceptance of the new member, and his or her name is added to the membership records. Membership in the monthly meeting also confers membership in the regional meeting and Intermountain Yearly Meeting, as well as in the worldwide body of the Religious Society of Friends.

8.   The meeting provides a warm welcome into the community for the new Friend.

9. Some meetings retain a tradition of having members of the clearness committee remain available to the new member for continued support and enfoldment into the community.

Children and Membership

From birth, all children of the meeting are under its care. Intermountain Yearly Meeting has no provision for *birthright membership*, although *birthright Friend* remains a term used by some in Intermountain Yearly Meeting for children raised within the meeting. Each monthly meeting has different ways of designating the children and young people in the community. In some, they are given the designation of junior or associate Friends either at birth or upon the request of their parents. Regardless of the terminology applied to children in individual meetings, all children of the yearly meeting are equal and to all are due the same consideration and care.

Meetings are responsible for helping young Friends assess their spiritual development, understand the faith and practice of Friends, and discern their relationship with and readiness for membership in the Society. Children and young adults may apply for membership according to the meeting's regular procedures. Meetings are urged to treat a young applicant with tenderness and care. The clearness committee is charged with ensuring that the applicant understands the meaning of membership and feels not only welcome but also prepared to participate fully in the life of the meeting.

Many young people wish to be acknowledged as part of the community of Friends for the purposes of support in conscientious objection to military service or upon application to Friends colleges, universities, or agencies. When these individuals have been under the care of the meeting and active in the community, demonstrating their unity with Friends' principles and beliefs, such written acknowledgment should be provided regardless of their official designation regarding membership.

Sojourning Membership

Membership is generally held in a meeting near the member's primary residence. Friends who expect to be residing temporarily near a different monthly meeting may ask their meeting for a minute of sojourn. This minute, written and signed by the home meeting's clerk, customarily outlines the reasons for and the probable duration of the member's sojourn. If the home meeting approves, a minute of sojourn is written for each family member and sent to the new meeting.

Typically, a sojourning Friend may participate fully in the life of the visited meeting. Meetings are encouraged to welcome sojourning Friends warmly and to extend to them the same care due a member. A sojourning membership terminates when the sojourner leaves the visited meeting. The clerk of the visited meeting notifies the home meeting of the sojourning Friend's departure, returning the sojourning minute to the home meeting. Friends who find that their stay will be prolonged should consider transferring their membership.

Transfer of Membership

Ideally, an individual holds membership in the meeting he or she regularly attends. Attending one meeting while holding membership in another can result in a loss to the individual and to the meetings involved. The member may not receive adequate support from either meeting. Likewise, the member may fail to assume the responsibilities of membership in either meeting. Although membership is based primarily on spiritual ties, it also assumes a willingness to share in the responsibilities of a meeting. When a Friend moves to the vicinity of another monthly meeting, the clerk of the original meeting should write promptly to the clerk of the new meeting recommending the member to its fellowship.

When a member desires to transfer membership, that member must request a letter of transfer from the home meeting. If the transfer is accepted, the receiving meeting sends a letter to that effect to the former meeting. A clearness committee can be offered or requested; clearness committees are available to anyone requesting a transfer.

Membership of Distant Friends

Occasionally, a person may seek membership in a meeting that is at some distance from their residence. When a meeting is willing to make a genuine, practical, and lasting commitment to maintaining supportive contact, membership may be appropriate. When a Friend who is a member moves to an isolated area, the Friend and the home meeting should try to locate a meeting in that area. Resources available to those living at some distance from a meeting include Friends' publications, webpages, the other branches of Friends throughout the country, and the Wider Quaker Fellowship. Attendance at the yearly meeting, retreats, the Annual Gathering of Friends General Conference, and workshops offered through Pendle Hill or Ben Lomond should be encouraged, as they can provide opportunities for fellowship.

Dual Membership

Monthly meetings within Intermountain Yearly Meeting vary in their acceptance of dual membership. Friends are advised to avoid contradictions and to maintain honesty and integrity in their affiliation with any religious body or organization. Should a member of the meeting be drawn to join another religious organization, the use of a clearness committee is recommended.

Applicants from Preparative Meetings and Worship Groups

When an attender of a preparative meeting or worship group wishes to become a member of the Religious Society of Friends, he or she does so by applying for membership in the overseeing monthly meeting, following the procedure for membership outlined above. The responsible monthly meeting appoints a clearness committee, which includes people from both the monthly meeting and the preparative meeting or worship group, if possible. The responsible committee of the monthly meeting may ask the worship group or preparative meeting's responsible committee to comment on a membership application.

Most of the responsibility for membership applications rests with the overseeing monthly meeting during the early development of a preparative meeting. As the preparative meeting matures, its responsibility increases. Only a monthly meeting can accept members, however.

When a preparative meeting becomes a monthly meeting, the clerk of the new meeting sends the former overseeing meeting a list of all those desiring transfer of their membership to the new meeting. These transfers are made promptly, not needing to follow the usual clearness committee process.

Termination of Membership

Termination of membership in a monthly meeting simultaneously ends membership in the Religious Society of Friends. Termination of membership may be initiated either by a member or by the monthly meeting. Membership ceases formally when the termination is minuted by the meeting for business.

On the Initiative of a Member

A member may resign from the Religious Society of Friends by writing a letter to the clerk of the monthly meeting. Any member considering ending her or his membership is encouraged to request a clearness committee to examine the motivations for termination. Is she or he no longer in accord with the faith and practice of Friends? Has she or he not been involved actively in the monthly meeting over a significant period of time? When the monthly meeting minutes acceptance of the Friend's resignation, acknowledging that it is at the member's request, the meeting sends a letter to the resigning member that includes a copy of the meeting minute. Meetings are encouraged to send correspondence regarding termination of membership by certified mail with return receipt requested. Letters written in acceptance of a resignation customarily manifest considerate regard for the person leaving membership.

When a member resigns without seeking clearness, the meeting is not absolved from further care. Customarily, the monthly meeting appoints a committee to visit with or otherwise contact the Friend and inquire about the reasons for the resignation.

If a member resigns out of a desire to join another religious body, the monthly meeting will, at the request of the member, write a letter to the other denomination indicating that the individual is no longer a member of the Religious Society of Friends.

On the Initiative of a Monthly Meeting

A monthly meeting may remove from membership an individual who (1) exhibits a persistent lack of interest in or responsibility toward the obligations of membership, (2) fails repeatedly to reply to communications from the meeting, (3) cannot be located by conscientious effort, or (4) exhibits repeated disregard for Friends' principles.

Customarily, monthly meetings periodically contact long-absent members. Meetings need to keep in mind that some Friends may go through periods—sometimes prolonged—when their association with the life of the meeting is tenuous due to difficult life circumstances, illnesses, or other crises. Meetings should make every effort to clarify the circumstances of a member's absence as well as the relationship between the member and the Religious Society of Friends.

If the monthly meeting—after conscientious effort over an extended period of time—receives no response from and cannot locate a member, it may consider termination of membership for that person. If the monthly meeting unites regarding the termination, it minutes the circumstances and ends the membership. The monthly meeting sends a letter that includes a copy of the minute to the former member, preferably by certified mail with return receipt requested. When the address of a member is unknown and the above procedure has been followed, the returned letter should be attached, unopened, to the meeting copy and filed in the membership record for former members.

If a Friend, by conduct or publicly expressed views, appears to be disregarding the faith and practice of the Religious Society of Friends or to be misrepresenting Friends so that the meeting or its undertakings are harmed by the person's membership, the concern should be communicated to the committee charged with ministry and counsel.

1. If the committee finds warrant in the concern, it can meet with or appoint a clearness committee to meet with the member and any other individual involved, seeking through a spirit of loving concern to understand the member's views and actions. This process must be handled with sensitivity and may need to be carried out in confidence. The clearness committee brings its findings and a recommendation to the originating committee. If the clearness committee finds insufficient grounds for removal, it is encouraged to make recommendations on how to facilitate reconciliation. If there appears to be no hope of restoring unity between the member and the meeting, the clearness committee recommends termination of membership. If action by the monthly meeting is recommended, a minute is sent to the clerk of the monthly meeting to this effect.

2.   When the clerk places the recommendation on the agenda of the monthly meeting, a letter is sent to the person concerned, inviting his or her presence and offering time to speak in response to the minute. This letter, sent preferably by certified mail with return receipt requested, must be received in sufficient time to allow the person to respond in person or in writing.

3.   The minute is read at the monthly meeting. The individual whose membership is under consideration may address the meeting regarding the proposed action and related circumstances. After adequate seasoning, no sooner than at the following meeting for business, the monthly meeting may unite in a decision. The individual concerned, if present, is asked to stand aside when the decision is made. The decision of the monthly meeting is minuted and sent to the individual, again preferably by certified mail with return receipt requested.

A monthly meeting or member may request assistance from a nearby meeting to help find clearness if problems arise regarding ending a membership. Procedures designed to promote clarity amid difficult circumstances are not intended to displace kindness and loving care for an individual's spiritual life.

A person whose membership has been terminated either by resignation or by action of the monthly meeting and who desires to rejoin the same or a different monthly meeting may do so by following the procedure outlined earlier for application for membership.

Record Keeping

Membership rolls should be kept current. Accurate accounting of new memberships and transfers, deaths, and removal of members should be recorded and reported in the yearly meeting census. Customarily, regular attenders are listed along with members in a meeting directory.

Suggested Queries and Topics for Use by a Clearness Committee on Membership

The test of membership is not a particular kind of religious experience, nor acceptance of any particular religious, social or economic creed. Sincere religious experience and right religious belief are both important, but develop in the course of participation in the ac-

tivities of the meeting. Anyone who can become so integrated with a meeting that he helps the whole and the whole helps him is qualified to become a member.

Howard Brinton
Friends for 350 Years, Pendle Hill Publications, 2002

The queries and topics listed below often arise naturally in the course of a clearness committee meeting with an applicant for membership. They are intended to clarify any questions the applicant may have about membership and the workings of the meeting, to help committee members become acquainted with the applicant on a deeper level, and to enable the committee members to share the experience of their spiritual lives with the applicant. All clearness committee meetings are held in a worshipful manner of openness and caring. It may be appropriate to hold several meetings.

- What are some milestones along your spiritual journey?
- How do you expect membership in the meeting to contribute to your spiritual journey?
- How have you experienced and come to understand the Light?
- How do you quiet yourself and open yourself to the Holy Spirit?
- How does the Religious Society of Friends meet your needs for worship and fellowship?
- How is Quakerism a "way of life" for you?
- How does your association with the Religious Society of Friends test you?
- What attracted you to Friends' articulated faith and practices? Are there some that you find puzzling or disturbing? In what ways do the advices and queries speak to you?
- Which of the testimonies of Friends speak most strongly to you? Which testimonies most confront your present life?
- How do you respond to the fact that Quakerism is rooted in Christianity but Friends differ in their views of Jesus and the role of Biblical scripture?
- How does the variety of religious language and expressions describing Friends' spiritual experiences fit or differ from your own? How might differences between the views you hold and the views held by other Friends affect your spiritual life and the life of the meeting?

- How do you feel you can contribute to the meeting's conduct of business?
- How do you envision the meeting supporting and contributing to your faith and spiritual development?
- How might you contribute to the faith and spiritual development of others in the meeting?
- How do you envision supporting the nurture and religious education of the meeting's children?
- What is your experience with the wider family of Friends, including the regional meeting, Intermountain Yearly Meeting, Friends General Conference, Friends Committee on National Legislation, Friends World Committee on Consultation, and the American Friends Service Committee, among other groups?
- How do you know that you are led to make this meeting your spiritual home?
- What, in your experience, contributes to manifesting qualities of worship while business is conducted? What interferes with business being conducted in a worshipful manner? What is your experience of the process and outcome of decision making among Friends?
- What is your understanding of the financial practices of the monthly meeting?
- How do you anticipate that your membership in a Friends meeting may affect your family relationships?
- Do you have any questions or other matters you want to discuss with us?

Young People
in the Religious Society of Friends

I was not "christened" in a church, but I was sprinkled from morning to night with the dew of religion. We never ate a meal together which did not begin with thanksgiving; we never began a day without "a family gathering" at which my mother read a chapter from the Bible, after which there would follow a hush of weighty silence. . . . My first steps in religion were thus acted. It was a religion that we did together. Almost nothing was said in the way of instructing me. We all joined together to listen for God, and then one of us talked to him for the others. In these simple ways my religious disposition was being unconsciously formed and the roots of my faith in unseen realities were reaching down far below my crude and childish surface thinking.

Rufus M. Jones, 1926

If the vigor of the meeting lives in its young people, and the wisdom of the meeting lives in its elders, then the strength of the meeting lies in interaction between the two.

Todd Swanson, 2005

Children

Children of Friends are born into or join their home family first of all, but they also become part of the spiritual family of their meeting. This spiritual family is entrusted with a significant role in their upbringing. Like parents and loving caretakers, the meeting shares responsibility for fostering the emerging spiritual life of its children—recognizing and nurturing their individual gifts, nourishing and guiding them as they experience the world and begin to assume the increasing responsibilities that are part of growing older.

In a number of monthly meetings, Friends gather to celebrate the birth of a baby or to welcome a child into the fellowship of the spiritual community. Because the first months of a child's life are sometimes very difficult—including for the new parents—it is important for the meeting to remember that the new family may need and welcome various kinds of help.

As children grow older, as they grow into being themselves, it matters that both parents and Friends in the meeting community try to be aware of changes as they take place, to be receptive to the chil-

91

dren's daily experiences, and to listen attentively to what children attempt to communicate of happiness, need, sadness. It is important that children have a sense that they have value, that they are loved by those around them, and that however young they are, their lives have meaning.

The child's home family is the environment in which Quaker values can be most strongly fostered early in life, where he or she can learn how to listen for the inner voice that offers guidance in choosing and doing good actions. The home can be the safe place where a child finds out how to seek understanding of truth and to test it, rather than accepting things passively. A Quaker home affirms for a child, long before the realization becomes conscious, that worship and work are parts of the same life and that although outward circumstances of our society and our culture may change with the times, the foundation of our lives in the Spirit remains unchanged.

As a child begins to be aware of the spiritual world beyond the home, both the parents and the meeting need to find ways to talk about the mystery at the core of Quakerism. Because silence is at the heart of the way Quakers worship, it is especially hard to communicate with children about the sometimes difficult and demanding journey of a spirit seeking God. It may make the mystery easier to grasp if we tell stories from our history about how Quakers have tried to live in accordance with their beliefs. In addition, hearing adults' vocal ministry in meeting for worship may slowly lead children toward understanding.

Most meetings foster Quaker values in their children by providing First Day school classes during all or part of the adult meeting for worship. Although in smaller meetings and worship groups such an arrangement is not always possible, care is taken to give children a sense of comfort, understanding, and safety during the time they are at meeting.

Friends need to be aware that we are just as susceptible as any other group—despite our self-image as peaceful people striving for good—to danger toward our children from those who would take advantage of their young age. Situations of trust can provide openings for abuse. We are responsible for ensuring the safety of children in our communities. Meetings are encouraged to educate themselves regarding the indicators, prevention, and handling of incidents of abuse.

> *Children can and do understand, have trusted and stood strong in their faith. It is heartening to read about the children, ten to twelve years old, who, in the 1600s "kept up their meetings regularly, and with remarkable gravity and composure" when their parents were being held in prison because of what they believed, even suffering beatings and the threat of prison, despite their tender age.*

> Britain Yearly Meeting, *Faith and Practice*, 19.35

Youth

As boys and girls become adolescents, they enter another stage of life. For many of them, this is an especially risky period of transition, during which they work out a degree of independence from their immediate family. When they try on unfamiliar trappings of maturity, their behavior and ideas may challenge those of the adults in their lives. Parents may need to take a step back, to move away from being the center of their child's experience. Yet at the same time it is important that they continue to offer their trust, the comfort of familiar values, and an unfailing sense of loving security that the youth can rely on.

Youths, meanwhile, are engaged in the difficult job of adjusting to the world beyond their own home, where values, standards, and expectations are often quite unlike those they've grown up with. Yet it is precisely at the same time as young people are confronting life-affecting decisions about education and occupation that our society lays upon them the burden of making important choices about fundamental social issues. Chief among these is the question of registration for or enlistment in the military. It is important that the meeting counter the recruitment efforts and claims of the military, assist individual young Friends in documenting their conscientious objection to war, and make known to our young people the full range of options open to them. Clearness committees may help them find clarity about and security in their own deeply held values during this critical time of special vulnerability to society's expectations.

It is no easy task for adolescents to live up to their ideals while trying to find a place in the world among people of their own age group who do not share those ideals. Family meetings that engage everyone in the household and during which issues important to youth are openly and honestly discussed can be a source of mutual inquiry, support, and learning. It is important that young and old listen to each other. What matters most at these times is keeping the lines of communication open so that the young person does not feel lost and isolated as he or she goes through the changes—intellectual, emotional, physical, and spiritual. It is also important to remember that growing up does not happen at the same age and in the same way for all adolescents. Some young people at the age of sixteen may be more mature than others who are twenty.

Friends from the meeting, as well as parents, may be able to offer support, guidance, and sympathy to adolescents. The meeting can express its trust in the gifts of its young people by asking them to join in the work of meeting committees and thereby to take on some of the responsibilities of being a Friend. This is not difficult if the meeting has made a practice over the preceding years of clarifying for their younger members the various ways of contributing to the meeting. It is an especially easy transition if young people and elders have shared intergenerational activities in the past. When younger and older Friends are comfortable with one another, the elders can serve as role models or mentors that the young people may feel they need to counterpoise the pressure from their peers at school. The meeting's elders have "been there and done that." If they are true friends of the young, they can be a great help. Likewise, it stands to reason that if the young are true friends of those who are older, they too can be a great help. It's a two-way street.

It is important that meetings recognize that the needs of all age groups deserve consideration. Intergenerational activities, including worship sharing, may help ease the tentativeness that accompanies differences of age when such activities are the product of mutual consultation and are entered into willingly. Young people become aware of themselves as Friends not only through attending meeting for worship and receiving religious instruction, but also through friendships within their own age group and participation in the meeting. They need to be included in the structure of the meeting, and the meeting needs what they can offer. Such considerations add up to what is most important of all—a sense of belonging, which makes young people feel they are an integral spiritual part of meeting.

The Voice of Young Friends

This is a time of life when we can actually follow our dreams, be idealistic, explore our future, and shape our destiny as individuals and members of our generation.

It's hard to find a balance in our lives with so much going on.

For the first time, decisions we make in our lives may have large consequences.

Senior Young Friends, 2005

An essential way in which Intermountain Yearly Meeting Senior Young Friends and Young Adult Friends begin to develop their own sense of Quaker practice and living Quaker testimony is to create a fully developed Yearly Meeting under the auspices of the Yearly Meeting. At the Annual Gathering, Senior and Young Adult Friends choose, in unity, co- clerks, create a Ministry and Counsel Committee with representatives to the larger Ministry and Counsel, conduct meetings for Worship with a concern for Business, and grow in their understanding of the right order of Quaker process.

The Yearly Meetings of Senior and Young Adult Friends are nurtured by the care and mentorship of the adult meeting. The youth, in turn, enrich and inspire the larger community. Their untarnished idealism, often part and parcel of youth itself, sometimes serves to "elder" their elders.

Their most profound expression of growth into genuine maturity is the way in which they practice the "testimony of community." Many of them have often expressed that their feelings of trust, deep love and connection to one another stand at the core of who they are. This deep sense of community becomes a blessed gift they bring with them as they ultimately become integrated into the larger meeting.

Bearing in mind the usefulness of intergenerational communication, two youthful elders attempted to gain a sense of the concerns of Senior Young Friends at the 2005 gathering of Intermountain Yearly Meeting. The Senior Young Friends offered genuine responses to the questions posed. They expressed a need for "healthy meetings," a concern about questions relating to gender, and gratitude for the comfort and support that their parents had given them.

The Senior Young Friends selected a number of individual statements as reflective of their common concerns. These comments, quoted directly and slightly edited, appear below and in the lines above. They make up a "snapshot" of our young Friends in 2005.

To be a Quaker means to be constantly searching.

We want to change things but feel we are not old enough to have much of an effect.

It's hard to love someone when you genuinely dislike him or her.

When you are uncentered, it's easy to become angry.

We are not taught how to deal with anger.

Sometimes it's hard to remain nonviolent.

What about Hitler? What about terrorism?

It is important to listen to us, to get our opinions, and to include us in decisions.

We need room to grow, while knowing adults are there for us.

It's hard to know when to bring things to meetings of the adults when they're all over the map themselves.

We need more volunteers for our programs. It's hard when adults criticize youth and youth programs but are unwilling to invest their time.

Adults feel they should let you go, but they don't trust you.

There are occasions when we have a consensus that the adult meeting lacks or that they are not yet ready to accept.

It's hard to find adult mentors when things go wrong.

Adults in meetings need to be "healthy," to be centered, to know what they are looking for in order to help us in our search.

Sometimes we feel isolated when we can't find other Quakers our age.

Adults often treat you as equals in the spiritual journey, though they may need reminding every few years.

We're not told what to think; we're allowed self-discovery.

Marriage
and Other Committed Relationships

Introduction

Marriage has always been regarded by Friends as a religious commitment, not a civil contract. George Fox said, "Marriage is the work of the Lord, only." It is an awe-inspiring, lifetime commitment between a couple and God, without need for priest or magistrate. Quaker marriage is a testament to that belief. The marriage ceremony is a meeting for worship during which the couple reverently speaks simple vows in the presence of the Spirit and those who prayerfully sustain them in undertaking their commitment.

From the very early days, the Religious Society of Friends stressed the need for serious consideration prior to marriage, the clearness from all other engagements of those wishing to marry, the public announcement of the intention to marry, and the significance of the meeting for worship in which the declarations were made. The couple was held to high standards of love, fidelity, and discipline, bearing witness to the presence of the Spirit between them.

Our practice today must attest to the same high standards for our committed relationships. Although the standards for marriage remain essentially the same as they were among early Friends, the cultural and social contexts in which we live have changed dramatically. We joyfully acknowledge the sustaining, enriching presence of loving unions among us, and we want the meeting's strength to reinforce these commitments.

Recognizing that some meetings in Intermountain Yearly Meeting do and others do not accomplish marriages between same-sex individuals, that the legal status of these relationships may change over time, and that there are many committed relationships that are not marriages between individuals of different sexes, the term 'committed relationships' is intended to include all such unions.

We intend, through the care and ministrations of our meetings, that strong, resilient marriages and other committed relationships will flourish. We are encouraged to

grow in both our virtue and our capacity to love by the testing,
against the world and each other, of those weaknesses which by the

grace of God we can convert into strengths, and by the finding of those strengths and beauties in each other which we hardly dared suspect were there. But these are the rewards of unfolding years; years, not weeks or months. The glory of a great marriage lies in the surprises which loving support, acceptance, and graceful forgiveness can bring forth.

R. B. Crowell, *"Words at a Quaker Wedding,"*
Friends Journal, 1974

Relationships *Under the Care of the Meeting*

Before taking the couple under its care, a meeting, through a clearness committee, counsels with the partners, seeking to discern their clearness about what they are undertaking. If the committee so recommends, and the meeting agrees, the couple is taken under its care. This can be understood as an affirmation that a loving community stands ready to take action as necessary to support the well-being of the two partners, of the relationship itself, and of any children who may be, or may become, involved.

Monthly meetings within Intermountain Yearly Meeting vary in their concept of marriage and acceptance of same-sex unions. A few are able to find clearness to oversee only heterosexual relationships; many find clearness to oversee both same-sex and heterosexual unions. It is the strength and quality of the loving spirit between two people that always concerns the meeting.

Request *to the Meeting*

When two people wish to have their relationship taken under the care of the monthly meeting, they write a letter to the clerk of that meeting stating their intention and requesting that the meeting begin the clearness process. In the good order of Friends, a period of at least three months is usually needed between the sending of the request and the date of the marriage. It is expected that at least one of the partners be a member or regular attender of the meeting. If one of the partners holds membership in another monthly meeting, a letter of clearness or release should be obtained from that meeting.

In cases where the individuals are neither members of the Religious Society of Friends nor regular attenders at meeting for worship, the meeting may choose to assist the couple in having a celebration of marriage or other committed relationship after the manner of Friends. This could include having a clearness committee and/or an arrangements committee, but this relationship would not be considered to be under the care of the meeting.

Clearness Committee

When a request for oversight of a couple's relationship is received, a clearness committee is appointed by the monthly meeting or by its Committee on Oversight. It is important that members of the clearness committee be willing to devote the time necessary to give prayerful consideration to the right course of action and be amenable to providing counsel in the future. Clearness committees often meet more than once. The committee members should be well grounded in Friends' practice.

The couple and the clearness committee meet in thoughtful and prayerful discussion to seek clarity about God's will regarding the proposed union. Specific queries or topics may be presented by the committee or the couple to give direction to the discussion, or discussion may arise out of worship. It is important that those participating in the clearness process approach each meeting with open hearts and minds, that sufficient time be allotted for thorough understanding and seasoning, and that any encumbrance be explored to ensure that both persons are free of conflicting obligations. Thoroughness in the clearness process can be valuable to the couple in helping them examine the strength of their commitment to a lifelong relationship with each other.

Because practices differ from state to state, it is especially important that both the committee and the couple recognize and understand the laws, statutes, and regulations regarding marriage in their state so that the legal standing of their relationship will be clear. After meeting with the couple, the clearness committee meets separately to share their impressions or concerns about the proposed union.

Topics Suggested for Discussion During the Clearness Process

The topics listed below tend to arise naturally in the course of clearness committee meetings. It is preferable that prospective partners broach them themselves; it is also well for the committee to have topics in mind and to see that they are covered.

1. *Background and Acquaintance.* How well acquainted are the partners? What are their common values? How do they adapt to differences between them in background, religion, age, temperament, and interests? Can they react to their differences with humor, mutual respect, patience, and generosity? Do they have compatible world views?

2. *Religious Beliefs, Feelings, Aspirations.* Do they see commitment or marriage as a spiritual relationship? How do they propose to meet their religious needs? Does each seek to understand and honor the religious beliefs of the other?

3. *Growth and Fulfillment.* Do they think of themselves as trusted and equal lifelong partners, sharing responsibilities and decisions? Are they supportive of each other's goals for personal growth and fulfillment?

4. *Daily Living.* Have they considered how they will deal with issues and problems, which are bound to arise during the course of the marriage? Are they able to talk with each other about their sexual expectations? Have they discussed and worked through questions regarding the use and management of money? Have they considered ways to resolve anger when it arises within the relationship? Have they thought about differing needs for time alone as opposed to time together? Have they explored their attitudes towards holidays and gift giving? Have they discussed the surname each will use? Are they prepared to seek creative means of resolution when their problems seem insoluble?

5. *Relationships with Others.* Have they considered whether they desire children — the problems as well as the joys children would bring, and the responsibilities for nurturing and guiding them? How do they view their relationships with each other's families and their obligations toward society? How will already-existing relationships be treated: with ex-spouses and children, old friends, ex-parents-in-law, ex-grandparents-in-law? Are they prepared to honor that of God in all of these relationships?

6. *Relationship with the Monthly Meeting.* How do the partners expect the monthly meeting to support their relationship? What

do they expect their relationship to bring to the monthly meeting?

7. *Discharge of Prior Commitments.* Do they have personal or financial obligations that need to be met or discharged? Are they aware of each other's financial obligations, and have they discussed and reached agreement on how these would be met during the relationship? Are they aware of the need for changing names on documents, creating new wills, and making other arrangements for existing legal documents to reflect the new relationship?

8. *Attitudes of Others.* What are the views of their families and friends toward the prospective marriage or commitment? Are there ways the meeting can help the couple deal with these views?

9. *The Celebration.* Is the couple acquainted with and accepting of the form and implications of the Quaker celebration of marriage? Do they wish to join themselves in a religious commitment to a lifetime together? Do they welcome the oversight and support of the meeting community? It may be that unity in reaching clearness to move forward is not readily found. The committee and the couple may choose to continue seeking clarity about God's will in this matter, or they may choose to lay aside the request for a while or permanently.

When the couple and the committee are clear that the celebration or wedding should go forward, the clearness committee reports to the Oversight Committee, the committee overseeing membership and marriage, or directly to the monthly meeting for busi..ess, giving its recommendation and asking for the approval of the monthly meeting. Some monthly meetings choose to hold such matters over for a period of time, for seasoning. Once the request has been approved, the monthly meeting (or its appropriate committee) appoints an arrangements committee, taking into consideration the couple's suggestions about its composition.

Remarriage

Following the loss of a partner, the decision to undertake a new marriage or other committed relationship requires great faith, strength, and courage. The new relationship may be taken under the care of the meeting in the good order of Friends.

The processes of request, clearness, and oversight of the new relationship are identical to those outlined for first-time marriages and committed relationships. During the clearness process, however, special consideration is naturally given to issues pertinent to the changed circumstances. Where children or other relatives are involved, it is advisable for the clearness process to include them in some of the discussions. It is important that all parties hold one another in the Light.

Arrangements Committee

This committee, appointed by the monthly meeting or its appropriate committee, works with the couple to ensure that the couple's desires are met regarding the ceremony and that it is accomplished with simplicity, dignity, and reverence. The date, time, and place of the celebration are announced, and Friends are invited. (A small monthly meeting may choose to have one committee serve as both the clearness committee and the arrangements committee.)

Responsibilities of the Arrangements Committee for Weddings and Ceremonies of Other Committed Relationships

1. To see that the ceremony is accomplished with dignity, reverence, and simplicity.
2. To meet with the persons being joined together to discuss plans for the ceremony, including the choice of persons to (a) explain the format of a Quaker wedding near the beginning of the meeting for worship so that attendees unfamiliar with the practice are informed; (b) to carry a small table and the wedding certificate and pen to the couple for their signatures; (c) to read the certificate; and (d) to close meeting.
3. To see in advance that all legal requirements are met and that the couple has a marriage license, if that is their wish. The marriage license may need to be altered to reflect Quaker practice.
4. To facilitate the signing of the marriage certificate by all those present at the meeting for worship.

5.   To see that the marriage license is signed, usually by the clerk of the meeting, and that the document is filed with the county clerk or designated official.

6.   The monthly meeting minutes the celebration of each marriage or committed relationship at its business meeting. It is suggested that appropriate records be maintained in the meeting's archives.

The Couple's Responsibilities

1.   To read about, understand, and follow the marriage procedures of the Religious Society of Friends.

2.   To refrain from sending out wedding invitations until the clearness process is complete.

3.   To call together the arrangements committee, discuss their plans in a timely fashion, and keep the committee informed.

4.   To have the marriage certificate prepared in time for the ceremony.

5.   To obtain a state marriage license, if that is the couple's desire, and to ensure that all legal requirements are met.

Traditional Friends Ceremony

The meeting for worship for the celebration of a marriage or a committed relationship gathers in silence at the appointed time. The meaning and procedure of the meeting for worship may have been explained in the invitations or it may be explained early in the meeting itself. Out of the silent worship, the couple will rise and, taking each other by the hand, declare in words to this effect, each speaking in turn:

In the presence of God, and before these our Friends, I take thee, _____, to be my (wife, husband, partner), promising, with divine assistance, to be unto thee a loving and faithful (husband, wife, partner), as long as we both shall live.

or

In the presence of God, and before these our Friends, I commit myself to thee, _____, promising, with divine assistance, to be unto thee loving and faithful, as long as we both shall live.

After these declarations, the certificate is signed by the couple and is then read to those gathered by a person appointed for that purpose.

Worship continues, often with rich vocal ministry, and is closed by someone appointed to do so. After the close of worship, all those gathered for the meeting for worship, including the children, sign the certificate.

Variations upon this procedure may be used by the couple with the approval of the arrangements committee.

> *Marriage ... is for life; and the wedding is a declaration that it is so....To turn a wedding into worship is to recognize that marriage is bigger than we are; that it is not just a pleasant arrangement we have made for our own convenience, but a vocation into which we have been drawn by nature and by God.*
>
> Harold Loukes, 1962, *Faith and Practice,*
> *Britain Yearly Meeting,* 1995

The Traditional Friends Marriage Certificate

WHEREAS, A.B., of (city or town) _____, son/daughter of C.B., of (city or town)_____ and D., his wife, and E.F., of (city or town)_____, daughter/son of G.F., of (city or town)_____ and H. _____, his wife, having declared their intentions of marriage with each other to _____ Monthly Meeting of the Religious Society of Friends, held at (city or town) _____, (state) _____, according to the good order used among them, and having the consent of parents (or guardians), their proposed marriage was allowed by that Meeting.

NOW THESE ARE TO CERTIFY to whom it may concern, that for the accomplishment of their intentions, this _____ day of the _____ month, in the year of our Lord _____, they, A.B. and E.F., appeared in a Meeting for Worship of the Religious Society of Friends, held at (city or town)_____(state) _____, and A.B., taking E.F. by the hand, did, on this solemn occasion declare that he/she took him/her, E.F., to be his/her wife/husband/partner, promising, with divine assistance, to be unto him/her a loving and faithful wife/husband/partner so long as they both shall live (or words to that effect); and then, in the same assembly, E.F. did in like manner declare that he/she took him/her, A.B., to be his/her wife/husband/partner, promising, with divine assistance, to be unto him/her a loving and faithful wife/husband/partner so long as they both shall live (or words to that effect). And moreover, they, A.B. and E.F., according to the custom of marriage, did, as a further confirmation thereof, then and there, to these presents, set their hands.

A.B._____ E.B. or E.F._____

AND WE, having been present at the marriage, have as witnesses set our hands the day and year above written.

Variations on the traditional certificate may be prepared by the couple in consultation with the arrangements committee, or pre-printed traditional forms may be ordered from the Philadelphia Yearly Meeting Office, 1515 Cherry Street, Philadelphia, Pennsylvania 19102.

Marriage or Commitments Outside the Care of the Meeting

If a member is married or celebrates a commitment outside the care of the meeting, the Oversight Committee should arrange for someone to visit the new couple as an expression of the meeting's interest in them. It is assumed that the member will continue to be active in the meeting and that the non-member partner will be made welcome and invited to attend Meeting.

Meeting's Care for the Relationship

Friends are reminded that the meeting's oversight and care of a relationship does not end with the celebration but endures throughout the life of the relationship.

The clearness committee should plan to meet with the couple approximately a year after the ceremony to confirm the committee's continuing interest, care, and availability.

Meetings have an important role in nurturing, supporting, and celebrating the couples under their care. In a loving community of persons of similar religious values, couples can be sustained and guided in their efforts to build an enduring relationship. Communication among the members of the meeting is vital. Celebrations, workshops, and supportive discussion, as well as meetings for worship, are important for couples in all stages of their relationship. Couples often appreciate the feeling of oversight that the meeting offers when times are easy; they are encouraged to access the oversight process during difficult times.

Although it is true that Friends sometimes have a strong sense of privacy that makes them reluctant to bring forth personal problems, individuals and couples are encouraged to seek the care of the meeting in times of conflict. The meeting provides guidance and support for the couple and any children, including possible referral to trusted professionals for additional assistance. Couples are urged to go to the Oversight Committee, their clearness committee, or a person whom they particularly respect, to seek together a solution when they have difficulties or unresolved conflicts.

Advice in Periods of Difficulty

> *We would counsel Friends to take timely advice in periods of difficulty. The early sharing of problems with sympathetic Friends or marriage counselors can often bring release from misunderstandings and give positive help towards new joy together. Friends ought to be able to do this, but much will depend on the quality of our life together in the Society. If marriages among us fail, we are all part of that failure. We need to be more sensitive to each other's needs, knowing one another in the things which are material as in the things which are eternal.*

Marriage & Parenthood Committee, 1956
Faith & Practice, London Yearly Meeting, 1972

Although marriages and other committed relationships are intended for life, with deep sorrow we acknowledge divorce among members. Meetings hold both parties tenderly and give special care to the children affected in these separations. No marriage or other committed relationship should be terminated lightly or quickly. If, after thoughtful and prayerful consideration and a period of seasoning, the couple finds that serious contemplation of separation or divorce is advisable, they are encouraged to seek clearness through their meeting's Oversight Committee. (In the event of an abusive relationship, a partner may decide that immediate separation is necessary.) A dissolution moves forward when the couple, the clearness committee, and God's leading make it clear that the marriage or other committed relationship no longer exists.

When two members are faced with separation or divorce, one or the other, or both, may feel alienated from further participation in meeting. If there has been an active clearness process, the sense of alienation may be lessened and separation may proceed with tenderness and charity. A worship service on the occasion of the dissolution of the marriage may be made available to seek God's grace for all and to acknowledge the marriage and its termination within the loving community of the meeting. This gives meeting members an opportunity to deal with what is often a major change in the structure of their community. It alerts them to the needs of the divorcing members and their children, if any, and gives the divorcing members an opportunity to share their pain with the community and for the community to share its grief as well.

Queries Related to Separation and Divorce

1. How does the meeting acknowledge Friends who are contemplating divorce?

2. What is the meeting's role in caring for Friends undergoing separation or divorce? Does the meeting reach out to both of them?

3. Are Friends mindful of the meeting's responsibility to pay special attention to the children of separating parents, at a time when parents are perhaps less able than usual to nurture their children? Is the meeting mindful to be attentive to the needs of adult children when their parents divorce?

4. When separation/divorce has become a legal fact, how does the meeting publicly acknowledge and deal with it?

5. Is the meeting mindful of the lengthy disruption and readjustment period involved in divorce? Does the meeting follow up with the divorced parties six months or a year later?

Renewal of Vows

On occasion, after years of marriage or having been joined together outside of the meeting, a couple may desire to renew their
vows in the presence of the Divine and the loving community of
their meeting. A couple can request a Clearness Committee to explore the health of their relationship and to chart their future. The
celebration is a wonderful opportunity for the meeting to express its
loving support of the couple in a specially called meeting for worship.

> *We thank God, then, for the pleasures, joys and triumphs of [life
> together]; for the cups of tea we bring each other, and the seedlings
> in the garden frame; for the domestic drama of meetings and part-
> ings, sickness and recovery; for the grace of occasional extrava-
> gance, flowers on birthdays and unexpected presents; for talk at
> evenings of the events of the day; for the ecstasy of caresses; for gay
> mockery at each other's follies; for plans and projects, fun and
> struggle; praying that we may neither neglect nor undervalue
> these things, nor be tempted to think of them as self-contained and
> self-sufficient.*

Faith and Practice, **London Yearly Meeting, 1959**

XXXVI

> *I sing the praise of danger, for we chart*
> *A dangerous course, who would be man and wife:*
> *Danger that conflict may decay to strife,*
> *Or lambent passion harden into art;*
> *Danger that sneaking death too soon may part*
> *One from the other's lingering earthly life,*
> *Danger from tottering ladder, glancing knife,*
> *Insidious germ, or too much burdened heart.*
> *But what is danger? Freedom's eldest son,*
> *That marks us off from angel and from beast,*
> *For they live most who cling to life the least*
> *And gain the most who give what they have won.*
> *Safety is for the slave, not for the free:*
> *So will I walk with danger, and with thee!*

Kenneth Boulding, *Sonnets on Courtship, Marriage and Family,* **1990**

Aging, Death, and Bereavement

...To preside over the disintegration of one's own body, looking on as sight and hearing, strength, speed, and short-term memory deteriorate, calls for a heroism that is no less impressive for being quiet and patient. To watch the same process taking place in someone whom one loves requires another kind of heroism, expressed in patience, devotion, and care...

Let Evening Come: Reflections on Aging, Mary C. Morrison, 1998

Approach old age with courage and hope. As far as possible, make arrangements for your care in good time, so that an undue burden does not fall on others. Although old age may bring increasing disability and loneliness, it can also bring serenity, detachment and wisdom....

Are you able to contemplate your death and the death of those closest to you? Accepting the fact of death, we are freed to live more fully.

paraphrased from *Philadelphia and the Jerseys Yearly Meeting, 1694–1695,* by Philadelphia Yearly Meeting, 1997

There are two different aspects of preparing for death; the first is preparing for one's own death, and the second is preparing for the death of another — whether a beloved friend, or even a stranger — preparing in such a way as to be of greatest comfort and support for those who mourn, including yourself.

Preparation for Death, a handbook by Tempe Monthly Meeting

Knowing how quickly many are removed by death, it is weightily recommended, that care be taken by each monthly meeting, that Friends who have estates to dispose of, be advised to make their wills in time of health, and strength of judgment, and therein to direct their substance as in justice and wisdom may be to their satisfaction and peace; laying aside all resentment, though occasion may have been given, lest it should go with them to the grave; remembering we all stand in need of mercy and forgiveness. Making such wills in due time can shorten no one's days, but the omission, or delay thereof to a time of sickness, when the mind should not be diverted from a solemn consideration of the approaching awful period of life, has often proved very injurious to many, and been the occasion of creating animosities in families, which the seasonable performance of this necessary duty might have effectually prevented. – 1691, 1703.

Friends are earnestly recommended to employ persons skilful in the law, and of good repute, to make their wills, as great inconvenience and loss, and sometimes the ruin of families have happened through the unskilfulness of some who have taken upon them to write wills, being unqualified to act in a matter of such importance. And all Friends who may become executors or administrators are advised to make a full, clear and perfect inventory of the estate and effects of the deceased, early after the interment, as many difficulties and disputes have arisen, and sometimes injustice been done for want of it, or by deferring it too long. – 1782, 1801

from "Wills," *The Rules of Discipline of Philadelphia Yearly Meeting,* from *The Old Discipline*

For I am sure that neither death, nor life, nor angels, nor principalities, nor things present, nor things to come, nor powers, nor height, nor depth, nor anything else in creation, will be able to separate us from the love of God in Christ Jesus our Lord.

Romans 8:38–39

Preparation for Death

The contemplation of our own death requires us to face and accept our mortality, grieve actively all our losses, and, through a review of our life, uncover and complete the unfinished business of forgiveness and reparation.

Death is no more than a turning of us over from time to eternity.

William Penn, 1693

I have arrived. I am at home in the here and in the now.
I am solid, I am free. In the infinite I dwell.

Thich Nhat Hanh, *Guide to Walking Meditation,* 1985

The catastrophic and devastating losses we suffer may occur at any time. We try to prepare ourselves in ways both practical and spiritual for what we know may come, yet we recognize that we cannot always foresee the time of their coming. Death may cut life short at any time. Not every danger can be foreseen. We do not expect accidents; nor the untimely loss of the young; nor even the death of those who knowingly place themselves at risk in war, in care of the diseased, or in other perilous situations. What we can do is foster an ever-present readiness in spirit for whatever may come.

Our Quaker experiences have, ideally, made us sensitive to the varieties of suffering that occur throughout life, and can, again ideally, help us make meaning of death and the diminishments that occur with aging. This sensitivity also allows us to release all that we love. Loss of independence—when we have to stop driving, leave our homes, or accept basic care for ourselves, for instance—strikes hard. Chronic pain or life-threatening illness challenges us utterly. Together, Friends may help us deal with many losses—our dreams and hopes, our mobility, our sight or hearing, our memory and mental acuity.

Spiritual preparation for death and loss is ongoing, modeled by wise elders and sometimes by children as well as in literature, music, and art. Much excellent material exists on preparation for death, dying, and bereavement, but the support of caring Friends is most valuable. A loving presence or practical offer of help matters more than eloquent words. Feelings of inadequacy should not keep us away from the dying and the bereaved.

Considering that the extraordinary medical advances of our time may sometimes extend life beyond our wishes, Friends are advised, as the end of life approaches, to consider ways of making their death their own. Worldly preparation for death includes legal and financial decisions such as wills, ethical wills, bequests, and powers of attorney for financial and health-care decisions. Couples, especially same-gender couples, who are not married in the eyes of the law are at special risk and need to take extra care that their legal papers reflect their wishes about end of life decision making and finances. Single people living alone may consider appointing a concerned Friend to look after and advocate for their interests and should make sure this person is aware of their wishes and knows the location of all relevant documents. Because death may come at any time, care should be taken by all adults, particularly those with children or those who place themselves at risk for conscience's sake, to make and communicate such decisions in a timely fashion. It is important that these decisions not be made under the influence of depression or chronic pain. Housing issues include how and when to move from independent to assisted living, to skilled nursing or home care, and finally to hospice. Friends may want to consider the choice between burial or cremation and may have joined a memorial society to preserve the most simplicity possible at the time of death. We may also wish to donate our bodies to research or our usable organs for reuse.

Bereavement

> *Blessed are they that mourn: for they shall be comforted.*
>
> *Matthew 5:4*

For ourselves, our own death is a transition; for those who love us, it is a deep loss.

In bereavement, give yourself time to grieve, recognizing that in some sense, grief for the loss of a loved one never ends. When others mourn, let your love embrace them.

It is important to realize that grief does not follow any particular pattern and that each person handles grief in his or her own way. The ways and the times grief manifests itself are often surprising. Support to the bereaved from individual Friends and the meeting may need to continue well beyond the initial period of bereavement. Bereaved children may need special attention and opportunities to express their grief — through art, journals, and special storybooks, for example.

Responsibility of Meetings to the Aging, the Dying, and the Bereaved

The monthly meeting Ministry and Oversight Committee or a special committee for Pastoral Care or specifically for Death and Bereavement may take on as appropriate these tasks in support of aging, dying, and bereaved Friends:

• Making the meeting space safe, comfortable, accessible, and with modifications for hearing and low vision.

- Providing for ongoing involvement in the meeting. Types of assistance may include rides to meeting, phone checks, visits, or occasional worship at their site.
- Discerning the need to revise or end the ill or aging person's level of meeting work.
- Coordinating visitation; helping with life tasks, financial aid, or transportation.
- Considering the formation of a Pastoral Care Committee if Ministry and Oversight Committee becomes overburdened.
- Providing support for the dying, the bereaved, or others in need, with referrals to qualified professionals as necessary. Clearness committees could also be provided for adult children of aging parents who may be resisting making the necessary decisions.
- Assisting with the planning and holding of a memorial meeting (see below).
- Holding ongoing or occasional worship sharing sessions or discussions on the topics of awareness of our mortality, the stages of grief, legal and financial matters, memorial societies, organ or body donation, and the many eventualities of end-of-life planning.[1]
- Adding to the meeting library any locally relevant legal materials and community resource lists as well as appropriate books on end of life and bereavement, including materials for children.
- Storing records of wills, last wishes, contacts, and other relevant information. Records clerks are often appointed by monthly meetings to annually update such records.[2]

Memorials

Friends usually hold a memorial meeting—a meeting for worship on the occasion of death—at a suitable time and place. In planning this event, the responsible committee consults the wishes of the family and those of the deceased Friend if these are on record. The memorial meeting is for those left behind and is encouraged.

A committee appointed by the meeting traditionally prepares, often in consultation with the bereaved, a memorial minute, separate from an obituary, which is customarily read at the memorial meeting. In addition to information from the obituary, the memorial minute might include such items as membership in meeting(s), work on committees or other activities within the Society of Friends, or use of

Quaker values in the wider community. If the family desires such assistance, a Friend, usually from the Ministry and Oversight Committee, notifies the local newspapers and distant friends and relatives of the time and place of the event. The meeting provides for the venue and adequate seating. It is usual for the clerk or other Friend to give a brief introduction explaining Quaker memorial customs, especially if the gathering includes many non-Friends. After all who wish to speak have spoken out of the silence and the memorial minute has been read, the meeting comes to a close and refreshments are served.

The memorial minute is sent promptly to the clerk of Intermountain Yearly Meeting for distribution and reading in the meeting for worship for memorials held during the yearly meeting session. It should also be forwarded to *Western Friend, Friends Journal,* and other such publications as seem appropriate. The memorial minute should also be sent to family members of the deceased Friend.

Monthly meetings may also hold occasional memorial meetings in which Friends speak about and honor all those for whom they grieve, and for all they have lost, both within and outside of their own circle of Friends.

---

[1] Some meetings have a handbook (see References section).

[2] See form, Appendix 7.

Advices and Queries

Introduction

A few years after its founding, The Religious Society of Friends realized that, to assess the health and progress of their Society, certain information was needed. Focused questions were formulated to gather that information. The first set of questions posed to each monthly meeting was as follows:

> *Which Friends in service to the Society, in their respective regions, departed this life since the last Yearly Meeting?*
> *Which Friends, imprisoned on account of their testimony, died in prison since the last Yearly Meeting?*
> *How, among Friends, did Truth advance since last Yearly Meeting and how do they fare in relation to peace and unity?*

By 1700, Friends had begun the practice of preparing written responses to these questions. The focused questions, now called queries, were expanded and designed to ensure consistency of conduct among Friends as well as to obtain information about the state of the Society. The first general advices were adopted in 1791; periodic revisions were made thereafter by the various yearly meetings.

As Friends became more involved in the public and social life of the times, queries and advices were developed regarding discipline, evangelical soundness, moral and spiritual instruction, social responsibility, and ministry. Advices and queries have represented a continuing exploration of our common faith and practice and continue to serve as a reminder of the insights of the Society.

Advices and queries help us see if we are living our faith in Truth. We must be honest with ourselves. Do we actively seek to act out that faith in our lives? At times, we may become disheartened when the ideal of following the Light seems impossibly demanding. Advices, however, help us stay the path, and the queries help us assess the rightness of our direction. Spiritual knowledge serves as a framework for our lives; advices and queries help with building that framework. Together, they remind us of the faith and principles held to be essential to the life and witness of the Religious Society of Friends. As members of the Religious Society of Friends, we commit ourselves not just to words but also to a way of life.

Intended for use by individuals as well as by monthly meetings, the advices and queries may serve the needs of Friends in several ways. Many meetings read and consider one or several of the queries, along with the related advices or other material, once a month during business meetings or in other forums. Meeting committees may find certain queries to be especially helpful in evaluating their activities. Meetings often publish the queries regularly in their newsletters. The advices and queries can also be the basis for a monthly meeting's annual state of the Society report.

For convenience, the advices and queries are divided into categories. Friends are reminded that each section is but a part of the whole. It is for the comfort and discomfort of Friends that we offer these advices and queries.

> *Watch how we live and you'll know what we believe.*
>
> saying from Iowa Conservative YM, reported by
> Deborah Fisch and Rebecca Henderson, circa 2002

Worship

> *One powerful way revelation occurs is in silent waiting, which can be described as the amazing fact of Quaker worship.*
>
> Elizabeth Bailey, circa 1999

Advices

1.   The heart of the Religious Society of Friends is the meeting for worship. It calls us to offer ourselves, body, mind, and soul, to wait in active anticipation for the revelation of the Spirit.

2.   It is in silence that we still our hearts and minds so that the Spirit of God may enter. This silencing, this waiting in expectancy, this listening for that which is deepest within—this is what Friends call worship. We seek a gathered stillness in our meetings for worship so that all may feel the power of God's love leading us and drawing us together.

3.   Worship is our response to an awareness of God. We can worship alone, but when we join with others in expectant waiting, we discover a deeper sense of the Presence. When we worship together in awareness that each of us is expecting communication with the Spirit, the power of a meeting for worship is magnified.

4.   When the meeting for worship has a central place in our lives, regular and punctual attendance occurs. When we arrive at meeting for worship on time, we help ourselves and others in the gathering wait upon the Spirit. Seeking the Spirit together, we may become aware of a willingness to give as well as to receive. Whether by speaking or by listening, each person contributes to and shares responsibility for the meeting's sense of worship. We thereby strengthen one another and refresh ourselves in the life of the Spirit.

5.   It is in the rhythm of waiting and listening throughout the meeting for worship that we are enabled to sense the Inward Light and to discern its leadings. When we become preoccupied or distracted in meeting, we need to let such restless thoughts give way to our awareness of the Light among us. By so doing, we prepare ourselves to tenderly receive vocal ministry. As we reach for the meaning deep within a message, we need to recognize that even though it may not be God's word for us, it may be so for others.

6.   Do not assume that vocal ministry is never to be your gift. Faithfulness and sincerity in speaking, even briefly, may open the way to fuller ministry from others. When prompted to speak, wait patiently to know that the leading and the time are right, but do not let a sense of your own unworthiness hold you back. Pray that your ministry may arise from the Spirit, and trust that words will be given to you. Speak clearly and simply, speaking neither predictably, at too great a length, nor too often. When children are present, bear in mind their understanding and experience. After a message has been given, Friends allow time to ponder and absorb its meaning before another speaks. It is important to maintain sensitivity to what is sacred.

7.   We deepen our contribution to communal worship when we open ourselves to the Light in our daily lives. Our spirits are enriched when nourished by means of various spiritual practices, and

we inevitably bring those benefits with us to the corporate meeting for worship.

8.   From the very beginning, a fundamental practice of Friends has been to assemble publicly for the purpose of worship held in expectant waiting for divine guidance. By worshiping together, we continue to demonstrate our belief in and dependence upon the Holy Spirit. It is important, therefore, that we attend meetings for worship seeking that Spirit that enables us to be fully aware of the divine power of God within as we find our way through the disillusionments and disturbances of the world. It may be helpful to remember that the Religious Society of Friends originated during times of great disturbances. Our belief is in the power of God to lead us out of the confusions of outward violence, inner conflicts, and all forms of willfulness.

Queries

1.   How do I prepare myself for worship? Do I set aside time during the week to strengthen my spirit? What is it that I bring to the meeting for worship?

2.   When in meeting for worship, do I clear my mind so that the Spirit has a place to enter? Do I wait in great expectancy for the Spirit to speak—through me or through another? Do I put my trust in the still small voice that I may hear?

3.   How do I discern the source of a leading? How do I know when to speak? Do I hold myself back when moved to speak, or do I trust in the Light to lead me? Am I careful not to speak at undue length or beyond my light? Am I aware of a sense of "rightness" after I speak?

4.   Does attendance at meeting for worship strengthen my spirit for the week ahead? What brings me back to center—back to my inner wisdom, home to myself—and how can I make that a regular practice?

5.   Are meetings for worship regularly held, and is each one of us faithful and punctual in attendance? How do we encourage attendance at meeting for worship? How do we greet newcomers so as to encourage their continued attendance?

6.   Do our meetings for worship give evidence that Friends come with hearts and minds prepared and open to the experience of God? How does the meeting help individuals and the group become gathered?

7.   Are we careful to ensure that we leave time between spoken messages so that they may be absorbed by those for whom they are intended? How do we encourage and foster the spiritual gifts of those who attend our meeting?

8.   Are our meetings for worship held in expectant waiting for divine guidance and openness to the Inner Light? Is there a living silence in which we feel drawn together by the power of God in our midst? In what ways do our meetings for worship provide a source of strength and guidance to those present?

Monthly Meeting

I always go to monthly meetings because if I don't, they usually end up doing some darn thing or other.
> Barney Aldrich, as remembered by Phyllis Hoge, 2002

For it is the corporate Truth or Light for which Friends labor together, not the proof or justification of the rightness of any particular position.
> Nancy Springer in
> *North Pacific Yearly Meeting Faith and Practice*, 1991

Advices

1.   Friends' way of conducting business is of central importance to the very existence of the monthly meeting. It is the Quaker way of living and working together; it is the way that creates and preserves a sense of fellowship in the meeting community. Friends must be mindful to conduct the business meeting as a meeting for worship with a concern for business. Those present help the meeting by exercising a spirit of wisdom, forbearance, and love. The right conduct of business meetings, even in routine matters, is a vital part of the worship experience. Individuals' submitting themselves to the corporate revelation of Truth forms the basis of Friends' approach to unity.

2.   All members are encouraged to attend meetings for business and to be faithful in the service of the meeting's affairs. Appointments of office holders and committee members are most successful when made with careful consideration of the qualifications of the nominees and of the opportunities for growth that may be afforded. This is especially important when considering young Friends. In our meetings for business and in all the duties connected with them, we are charged to make conscientious use of our gifts.

3.   In meetings for business, work and worship together with patience and warm affection for each other, aware of the peaceable spirit of the light of Truth. A majority decision or even consensus is not the goal. In waiting patiently for divine guidance, Friends' experience is that the way that leads to unity will open.

4.   Those who speak in meetings for business are advised to feel free to express their views but to refrain from pressing them unduly, avoiding contentiousness, obstinacy, and the urge to control. Seek the leadings of the Light and admit the possibility of error. A "third way" may be needed in order for Truth to emerge and a sense of the meeting to be reached.

5.   A deep and seeking silence can help reconcile seemingly opposing points of view. Be willing to wait upon God as long as may be necessary. By holding division and disruption in the Light, meetings may shift toward stronger and more creative solutions.

Queries

1.   Are our monthly meetings held in the spirit of a meeting for worship in which we, in love and mutual respect, seek divine guidance?

2.   How well do our meetings for business lead to a corporate search for and revelation of the Light?

3.   How effectively do members of the meeting temper and strengthen individuals' leadings?

4.   As difficult problems arise, are we careful to meet them in a spirit of love and humility with minds receptive to creative solu-

tions? Do we avoid pressure of time, neither unnecessarily prolonging nor unduly curtailing full discussion?

5.　　　Are we aware that we speak through inaction as well as action?

6.　　　Are we prepared to let go of our individual desires and let the Holy Spirit lead us to unity? Do we accept with grace a decision of the meeting with which we are not entirely in agreement?

Participation in the Life of the Meeting

There are varieties of Gifts, but the same Spirit. There are varieties of service, but the same Lord. There are many forms of work, but all of them, in all men, are the work of the same God. In each of us the Spirit is manifested in one particular way, for some useful purpose. One man, through the Spirit, has the gift of wise speech, while another, by the power of the same Spirit, can put the deepest knowledge into words. Another, by the same Spirit, is granted faith; another, by the one Spirit, gifts of healing, and another miraculous powers; another has the gift of prophecy, and another the ability to distinguish true spirits from false; yet another has the gift of ecstatic utterance of different kinds, and another the ability to interpret it. But all these gifts are the work of one and the same Spirit, distributing them separately to each individual at will.

1 Corinthians 12:4–11

We are the Monthly Meeting, the Regional Meeting, and Intermountain Yearly Meeting. Each functions best when each of us contributes what gifts we have…we cannot expect others to serve these to us.

Adapted from Ross Worley, 2003

Giving is not buying. God asks us to give because it is good for us, not because it is good for the person or cause to whom we give it.

Chris Viavant in Continuing Committee, IMYM, 2005

Advices

1.   The vitality of our meetings depends upon the many and varied gifts of those who take part in their activities. When each member and attender participates actively, the whole meeting is enriched. The Holy Spirit moves through us as we speak in meeting, care for one another, teach First Day school, work on committees, and testify to our lives in the Light. Each one of us has a responsibility for the financial support of the monthly meeting as well as for participation in the structure and function of its programs. When deciding whether to accept a service to which one is nominated, Friends are advised to understand the responsibilities required, to feel a leading to go forward, and to be willing to grow into the task. A meeting functions best when its members take their service to it seriously. Nominations are neither to be accepted, nor to be refused, casually.

2.   Our capabilities and possessions are not held as ends in themselves but are God's gifts entrusted to us. They are ours to share with others and to be used with humility, courtesy, and affection.

3.   In service to our meetings, we are to be careful to guard against contentiousness and the allure of power, and to be alert to the personalities and needs of others.

4.   We encourage those who attend our meetings to become acquainted with Friends' ways. When it is evident that the meeting has become a spiritual home for an individual, we encourage him or her to apply for membership.

5.   Those unable to attend meeting by reason of distance, infirmity, imprisonment, or other stresses are to be remembered and held in the Light. Visits to these Friends are encouraged.

6.   Friends show a loving consideration for all living things, cherishing the beauty and wonder of God's creation.

Queries

1.   What are we doing to recognize the varied skills and spiritual gifts of the members, attenders, and children among us? Are we

tender and loving toward those with gifts different from the commonplace?

2.   Does each of us take our right share of responsibility in work and service for the meeting? What gifts do we offer? What do we hold back from offering? What do we have tied up that God has need of?

3.   How welcoming is our meeting to newcomers? When attenders request information about Quakerism, what resources do we share with them to increase their knowledge?

4.   Are younger Friends, new members, and attenders encouraged to take part in committees and to attend meetings for business? Do we encourage their participation in the meeting's activities? Do we encourage them to pursue membership when they are ready?

5.   What are we doing as individuals and as a meeting to encourage the use of members' and attenders' gifts?

Mutual Care

The spiritual welfare of a meeting is greatly helped if its social life is vigorous and its members take a warm personal interest in one another's welfare. . . . It is our duty and privilege to share in one another's joys and sorrows.

Faith and Practice, London Yearly Meeting, 1960

Advices

1.   The Religious Society of Friends is a community of people who strive to care for one another. Friends are advised to maintain love and unity, to avoid tale-bearing and detraction, and to settle differences promptly in a manner free from resentment and inward violence. Live affectionately as friends, entering with sympathy into the joys and sorrows of one another's daily lives. Visit one another. Be ready to both give and receive help. Bear the burdens of one another's failings; delight in one another's strengths. Seek to know one another in the things that are eternal. Make the meeting a channel for God's love and forgiveness.

2.   Cherished friendships grow in depth of understanding and mutual respect. In close relationships there is a risk of finding pain as well as joy. Open yourself to the workings of the Light within when experiencing or witnessing great happiness or great hurt.

3.   Each of us has a particular experience of God, and each must find the way to be true to it. When another's words are strange or disturbing to you, seek to understand where they come from. Listen patiently and seek the truth that other people's thoughts may contain for you. Avoid hurtful criticism and provocative language. Be careful not to be too firm in your position; allow for the possibility that you may be mistaken.

4.   Different ways of understanding the Divine are present in Intermountain Yearly Meeting. It is important that these differences not be ignored for the sake of superficial agreement. When they are recognized and understood, a deeper and more vital unity can be reached. From the wide diversity among us we can broaden our awareness of the spirit flowing through and among us. We are reminded to refrain from applying our prejudices to the life journeys of others. Our community is maintained through faith and fellowship with each other as we wait in the Light for the unity that draws us together.

Queries

1.   Do we trust sufficiently the goodwill of our meeting members and attenders to make our needs and concerns known? Do we love one another as becomes the followers of the Light, even to the point of sharing one another's burdens? Do we care for one another so deeply that each other's needs are recognized and addressed? As members of a spiritual community, do we actively work to maintain love and unity?

2.   Is our meeting a loving, spirit-centered community in which each person is accepted and nurtured and strangers are welcome? In what ways do we incorporate people of different generations, members and attenders, and married and single adults into our community? On what occasions do we visit one another in our homes? How do we keep in touch with distant members?

3.   To what extent does our meeting ignore differences merely to avoid possible conflicts? When conflicts exist, are they discussed calmly and patiently in an attempt to arrive at a creative resolution? Does our meeting, in appropriate ways, counsel any member whose conduct or manner of living gives cause for concern? Are we charitable with each other, being careful not to sully the reputations of others?

4.   How well do we respect that of God in every person, even though the Spirit may be expressed in unfamiliar ways or be difficult to discern? In what ways do we welcome diversity of culture, language, and expressions of faith in our monthly meeting, yearly meeting, and the world community of Friends? Do we seek to gain from the range of rich heritages and spiritual insights that diversity presents?

Family

The bond that links your true family is not one of blood, but of respect and joy in each other's life.

Richard Bach, *Illusions*, 1977

Advices

1.   Ideally, a family is held together by emotional and spiritual ties. It is a precious and sometimes tenuous bonding of people that may arouse anguish as well as joy. A family unit is usually thought of as consisting of parents and children. But a family may include aging parents in need of care or persons not related by blood who are intimately connected with one's household. Families also include single parents and their children, couples without children, and couples (heterosexual or homosexual) living in committed relationships. For individuals living alone, including those who are single as a result of the death of, or divorce or separation from, a partner, the meeting may provide a sense of family.

2.   In our homes, we have the opportunity to practice living in a way that expresses the Quaker way of life. Irrespective of the type of family unit, the same opportunity exists — to nurture and cherish the seed of God. In the family setting, individuals can become aware of

the Spirit living in them and in the world. It is important that adults and children share the experiences they find precious—of people, books, art, music, drama, dance, poetry, and the Divine.

3. The meeting can nurture, but cannot replace, the family unit. Every member of a meeting is responsible in some measure for the care of families, both adults and children. In this environment of common concern, our families may gain a sense of belonging and commitment to the expanded family of Quakers and to our Quaker heritage.

Queries

1. Do we uphold Friends in their efforts to develop stable, loving relationships? Do we acknowledge and support all relationships that are based on love and commitment? Do we offer strength and comfort to the aging, the widowed, the separated or divorced, and others—including children—in families that have been affected by disruption or sorrow?

2. Does our home life nourish the need both for a sense of personal identity and for fully shared living? Are our homes places of friendliness, peace, and renewal, where the Light is real for those who live there and those who visit? Do we take care that our commitments outside the home do not encroach upon the time and loving attention the family needs for its health and well-being?

3. Is there a climate of trust in our meeting that invites all members and attenders to be open about individual and family lifestyles, including their satisfactions and problems? Does there exist in our meeting a sense of spiritual kinship for those who participate in it?

4. Are religious education offerings adequate to family members' needs? Do families support the First Day school through their children's regular attendance? Do adults in meeting help lead First Day school classes so that parents may attend meeting for worship?

Aging, Death, and Bereavement

Life, then, is a gift of time. For each of us the days are numbered. I am grateful for each day I have to walk this beautiful earth. And I do not fear the return to the earth, for I know . . . that it is part of myself.

Elizabeth Watson, *Guests of My Life*, 1979

Advices

1.   New opportunities present themselves at every stage of life. Approach the aging process with courage and hope. Honor that which you have been, welcoming new possibilities for wisdom, objectivity, and greater knowledge of the Spirit. Realize that as time passes, new ways of receiving and reflecting God's love will open.

2.   Inspect your finances while you are in good health, making whatever provisions are needed for the settlement of your affairs. Consider the value of a living will and other documents that express your wishes for your end of life. Make sure that those dear to you are well informed, so that you and they are freed to live more fully. Friends are advised to review these documents annually.

3.   Aging may bring increased disability and loneliness, so care for yourself tenderly, being aware that exercise, nutrition, and medical care are important. Determine who will help you should a need arise, and make arrangements for your care such that undue burdens do not fall on any one person.

4.   Tragedies can occur at any time in our lives; death does not always announce itself. Friends of any age can prepare themselves for the loss of a dear one. It is as important to prepare for the end of our life as it is to prepare for other important events. Bookstores are filled with books that describe stages of life, death, and dying. It is helpful to know what lies ahead and to be ready for it.

5.   Children's grief is frequently unseen. We need to be mindful that their sorrow is as real as adults' sorrow and needs to be equally expressed and accepted. Other losses, such as that of a beloved pet, impart sorrow as well. Friends must be careful not to minimize the extent of heartache that such losses cause. The meeting can be especially helpful to children when their parents are also grieving.

6.   Meetings need to let members and attenders know whom to contact in time of serious illness or death. It is useful for Meetings to have information available on the laws of their state regarding burials and cremation as well as which funeral homes and cemeteries are sympathetic to Friends' wishes for simplicity.

Queries

1.   Are we aware of those in our meeting who endure tragedy or loss? Do we seek to understand their needs and to comfort them? Do we, in loving concern, extend assistance to those who require it?

2.   Have I prepared for my own death and for the deaths of those I love with the same care as for other events in my life? Have I learned what I can about the aging and dying process? If not, what prevents me from learning about these topics? Do I fully discuss and share this information within my family?

3.   Are my personal papers and finances up to date and in good order? Have documents been prepared that will help those I love in the event of my serious illness or death: a will, a living will, powers of attorney, and a description of the type of care I desire in the case of a serious, debilitating event or illness? Have I discussed these matters with those close to me?

4.   Should my vision, hearing, balance, or thought processes deteriorate, what steps will I take to prevent having an accident? When will I be willing to relinquish my car keys?

5.   How can the meeting help me find clearness about the difficult questions surrounding aging and dying? Do I know whom to contact when I am in need of spiritual support or material assistance? What am I willing to ask of the meeting? Am I willing to accept what the meeting has to give?

Religious Education

When we find ourselves teaching . . . can we draw upon that respect for one another and faith in one another's potential that will enable the other to feel taller and more capable? At Rufus Jones's memorial meeting, one of his students simply said: "He lit my candle." That is a high aim for us all to aspire to in educating ourselves and our young people.

Barbara Windle, 1988

in *Quaker Faith & Practice of Britain Yearly Meeting,* 1993

Advices

1.   The Bible and other religious literature is the rightful heritage of us all. The study of sacred books expands and deepens our awareness of our own spiritual heritage and that of others. What we read means little unless it helps us understand our own personal religious experience, the work of the Spirit behind the words. It helps to know that our search for truth can include a multitude of experiences.

2.   It is essential that children be taught the meaning of silence and vocal ministry in meeting, and the history of the Religious Society of Friends. Knowledge of our testimonies and their evolution is equally important to their religious education. Work camps, community activities, and opportunities to serve others enhance their experience. We must be gentle and respectful as our children seek their own spiritual truths, appreciating whatever insights they bring to us.

3.   All adults in meeting can benefit from religious education in the form of Quaker Studies programs, spiritual formation groups, prayer groups, worship-sharing groups, or adult First Day school classes. Like a garden, the spirit within must be tended and nurtured. The meeting is enriched when all those participating care for their own spirits.

Queries

1.   In what ways does our meeting help develop the spiritual lives of our children and adult members and attenders? Do we provide our children and young adults with a framework for active, ongoing participation in meeting? Do we welcome their presence among us?

2.　　How does our meeting educate its members of all ages about the Bible, other sacred writings, our Christian heritage, and the history and principles of Friends?

3.　　Do we encourage our children to participate actively in meetings for worship and meetings for business? Are they aware of the meaning of membership in the meeting and the importance of service to the community?

4.　　How do we share our deepest beliefs with our children and with one another? What inspires us to develop our spiritual and religious life?

Integrity

The Inner Light does not lead men to do that which is right in their own eyes, but that which is right in God's eyes.

Ellen S. Bosanquet, 1927
in *Quaker Faith & Practice of Britain Yearly Meeting,* 1995

Nor do men light a lamp and put it under a bushel, but on a stand, and it gives light to all in the house. Let your light so shine before men, that they may see your good works.

Matthew 5:15–16, RSV

Advices

1.　　Our witness to the world comes from our perception of the Divine Spirit moving through us. The reliability of our words, essential to all communication between one person and another and between one person and God, has always been important to Friends. Friends profess a genuineness of life and speech that leaves no room for deceit or artificiality. Throughout our history, therefore, we have borne witness against judicial oaths as suggesting a double standard of truth. Devotion to what is true and eternal requires openness, honesty, and careful speech in social, business, and family relationships. As early Friends took care to avoid flattering titles and phrases, modern Friends need to discourage the insincerities and extravagances prevalent in our society. It is also advisable to avoid hurtful criticism and provocative language. With courtesy and kindness, Friends are called to speak the truth, in love.

2.   As Friends, we must not waver in making our faith evident, in words or deeds. Recognizing the oneness of humanity in God, we affirm fellowship with all people. The various experiences of those whose circumstances differ from our own can help us discover what is true in our lives and can lead us into a more honest kinship. In our dealings with others, humility and a willingness to learn help us transcend differences. When in discussion with others, we must not allow the strength of our convictions to betray us into making misleading or contentious statements.

3.   Our witness is most effective when we are in touch with the Spirit within. Each of us has a particular experience of God; each must find the ways to be true to it. There are times when we may need to remember that the truth is greater than the knowledge any one of us has of it. God did not put all the fruit on one tree.

4.   Bear witness to the humanity of all people, including those who break society's conventions or laws. Seek to understand the causes of injustice, social unrest, and fear. As members of the Religious Society of Friends, we commit ourselves not to words, but to a way of life.

5.   Friends keep to the simplicity of truth, discerning its manifestations through prayer, reading, the arts, and all experiences of daily life. In accepting guidance as to what is true and eternal, we are required to be open, honest, and careful of speech and actions in all situations.

Queries

1.   Do we keep to a single standard of truth? Are we punctual in keeping promises, prompt in the payment of debts, and just and honorable in all our dealings? Do we exercise moderation and honesty in our speech, our manner of living, and our daily work?

2.   How are we prepared, both as individuals and as a meeting, to resist pressure to lower our standard of integrity?

3.   How do I strive to maintain the integrity of my inner and outer lives—in my spiritual journey, my work, and my family responsibilities?

4.   In what ways do we cooperate with persons and groups who share our beliefs and concerns? How does our connection to the Spirit inspire and challenge us?

5.   Do we search diligently for ways to assure the right of every individual to be loved, cared for, educated appropriately; to obtain useful employment; and to live in dignity?

6.   When the meeting receives multiple requests for funds or action, how do we determine which are most pressing?

7.   What are we doing individually and corporately to share the experience of our faith? Do we let others know about the source of our convictions? What are we doing to make the larger community aware of our Friends meeting?

Peace

> *A good end cannot sanctify evil means; nor must we ever do evil, that good may come of it. . . . It is as great presumption to send our passion upon God's errands, as it is to palliate them with God's name. . . . We are too ready to retaliate, rather than forgive, or gain by love and information. And yet we could hurt no man that we believe loves us. Let us then try what Love will do: for if men did once see we love them, we should soon find they would not harm us. Force may subdue, but Love gains: and he that forgives first, wins the laurel.*

> William Penn, 1693,
> in *Quaker Faith & Practice of Britain Yearly Meeting*, 24.03

Advices

1.   We affirm that our first allegiance is to our experience of the Divine. If this conflicts with any compulsion of the state, our country is served best when we remain true to our higher loyalty. Over the centuries, Friends have valued their part in shaping the laws of our country so as to achieve a more just and evenly balanced social or-

der. The peace testimony of the Religious Society of Friends is a positive expression of goodwill in human relationships, not just a negative statement calling us to abstain from all that leads to war.

2. As Friends, we are urged to identify the seeds of war within ourselves individually and in our way of life. Any element of fear, restlessness, discontent, unhappiness, and poverty of spirit can lead to violence and war. We are cautioned not to bury these feelings, but to acknowledge their presence, pinpoint their sources, and transform pain and anger into the power of positive action. Thus, we heal ourselves and become free and able stewards in the healing of others.

3. When working toward peace in the broader community and wider world, we look to change the conditions that spark violence in others—poverty, despair, fear, hopelessness, dehumanization, and hunger, among others. We return to our roots in the truth to establish secure conditions where cooperation, equality, justice, and freedom can flourish. We work toward improving the environment and toward right sharing of the world's resources.

4. We refuse to join in actions that denigrate others or lead to their victimization. Friends are also advised not to join in actions that lead to destruction and death. We actively seek ways to strengthen the bonds of unity, refusing to participate in conduct that makes for war. We teach our children that it is possible to overcome evil with good, to love the persecutor, and to find alternative ways to resolve conflict.

5. Friends actively support movements that substitute teamwork and justice for coercion and dishonesty, encouraging all efforts to overcome prejudices based on race, nationality, class, and other characteristics. Friends are encouraged to use and teach nonviolent communication.

6. Our responsibilities to God and our neighbor may lead us to take unpopular stands. In carrying out principled decisions and actions, we may struggle against the desire to be sociable, the fear of seeming different or peculiar, or the fear of possible consequences.

7. If, by divine leading, we focus on a law contrary to our perception of divine law, we proceed with care. It is important to seek

clearness before taking action. Consultation with other Friends helps us consider the views of those who might be affected by our decision and see more clearly what actions are needed. When clarity is reached, we act with conviction. If our decision involves disobedience of the law, we make the grounds for our action clear to all concerned. If there are penalties, we face them without evasion. When a meeting supports a member's leading to engage in civil disobedience, the meeting has an obligation to assist the member in dealing with the consequences.

Queries

1.   Do we live in the awareness of the presence of God? How do we center ourselves and practice living in unity with the Spirit? Does our meeting help individuals find such unity?

2.   To what extent is our personal life in accord with Friends' principles? Do we "live in the virtue of that life and power that takes away the occasion of all wars"? How would others recognize that? Where there is animosity, division, and conflict, do we facilitate healing and reconciliation? Do we care for our own health so that we are more able to help others care for theirs? Does the meeting support us in this work?

3.   When those among us disclose opinions that differ greatly from our own, are we able to listen to them without judgment or derision? Are we able to support tenderly those whose views differ from our own, knowing that the Light shines in them also? When unpopular or even illegal stands are taken by Friends, are these held in the Light for discernment by the meeting?

Equality

Then that little man in black there, he says women can't have as much rights as men, 'cause Christ wasn't a woman! Where did your Christ come from? Where did your Christ come from? From God and a woman! Man had nothing to do with Him.

Sojourner Truth, 1851

Until we as a Religious Society begin to question our assumptions, until we look at the prejudices, often very deeply hidden, within our own society, how are we going to be able to confront the inequalities within the wider society?

Susan Rooke-Matthews, 1993
in *Quaker Faith & Practice of Britain Yearly Meeting,* 1993

Advices

1.   Since the time of George Fox, Friends have believed that all people are spiritually equal before God. Believing that, it is important that Friends everywhere question the prejudices (often deeply hidden) within the Religious Society of Friends and challenge the assumptions we make about others. In the past, Quakers helped foment vast societal changes by challenging the oppression they saw. Today our voices do not ring as loudly nor are they as unified when we confront oppression and inequality. For example, we are deeply divided among ourselves regarding same-gender marriage.

2.   Friends need to be mindful that continual reflection is required to recognize that our race, gender, nationality or economic status may grant us privileges which separate us from those different from us. At the same time, those among us who do not have such privileges must be careful not to empower that sense of privilege by acknowledging the inequality.

3.   Friends must bear in mind that any perceived inequality gets in the way of relating to that of God in one another.

Queries

1.   Do we believe that God speaks to us through others? Do we look for and recognize "that of God" in all others? Do we love our neighbor as ourselves? Do we value diversity and acknowledge the enrichment that comes from sharing differences? How do we encourage those we know to consider people as individuals rather than as stereotypes?

2.   Do we work individually and as a meeting to bring about a just and compassionate society that allows all people to develop their capacities and fosters their desire to serve? Are we alert to prac-

tices in our own country and throughout the world that discriminate against people on the basis of who or what they are or what they believe? What are we doing as individuals and as a meeting to promote equal social and economic opportunity for those who suffer discrimination for any reason whatsoever?

3.   Do we take the risks that right action demands?

Simplicity

The rush and pressure of modern life are a form, perhaps the most common form, of its innate violence. To allow oneself to be carried away by a multitude of conflicting concerns, to commit oneself to too many projects, to want to help everyone with everything is to succumb to violence. More than that, it is cooperation with violence. The frenzy of the activist neutralizes his or her work for peace. It destroys her or his capacity for peace. It destroys the fruitfulness of the work because it kills the root of inner wisdom, which makes the work fruitful.

Thomas Merton, in *Letter to a Young Activist*, 1960s

Advices

1.   Ever-expanding knowledge, communication, and technology have made the world far more complex than it was for early Friends. What may be simple for one is problematic for another. We believe in the wholeness of the Spirit, a Spirit that knows and comprehends all things, simple and complex. As we wrestle with the demands of society, we would do well to be aware that expressions of simplicity vary considerably and not to judge those whose expressions differ from ours.

2.   It is important to ensure that our lives are not so full that we lose sight of the Light within. By consulting the Light, we are able to discern whether to take up or turn down responsibilities without indulging our pride or our guilt. We are advised to consider our capabilities and possessions not as ends in themselves but as God's gifts entrusted to us. We are to share them with others, using them with humility, courtesy, and affection.

3.   Friends are advised to distinguish between ways to happiness offered by society that are truly fulfilling and those that are potentially corrupting and destructive. We are responsible for the manner in which we acquire, use, and dispose of our possessions. This does not mean our lives are to be poor and bare, destitute of joy and beauty. Do not be persuaded into buying what you do not need or cannot afford. All that promotes fullness of life and aids in service for God is to be accepted with thanksgiving. A simple lifestyle freely chosen is a source of strength. Each person must determine, based on the Light given to them, what promotes and what hinders their search for truth.

4.   From early days, Friends have deplored and avoided the gambling spirit that permeates our society—in finance and commerce, sports and recreation, for example. It is best to refrain from hazardous speculation and from engaging in business that may be questionable. Such indulgence has caused the material ruin of many, as well as dwarfing their moral and spiritual lives. It is advised that our recreations not become occasions for self-centeredness and that we avoid amusements that debase the emotions by playing upon them.

5.   We are advised to be aware of and to take a stand against the great waste of human and economic resources resulting from all forms of addiction, knowing that they lead to self-absorption and to forgetfulness that each person's humanity is shared by all persons. It is the experience of Friends that feelings of emptiness and a failure to listen for the voice of God can lead to addiction. In addition to self-destructive behavior such as drunk driving, addiction is commonly associated with outwardly destructive acts such as domestic violence and child abuse. Friends are reminded that being a Quaker is no absolute defense against having these problems. We must be ready as a community to intervene when necessary. When our lives are filled with the Spirit, there is no need to indulge in excessive and addictive use of tobacco, alcohol, or other drugs, or to engage in gambling and other addictive behaviors. Let us remember to live and work in the spirit of a true follower of the Light.

6.　　In our daily work, let us avoid involvements and entanglements that separate us from each other and from God. In the context of our complex lives, let us strive to maintain our ideals of sincerity and simplicity, to keep before us the essential truths, and to measure our lives by those truths. Be diligent in seeking the faith that is the foundation for the inner peace that holds firm in the face of outward confusion.

Queries

1　　Is the life of our meeting ordered so as to help us simplify our personal lives? Does the meeting help us center ourselves in the awareness of the presence of God so that all things take their rightful place?

2.　　Do we structure our days so as to provide space to nourish our spiritual growth? Do we center our lives in the awareness of the presence of God so that all things take their rightful place? Does our way of life nourish our spiritual growth and that of our families? In our daily lives, are we aware of pressures that separate us from each other and from the Divine?

3.　　Do we avoid commitments beyond our strength and Light as well as a clutter of multiple activities? Are we careful how we choose to use our time and energy?

4.　　Do we choose recreations that strengthen our physical, mental, and spiritual lives and avoid those that may prove harmful to ourselves and others?

5.　　In our relations with those who have problems with addiction to a substance or a behavior, are we careful to be guided by compassion for the individual rather than by others' opinions or attitudes?

Stewardship

> *Quakers often talk about being led. . . . We are all led. The question is not whether we are led, but what leads us.*
>
> Robert Griswold, 2005

In the biblical tradition, the foundation for human governance is stewardship rather than ownership; we care for life's homeplace as servants, not as the lords of the earth.

Jim Corbett, *Sanctuary for All Life*, 2005

Advices

1.   We must be grateful for all that we have, neither reveling in our own gifts nor coveting those of others.

2.   The principle of stewardship applies to all that we are given and to who we are as individuals, members of groups, and inhabitants of the earth. We are each obliged to use our time, abilities, strength, money, material possessions, and other resources in a spirit of love, aware that we hold these gifts in trust and that we are responsible for using them wisely. We need to be aware of pollution, overpopulation, and all forms of wastefulness.

3.   As Friends, and as members of other groups, we seek to apply the same spirit to the use and contribution of our corporate resources. We are obliged to cherish the earth and to walk gently upon it, recognizing that it is not ours to own or to dispose of at will. We are to protect all its resources in a spirit of humble stewardship, committed to the right sharing of these resources among all peoples and creatures of the world.

Queries

1.   Do we regard our time, talents, energy, money, material possessions, and other resources as gifts from God, to be held in trust and shared according to the Light we are given? How do we witness to this conviction in our lives? Do we investigate the companies in which our money is invested, avoiding investing in those whose practices undermine Quaker testimonies and values?

2.   Do we practice and encourage thoughtful family planning? What are we doing to ensure adequate water, food, shelter, education, and respect for those who do not have ready access to these blessings? Are we informed about the effects of our lifestyle on the global economy and the environment?

Harmony with Nature

A holistic or hallowing way of life doesn't grow out of right views. It is born from life in the land rather than ecology; only those who live by fitting into the land can learn to fit into the land harmoniously.

Jim Corbett, *Sanctuary for All Life*, 2005

The environmental crisis is at root a spiritual and religious crisis; we are called to look again at the real purpose of being on this earth.

London Yearly Meeting, 1988
in *Quaker Faith & Practice of Britain Yearly Meeting,* 1993, 25.02

Our concern for peace and the environment arises from the recognition of the sacredness of all creation and the presence of the Divine in each person. We are called to embrace, cherish, and protect all of creation.

Genie Durland, 2006

The produce of the earth is a gift from our gracious creator to the inhabitants, and to impoverish the earth now to support outward greatness appears to be an injury to the succeeding age.

John Woolman, 1772
in *Quaker Faith & Practice of Britain Yearly Meeting,* 25.01

Advices

1.   Implicit in our testimony on simplicity is an understanding that we will not take more than we need — particularly if it means depriving others, including future generations, of their basic needs.

2.   The earth is not in bondage to us nor are its riches ours to dispose of at will. We recognize that we are part of the natural world. Humankind is not a species to which all of creation is subservient. Rather, it is one of many interrelated and interdependent facets of a creation more vast than human understanding can grasp.

3.   Part of understanding one's place in the world is forming right relationships with things. Such relationships are as much a consequence of observation as they are the product of activity. Let us exercise our power over nature responsibly, with due reverence for

life. Let us strive to show loving consideration for all creation and seek to enhance the beauty and variety that surrounds us.

4.		Truth is revealed in diversity if we give way for its expression. Rejoice in the splendor of the earth's continuing creation, for it is that of God speaking.

Queries

1.		How do we inform ourselves about how our style of living affects the global economy and the environment?

2.		How do we exercise our respect for the balance of nature? Are we careful to avoid poisoning the earth, the air, and the water? Do we use the world's resources with care and consideration for future generations and with respect for all life? Do we recycle all that we can?

3.		How do we encourage environmental responsibility within our community?

4.		How do we live in accord with our sense of God in all creation?

Service

> Is this not what I require of you as a fast:
> > to loose the fetters of injustice,
> > to untie the knots of the yoke,
> > to snap every yoke and set free those that have been crushed?
> Is it not sharing your food with the hungry,
> > taking the homeless into your house,
> > clothing the naked when you meet them,
> > and never evading a duty to your kinfolk?
> Then shall your light break forth like the dawn
> > and soon you will grow healthy like a wound newly healed;
> your own righteousness shall be your vanguard,
> > and the glory of the Lord your rear guard.
> Then if you call, the Lord will answer.
> If you call to him, he will say, "Here I am."
>
> *Isaiah 58:6–9 (NEB)*

We recognize a variety of ministries. In our worship these include those who speak under the guidance of the Spirit and those who receive and uphold the work of the Spirit in silence and prayer. We also recognise as ministry service on our many committees, hospitality and childcare, the care of finance and premises, and many other tasks. We value those whose ministry is not in an appointed task but is in teaching, counseling, listening, prayer, enabling the service of others, or other service in the meeting or the world. The purpose of all our ministry is to lead us and other people into closer communion with God and to enable us to carry out those tasks which the Spirit lays upon us.

London Yearly Meeting, 1986
in *Faith & Practice of Philadelphia Yearly Meeting*

Advices

1.   The Religious Society of Friends challenges each of us to live a life reflective of our beliefs. We take our faith into the broader community in many ways. Some are led to do acts in full view of society; others are led to work where their service is less visible but no less valuable. Each of us holds a part of the whole. None of us could consistently do what we do, no matter how little, without drawing from the well of our faith. Among us all, we make a greater impact than we may realize as individuals.

2.   Quaker service springs from our deepest convictions and is the natural expression of our beliefs in justice, equality, and community. Our service may lead us to practice a profession in which we serve others; numerous opportunities exist for those of us whose professions are not directly service related. We can work with integrity on school boards and in community associations; we may influence our families and friends to examine their consumption of natural resources and to find various ways to recycle more fully; we may help rebuild devastated homes or lives; we may soothe and comfort those with wounded souls. It is important to discern whether our service is inspired and led by the Spirit so that we do not take on tasks beyond our strength or capabilities. By ever returning to the Light within, we can trust we will find ways in which we can...

be patterns, be examples in all countries, places, islands, nations, wherever you come, that your carriage and life may preach among all sorts of people, and to them; then you will come to walk cheerfully over the world, answering that of God in everyone.

George Fox, Journal, 1656

Queries

1. In what ways does your life reflect your faith? In what ways does your faith illuminate your life?

2. How do you distinguish between the leadings of the Divine and the pressures of the needy?

3. Do you give sufficient time to sharing with others in the meeting, both newcomers and long-time members, your understanding of service and commitment to Quaker witness?

4. Mindful that the light leads us in different ways, how do you demonstrate your respect for others' modes of service?

III. Friends Speak

Introduction

Without a divinely ordained authority beyond the Inward Light, Friends have always valued the meaningful experiences of those who share our journey. This chapter contains a small selection of Friends' words—from vocal ministry, journals, articles, letters, and comments heard and overheard—to show some of the depth and breadth of Friends' experiences and insights.

Friends' Experiences

1.01   As I had forsaken all the priests, so I left the separate preachers also, and those called the most-experienced people. For I saw there was none among them all that could speak to my condition. And when all my hopes in them and in all men were gone, so that I had nothing outwardly to help me, nor could tell what to do, then, oh then, I heard a voice which said "There is one, even Christ Jesus, that can speak to thy condition," and, when I heard it, my heart did leap for joy. Then the Lord did let *me* see why there was none upon the earth that could speak to my condition, namely, that I might give him all the glory. For all are concluded under sin and shut up in unbelief, as I had been, that Jesus Christ might have the preeminence, who enlightens, and gives grace and faith and power. Thus, when God doth work, who shall let it? And this I knew experimentally.

George Fox, 1647

1.02   At last after all my distresses, wanderings and sore travels, I met with some writings of this people called Quakers, which I cast a slight eye upon and disdained, as falling very short of that wisdom, light, life and power, which I had been longing for and searching after. . . . After a long time, I was invited to hear one of them. . . . When I came, I felt the presence and power of the Most High among them, and words of truth from the Spirit of truth reaching to my heart and conscience, opening my state as in the presence of the Lord. Yes, I did not only feel words and demonstrations from without, but I felt the dead quickened, the seed raised; insomuch as my heart, in the certainty of light and clearness of true sense, said: "This is he; this is he; there is no other; this is he whom I have waited for and sought after from my childhood, who was always near me, and had often begotten life in my heart, but I knew him not distinctly nor how to receive him, or dwell with him."

But some may desire to know what I have at last met with. I answer, "I have met with the Seed." Understand that word, and thou wilt be satisfied and inquire no further. I have met with my God, I have met with my Saviour, and he hath not been present with me without his Salvation, but I have felt the healings drop upon my soul from under his wings.

Isaac Penington, 1667

1.03   Not by strength of arguments or by a particular disquisition of each doctrine and convincement of my understanding thereby, came I to receive and bear witness of the Truth, but by being secretly reached by the Life. For when I came into the silent assemblies of God's people, I felt a secret power among them which touched my heart; and as I gave way unto it I found the evil weakening in me and the good raised up and so I became thus knit and united unto them, hungering more and more after the increase of this power and life, whereby I might feel myself perfectly redeemed.

Robert Barclay, 1676

1.04   Whenever we are driven into the depths of our own being, or seek them of our own will, we are faced by a tremendous contrast. On the one side we recognize the pathetic littleness of ephemeral existence, with no point or meaning in itself. On the other side, in the depth, there is something eternal and infinite in which our existence, and indeed all existence, is grounded. This experience of the depths of existence fills us with a sense both of reverence and of responsibility, which gives even to our finite lives a meaning and a power which they do not possess in themselves. This, I am assured, is our human experience of God.

John MacMurray, 1967

1.05   There is indeed One that speaks to my condition, but that One may not announce a name, or even speak a word; it may reveal itself as Light, or inner peace, or compassion for humanity. But whatever its manifestation, there is only One. If that One is perceived as a King, then that is a true perception; if it is perceived as a Mother, then that is also a true perception. If I call God "Holy Mother" and you call God "Divine King," does that mean there are two Gods? No, there is only One.

That of God within every person is sometimes recognized as the Spirit of Christ, or the Holy Spirit, or the Inner Light. As Friends we accept and respect that Spirit, however perceived, in all people, and particularly in each other. We can give testimony to our own experience, as honestly and faithfully as possible, but we cannot alter another's spiritual condition. Let us receive Light as it is given to us, and share it as we are able, and trust in the One that can speak to the condition of all people, to care for and guide us all.

Helen Park, 1979

1.06   When we turn inside or beyond ourselves to grasp some understanding of the divine, we discover through encounter that what we need to find we will find: a something creative and renewing, overwhelmingly strong and passive, completely wise and innocent, living and dying, feminine and masculine.

Our father, our mother, our light, which is in heaven and earth, holy is your name. Come.

Patrice Haan, 1983

1.07   I am just now beginning to feel comfortable with the realization of a Feminine Spirit as a personal presence. I will continue to work toward centering in Worship, to be open to the Light, its peace and comfort, and maybe then, its message through her voice. I do not search for her. I just know her as the source of my Light.

Molly Barnett, 1983

1.08   Around the age of seven I decided that what I wanted to be when I grew up was a saint. That didn't work out. I gave it my best shot at the time, but I lacked staying power.

Some years later, when I was eleven, there were several months when I thought I'd like to be a nun, in the belief that what the job required was good works, a predisposition to meditativeness, and a willingness to be isolated from the real world. I was wrong, of course, and it was just as well that that didn't work out either. I may have had what my loved father called "the necessary sap," but I wasn't a Roman Catholic, to begin with, and, more important, I lacked vocation.

I did, however, sense a spirit in things, in literal, tangible things, as well as in places, in houses, in people, trees, flowers, animals. When I felt its presence in the sky, in the stars, I called this spirit God. Even in the worst of times I never lost this feeling of Something Other. Moreover, those early personality traits, obscurely religious, persisted, and to this day I describe myself, roughly speaking, as a religious person.

Consciousness of the spiritual, of God — whatever that means — is at the heart of who I am. Yet I appear to myself and quite probably to those who know me as an ordinary, daily sort of person, as mundane, as worldly, as anyone else, living a life made up of bills, telephone calls, computers, car-washes, work, food, laundry and so on. Yet my life is aware of a spirit in things. But hardly ever do I so much as mention it.

The same is true for a very great number of people, and it is very likely that many whose characters are similarly constructed go through their days and nights whispering "Thank You," or "I need help," or "Please" — prayers, in short, to whatever is out there listening, holding the world together, binding the stars. As a consequence of this obscure sense of spirit, my life seems rich to me.

I seldom speak of it. I certainly do not mention God's name, whatever that may be, except in the context of mild swearing. But the sense of a spirit in things is what keeps me alive. I suspect such a recognition is common. I suspect many do not speak of what they deeply recognize as faith.

I believe that many lives as ordinary as my own are founded in a sense of the spirit. I believe that faith, consciousness of the unseen

Other, works constantly in ordinary lives like mine in a wonderful and mysterious way. Even though no one but the one who knows such faith may feel its power, I believe that in those who are silent faith may be profound and strong, may be the very force which brings about miracles of light.

Phyllis Hoge, 2005

1.09   There is a spirit which I feel that delights to do no evil nor to revenge any wrong, but delights to endure all things, in hope to enjoy its own in the end. Its hope is to outlive all wrath and contention, and to weary out all exaltation and cruelty, or whatever is of a nature contrary to itself. It sees to the end of all temptations. As it bears no evil in itself, so it conceives none in thoughts to any other. If it is betrayed, it bears it, for its ground and spring is the mercies and forgiveness of God. Its crown is meekness, its life is everlasting love unfeigned; and takes its kingdom with entreaty and not with contention, and keeps it by lowliness of mind. In God alone it can rejoice, though none else regard it, or can own its life. It's conceived in sorrow, and brought forth without any to pity it, nor doth it murmur at grief and oppression. It never rejoiceth but through sufferings; for with the world's joy it is murdered. I found it alone, being forsaken. I have fellowship therein with them who lived in dens and desolate places in the earth, who through death obtained this resurrection and eternal life.

James Nayler, 1660

1.10   Conscience follows the judgment, doth not inform it; but this light as it is received, removes the blindness of the judgment, opens the understanding, and rectifies both the judgment and the conscience. The conscience is an excellent thing where it is rightly informed and enlightened; wherefore some of us have fitly compared it to the lantern, and the light of Christ to the candle; a lantern is useful, when a clear candle burns and shines in it, but otherwise of no use. To the light of Christ then in the conscience, and not to man's natural conscience, it is that we continually commend men.

Robert Barclay, 1676

1.11   That which the people called Quakers lay down as a main fundamental in religion is this, that God through Christ hath placed a principle in every man to inform him of his duty, and to enable him to do it; and that those that live up to this principle are the people of God, and those that live in disobedience to it are not God's people, whatever name they may bear or profession they may make of religion. This is their ancient, first, and standing testimony. With this they began, and this they bore and do bear to the world.

William Penn, 1693

1.12   The unity of Christians never did nor ever will or can stand in uniformity of thought and opinion, but in Christian love only.

Thomas Story, 1737

1.13   In the love of money and in the wisdom of this world, business is proposed, then the urgency of affairs push forward, nor can the mind in this state discern the good and perfect will of God concerning us. The love of God as manifested is graciously calling us to come out of that which stands in confusion; but if we bow not in the name of Jesus, if we give not up those prospects of gain which in the wisdom of this world are open before us, but say in our hearts, "I must needs go on, and in going on I hope to keep as near to the purity of Truth as the business before me will admit of," here the mind remains entangled and the shining of the light of life into the soul is obstructed.

John Woolman, 1772

1.14   There is a principle which is pure, placed in the human mind, which in different places and ages hath had different names. It is, however, pure and proceeds from God. It is deep and inward, confined to no forms of religion, nor excluded from any, where the heart stands in perfect sincerity. In whomsoever this takes root and grows, of what nation soever, they become brethren in the best sense of the expression.

John Woolman, 1774

1.15   They fail to read clearly the signs of the times who do not see that the hour is coming when, under the searching eye of philosophy and the terrible analysis of science, the letter and the outward evidence will not altogether avail us; when the surest dependence must be on the light of Christ within, disclosing the law and the prophets in our own souls, and confirming the truth of outward Scripture by inward experience.

John Greenleaf Whittier, 1870

1.16   While seeking to interpret our Christian faith in the language of today, we must remember that there is one worse thing than failure to practice what we profess, and that is to water down our profession to match our practice.

Friends World Conference, 1952

1.17   The best type of religion is one in which the mystical, the evangelical, the rational, and the social are so related that each exercises a restraint on the others. Too exclusive an emphasis on mysticism results in a religion which is individualistic, subjective, and vague; too dominant an evangelicalism results in a religion which is authoritarian, creedal, and external; too great an emphasis on rationalism results in a cold intellectual religion which appeals only to the few; too engrossing a devotion to the social gospel results in a religion which, in improving the outer environment, ignores defects in the inner life which cause the outer disorder. In Quakerism the optimum is not equality in rank of the four elements. The mystical is basic. The Light Within occasions the acceptance or rejection of a particular authority, reason, or service.

Howard Brinton, 1952

1.18   Experience is the Quaker's starting-point. This light must be my light, this truth must be my truth, this faith must be my very own faith. The key that unlocks the door to the spiritual life belongs not to Peter, or some other person, as an official. It belongs to the individual soul that finds the light, discovers the truth that sees the revelation of God and goes on living in the demonstration and power of it.

Rufus M. Jones, 1927

1.19   For God can be found. . . . There is a Divine Center into which your life can slip, a new and absolute orientation in God, a Center where you live with him and out of which you see all life, through new and radiant vision, tinged with new sorrows and pangs, new joys unspeakable and full of glory.

Thomas R. Kelly, 1938

151

1.20   The Inward Light is a universal light given to all men, religious consciousness itself being basically the same wherever it is found. Our difficulties come when we try to express it. We cannot express; we can only experience God. Therefore we must always remember tolerance, humility, and tenderness with others whose ways and views may differ from ours.

Pacific Yearly Meeting, 1953

1.21   We must be alert that the warm coziness which we find enveloping us at Yearly Meeting and in our Monthly Meetings does not snare us into imagining that this is all of Quakerism. A vital religion is one which goes from an encounter with the love of God to an encounter in service to that love, no matter how hopeless the situation may be.

Pacific Yearly Meeting, 1967

1.22   This central affirmation, that the Light of the Christlike God shines in every person, implies that our knowledge of God is both subjective and objective. It is easy to misconstrue "Inner Light" as an invitation to individualism and anarchy if one concentrates on the subjective experience known to each one. But it is an equally important part of our faith and practice to recognize that we are not affirming the existence and priority of your light and my light, but of the Light of God, and of the God who is made known to us supremely in Jesus. The inward experience must be checked by accordance with the mind of Christ, the fruits of the Spirit, the character of that willed caring which in the New Testament is called Love.

It is further checked by the fact that if God is known in measure by every person, our knowledge of him will be largely gained through the experience of others who reverently and humbly seek him. In the last resort we must be guided by our own conscientiously held conviction—but it is in the last resort. First, we must seek carefully and prayerfully through the insights of others, both in the past and among our contemporaries, and only in the light of this search do we come to our affirmation.

Hugh Doncaster, 1972

1.23   For the mystery of faith is held in a pure conscience, that you may be led, guided, taught, and governed by this which cannot err, but is pure and eternal, and endureth for evermore.

Margaret Fell, 1668

1.24   This much is clear: Christians and the Universalists need each other. Our culture is grounded in ancient Christian symbols, which, if we listen, still quiver with dense ineffable meanings. In an effort to persuade us to listen to those meanings, Christians try to find words for them. The danger is that the words may become idols: creeds graven in stone. Universalists, alive to this danger, remind us that other cultures have other symbols which—could we but attune ourselves to their resonance—are just as fraught as ours. There are other ways of seeing. Here the danger is that we may abandon particularity altogether and find ourselves adrift on an ocean of light without stars, landmarks, or anchorage. Christians would call us back to terra firma lest we dissolve. Universalists would have us venture forth lest we petrify. The interplay of universal and particular must be as old as religion itself. Each has dangers which the other counteracts.

The Church Universal needs both its seafarers and its stay-at-homes. Why is that so difficult? Why have I myself never understood it until now?

Esther Murer, Faith & Practice of Philadelphia Yearly Meeting, 1986

1.25   We do not speak with one voice. We have so many elements, not only those which are differently organized, but with each group we go off on different lines and too often even criticize one another. We want no artificial unison, but the deeper we get to really central things, the deeper will be the harmonies that emerge.

Henry Hodgkin, Can Quakers Speak to this Generation?, 1933

1.26   Our differences are our riches but also our problem. One of our key differences is the different names we give our Inward Teacher. Some of us name that Teacher, Lord; others of us use the names Spirit, Inner Light, Inward Christ, or Jesus Christ. It is important to acknowledge that these names involve more than language; they involve basic differences in our understanding of who God is, and how God enters our lives. We urge Friends to wrestle, as many of us have here, with the conviction and experience of many Friends through our history that this Inward Teacher is in fact Christ himself. We have been struck this week, however, with the experience of being forced to recognize this same God at work in others who call that Voice by different names, or who understand differently who that Voice is.

We have wondered whether there is anything Quakers today can say as one. After much struggle, we have discovered that we can proclaim this: There is a living God at the centre of all, who is available to each of us as a Present Teacher at the very heart of our lives.

An Epistle to All Friends Everywhere, from 300 Young Friends from 34 countries, 57 yearly meetings, and 8 monthly meetings, under the care of Friends World Committee for Consultation, 1985

1.27   For those who believe in a personal God, that will mean developing a personal relationship with God—a feeling of being nurtured, cherished and personally guided. For others, it is a sense of beauty and appreciation for interconnectedness with all of life, caring for all creatures, a sense of mystery, of transcendence or of special meaning in ordinary living.

Cynthia Taylor, ed., "Religious Education Newsletter," Intermountain Yearly Meeting, Spring 1995

1.28   The field of my religious training presupposed a clear definite call to a particular kind of service. I must confess that this has never happened to me.... I have never aspired to a particular job or asked for one; nor have I been "stricken on the road to Damascus" as was Paul and had my way clearly dictated to me from the heavens. The entire course has been a maturing of family and personal decisions. In perspective, I should say in all humility that my life has been characterized by an inadequate, persistent effort to try to find a workable harmony between religious profession and daily practice.

Clarence E. Pickett, Faith & Practice of Philadelphia Yearly Meeting, 1966

1.29   I said to one of the Cuban Friends, "It must be hard to be a Christian in Cuba." He smiled. "Not as hard as it is in the United States," he said. Of course, I asked why he said that, and he went on, "You are tempted by three idols that do not tempt us. One is affluence, which we do not have. Another is power, which we also do not have. The third is technology, which again we do not have. Further-more, when you join a church or a meeting, you gain in social acceptance and respectability. When we join, we lose those things, so we must be very clear about what we believe and what the commitment is that we are prepared to make."

Gordon M. Browne, Jr., Faith & Practice of Philadelphia Yearly Meeting, 1989

1.30   Spiritual Discernment is at the heart of Quaker Spirituality and Practice. It's grounded in the central Quaker conviction of the availability to every person of the experience and guidance of God. . . . Discernment is the faculty we use to distinguish the true movement of the Spirit to speak in meeting for worship from the wholly human urge to share, to instruct, or to straighten people out.... It is the ability to see into people, situations and possibilities to identify what is of God in them and what is of the numerous other sources in ourselves—and what may be both. . . .

Discernment is a gift from God, not a personal achievement. . . . It is given for the building of the community and of relationship with God rather than for self-fulfillment or self-aggrandizement. . . . We all have been given some measure of the gift of discernment. In a life lived with other priorities, the gift may be left undeveloped. But as we grow and are faithful in the spiritual life, we may well be given more.

Patricia Loring, "Spiritual Discernment" 1992

1.31   In my experience, a leading is a persistent desire to do something that may not make much sense. It is beyond reason. It keeps asking for your attention; it doesn't go away. It may be inconvenient. It may be misunderstood by people you love. When you finally act on it, it is like stepping into a river and letting it carry you. Your fear doesn't go away, your confusion doesn't go away, you're not suddenly happy all the time. But you feel relief. There is a kind of knowing that comforts you.

Paula Palmer, 2005

The Scriptures

2.01   Concerning the Holy Scriptures, we do believe that they were given forth by the Holy Spirit of God, through the holy men of God, who (as the Scripture itself declares, 2 Peter 1:21) "spoke as they were moved by the Holy Ghost." We believe they are to be read, believed, and fulfilled (he that fulfills them is Christ) and they are "profitable for doctrine, for reproof, for correction, and for instruction in righteousness, that the man of God may be perfect, thoroughly furnished unto all good works" (2 Timothy 3:16).

George Fox, 1671

2:02   And the first words that he spoke were as followeth: "He is not a Jew that is one outwards, neither is that circumcision which is outward, but he is a Jew that is one inward, and that is circumcision which is of the heart." And so he went on and said, How that Christ was the Light of the world and lighteth every man that cometh into the world, and that by this Light they might be gathered to God, etc. And I stood up in my pew, and I wondered at his doctrine, for I had never heard such before. And then he went on, and opened the Scriptures, and said, "The Scriptures were the prophets' words and Christ's and the apostles' words and what as they spoke they enjoyed and possessed and had it come from the Lord." And said, "Then what had any to do with the Scriptures, but as they came to the Spirit that gave them forth. You will say, Christ saith this, and the apostles say this; but what canst thou say? Art thou a child of the Light and has walked in the Light, and what thou speakest is it inwardly from God?"

This opened me so that it cut me to the heart; and then I saw clearly we were all wrong. So I sat me down in my pew again, and cried bitterly. And I cried in my spirit to the Lord. "We are all thieves, we are all thieves, we have taken the Scriptures in words and know nothing of them in ourselves." ... I saw it was the truth and I could not deny it; and I did as the apostle saith, I "received the truth in the love of it." And it was opened to me so clear that I had never a tittle in my heart against it; but I desired the Lord that I might be kept in it, and then I desired no greater portion.

Margaret Fell, about 1652

2.03   How much the Bible has to teach when taken as a whole, that cannot be done by snippets! There is its range over more than a thousand years giving us the perspective of religion in time, growing and changing, and leading from grace to grace. There is its clear evidence of the variety of religious experience, not the kind of strait jacket that nearly every church, even Friends, have sometimes been tempted to substitute for the diversity in the Bible. To select from it but a single strand is to miss something of its richness. Even the uncongenial and the alien to us is happily abundant in the Bible. The needs of men today are partly to be measured by their difficulty in understanding that with which they differ. At this point the Bible has no little service to render. It requires patient insight into the unfamiliar and provides a discipline for the imagination such as today merely on the political level is a crying need of our time.

Further, the Bible is a training school in discrimination among alternatives. One of the most sobering facts is that it is not on the whole a peaceful book — I mean a book of peace of mind. The Bible is the deposit of a long series of controversies between rival views of religion. The sobering thing is that in nearly every case the people shown by the Bible to be wrong had every reason to think they were in the right, and like us they did so. Complacent orthodoxy is the recurrent villain in the story from first to last and the hero is the challenger, like Job, the prophets, Jesus, and Paul.

Henry Joel Cadbury, 1953

2.04   The quality of his life and the profound things he said drew me to him, not the myths of his birth and resurrection. His life and teachings commanded my allegiance then, and still do. If being a Christian means accepting Jesus Christ as Lord and Savior, then I am probably not a Christian. If being a Christian means accepting his teachings as the norm for my life, striving to live out those terribly difficult precepts, then I am a Christian.

Elizabeth Watson, 'This I Know Experientially,' 1977

157

Prayer

3.01   Prayer releases energy as certainly as the closing of an electric circuit does. It heightens all human capacities. It refreshes and quickens life. It unlocks reservoirs of power. It opens invisible doors into new storehouses of spiritual force for the person to live by and, as I believe, for others to live by as well. It is effective and operative as surely as are the forces of steam and gravitation.

Rufus M. Jones, 1918

3.02   One of these deep constructive energies of life is prayer. It is a way of life that is as old as the human race is, and it is as difficult to "explain" as is our joy over love and beauty. It came into power in man's early life and it has persisted through all the stages of it because it has proved to be essential to spiritual health and growth and life-advance. Like all other great springs of life, it has sometimes been turned to cheap ends and brought down to low levels, but on the whole it has been a pretty steady uplifting power in the long story of human progress. The only way we could completely understand it would be to understand the eternal nature of God and man. Then we should no doubt comprehend why he and we seek one another and why we are unsatisfied until we mutually find one another.

Rufus M. Jones, 1931

3.03   As taught and practiced by Jesus, prayer is communion with God, in which mind and heart become open to his sustaining power and gladly and humbly submissive to his directing will.

The Lord's Prayer is an example of the simple directness of the prayers of Jesus. One can meet God without an elaborate chain of words, even in the rush and tension of everyday life.

Prayer may be response to the beauty or grandeur of nature; to the courage and goodness sometimes revealed by the human spirit; to a desperate sense of need. Prayer may be inspired by joy and sorrow, illness and health, birth and death. Prayer may be without words or in the simplest phrases. Through prayer, daily or special, he who prays can find serenity, humility, strength, courage and direction amid the stresses as well as the joys of life.

Prayer is an exercise of the mind and spirit. Its efficacy is increased by conscious practice. Prayer can work miracles by making individuals sensitive to the will of God and, through obedience, strong to accept or surmount the natural conditions of life.

Philadelphia Yearly Meeting, 1972

3.04   Oh God, our Father, spirit of the universe, I am old in years and in the sight of others, but I do not feel old within myself. I have hopes and purposes, things I wish to do before I die. A surging of life within me cries. "Not yet! Not yet!" more strongly than it did ten years ago, perhaps because the nearer approach of death arouses the defensive strength of the instinct to cling to life.

Help me to loosen, fiber by fiber, the instinctive strings that bind me to the life I know. Infuse me with Thy spirit so that it is Thee I turn to, not the old ropes of habit and thought. Make me poised and free, ready when the intimation comes to go forward eagerly and joyfully, into the new phase of life that we call death.

Help me to bring my work each day to an orderly State so that it will not be a burden to those who must fold it up and put it away when I am gone. Keep me ever aware and ever prepared for the summons.

If pain comes before the end help me not to fear it or struggle against it but to welcome it as a hastening of the process by which the strings that bind me to life are untied. Give me joy in awaiting the great change that comes after this life of many changes. Let my self be merged in Thy Self as a candle's wavering light is caught up into the sun.

Elizabeth Gray Vining, Faith & Practice of Philadelphia Yearly Meeting, *1978*

Meeting for Worship

4.01   Be still in thy own mind and spirit from thy own thoughts, and then thou wilt feel the principle of God to turn thy mind to the Lord God, whereby thou wilt receive his strength and power from whence life comes, to allay all tempests, against blusterings and storms. That is it which molds into patience, into innocency, into soberness, into stillness, into stayedness, into quietness, up to God, with his power.

George Fox, 1658

4.02   When you come to your meetings, what do you do? Do you then gather together bodily only, and kindle a fire, compassing your-selves about with the sparks of your own kindling, and so please yourselves, and walk in the "Light of your own fire, and in the sparks which you have kindled?" . . . Or rather, do you sit down in the True Silence, resting from your own Will and Workings, and waiting upon the Lord, with your minds fixed in that Light where-with Christ has enlightened you, until the Lord breathes life into you, refresheth you, and prepares you, and your spirits and souls, to make you fit for his service, that you may offer unto him a pure and spiritual sacrifice?

William Penn, 1678

4.03   As iron sharpeneth iron, the seeing of the faces one of an-other when both are inwardly gathered into the life, giveth occasion for the life secretly to rise and pass from vessel to vessel. And as many candles lighted and put in one place do greatly augment the light and make it more to shine forth, so when many are gathered together into the same life, there more of the glory of God and his powers appears, to the refreshment of each individual.

Robert Barclay, 1671

4.04   I went to meetings in an awful frame of mind and endeav-ored to be inwardly acquainted with the language of the True Shep-herd. And one day, being under a strong exercise of spirit, I stood up and said some words in a meeting; but not keeping close to the Di-vine opening, I said more than was required of me. Being soon sen-sible of my error, I was afflicted in mind some weeks without any light or comfort, even to that degree that I could not take satisfaction in anything. I remembered God, and was troubled, and in the depths of my distress he had pity on me, and sent the Comforter. I then felt forgiveness for my offense; my mind became calm and quiet, and I was truly thankful to my gracious Redeemer for his mercies. About six weeks after this, feeling the spring of Divine love opened, and a concern to speak, I said a few words in a meeting, in which I found peace. Being thus humbled and disciplined under the cross, my understanding became more strengthened to distinguish the pure spirit which inwardly moves upon the heart, and which taught me to wait in silence sometimes many weeks together, until I felt that rise which prepares the creature to stand like a trumpet, through which the Lord speaks to his flock.

John Woolman, 1740

4.05   It is indeed true, as Friends have been accustomed to say, that we cannot expect "to eat the bread of idleness" in our silent meetings. Every individual spirit must work out its salvation in a living exercise of heart and mind, an exercise in which "fear and trembling" must often be our portion, and which cannot possibly be fully carried out under disturbing influences from without. Silence is often a stern discipline, a laying bare of the soul before God, a listening to the "reproof of life." But the discipline has to be gone through, the reproof has to be listened to, before we can find our right place in the temple. Words may help and silence may help, but the one thing needful is that the heart should turn to its Maker as the needle turns to the pole. For this we must be still.

Caroline E. Stephen, 1908

4.06   The first thing that I do is to close my eyes and then to still my body in order to get it as far out of the way as I can. Then I still my mind and let it open to God in silent prayer, for the meeting, as we understand it, is the meeting place of the worshiper with God. I thank God inwardly for this occasion, for the week's happenings, for what I have learned at his hand, for my family, for the work there is to do, for himself. And I often pause to enjoy him. Under his gaze I search the week, and feel the piercing twinge of remorse that comes at this, and this, and this, and at the absence of this, and this, and this. Under his eyes I see again—for I have often been aware of it at the time—the right way. I ask his forgiveness of my faithlessness and ask for strength to meet this matter when it arises again. There have been times when I had to reweave a part of my life under this auspice.

I hold up persons before God in intercession, loving them under his eyes—seeing them with him, longing for his healing and redeeming power to course through their lives. I hold up certain social situations, certain projects. At such a time I often see things that I may do in company with or that are related to this person or this situation. I hold up the persons in the meeting and their needs, as I know them, to God.

Douglas V. Steere, 1937

4.07   We are met in a great task when we meet in worship, no less than to realize the Divine Presence and to create an atmosphere in which that Presence and Power can touch us into fuller life. Once we remember this, we cannot but approach the occasion with reverent humility and the desire that nothing on our part may hinder or disturb.

It is something holy and wonderful we are trying to build up together — the consciousness of the Presence with us here and the reality of communion with God.

Quaker poster designed by FGC Press

4.08   Worship, according to the ancient practice of the Religious Society of Friends, is entirely without any human direction or supervision. A group of persons come together and sit down quietly with no prearrangement, each seeking to have an immediate sense of divine leading and to know at first hand the presence of the Holy Spirit. It is not wholly accurate to say that such a Meeting is held on the basis of Silence; it is more accurate to say that it is held on the basis of Holy Obedience. Those who enter such a Meeting can harm it in two specific ways: first, by an advanced determination to speak; and second, by advanced determination to keep silent. The only way in which a worshipper can help such a Meeting is by an advanced determination to try to be responsive in listening to the still small voice and doing whatever may be commanded.

Adapted from the statement prepared for a Friends meeting attended by delegates to the World Council of Churches, Amsterdam, 1948

4.09   The true practice of the essence of Quaker worship is to be free, fully open and responsive to a full range of leadings of the Spirit from deep silence to joyful singing and even to dance. Fearlessly and consistently following this path over the long term would eventually obviate all issues of multiculturalism, multiracialism and inclusiveness.

Friends Journal, October 2003

4:10   Waiting for the spirit to speak is like waiting for a dear friend to arrive. No noise escapes our attention. Even as we work on other things we are attuned to anything that is out of the ordinary. Every part of us is alert to the sound of its coming . . . and when it comes, we are there, listening.

Martha Roberts, 2004

Monthly Meeting

5.01   Being orderly come together, not to spend time with needless, unnecessary and fruitless discourses; but to proceed in the wisdom of God not in the way of the world, as a worldly assembly of men, by hot contests, by seeking to outspeak and overreach one another in discourse as if it were controversy between party and party of men, or two sides violently striving for dominion, not fellowship of God, in gravity, patience, meekness, in unity and concord, submitting one to another in lowliness of heart, and in the holy Spirit of truth and righteousness.

Edward Burrough, 1662

5.02   If you want to listen, then you hear; if you don't want to listen, God is working anyway.

Gusten Lutter, 2002

5.03   It is a weighty thing to speak in large meetings for business. First, except our minds are rightly prepared, and we clearly understand the case we speak to, instead of forwarding, we hinder the business and make more labour for those on whom the burden of work is laid.

If selfish views or a partial spirit have any room in our minds, we are unfit for the Lord's work. If we have a clear prospect of the business and proper weight on our minds to speak, it behooves us to avoid useless apologies and repetitions. Where people are gathered from far, and adjourning a meeting of business attended with great difficulty, it behooves all to be cautious how they detain a meeting, especially when they have sat six or seven hours and a good way to ride home.

In three hundred minutes are five hours, and he that improperly detains three hundred people one minute, besides other evils that attend it, does an injury like that of imprisoning one man five hours without cause.

John Woolman, 1758

5.04   The spirit of worship is essential to that type of business meeting in which the group endeavors to act as a unit. . . . To discover what we really want as compared with what at first we think we want, we must go below the surface of self-centered desires. . . . To will what God wills is . . . to will what we ourselves really want.

Howard Brinton, 1952

5.05   To be present is ... to penetrate the deeper dimensions ... to be open to influence and change; to be vulnerable, to be able to be hurt; to be willing to be spent and also to be awake, alive, and engaged actively in the immediate assignment that has been laid upon us.

Douglas V. Steere, "On Being Present Where You Are," 1967

5.06   Friends, both in individual worship and in meetings for worship and for business, continue to experience the presence of the living God not only as awe and healing but also as guidance for conduct. Like the prophets of Israel, they proclaim the unity of religious faith and social justice.

From the foreword in Faith & Practice of Philadelphia Yearly Meeting, *2002*

5.07   It seems to me to be a major issue for the Society of Friends . . . whether on the whole the emphasis is to be for a type of open, expectant religion, or whether it is to seek for comfortable formulations that seem to ensure safety, and that will be hostages against new and dangerous enterprises in the realm of truth. Are we charged with hope and faith and vision, or are we busy endeavoring to coin repetitive phrases and to become secure resting places for the mind?

Rufus M. Jones, Rethinking Quaker Principles, 1940

Membership

6.01   Now the Lord God hath opened to me by his invisible power how that every man was enlightened by the divine light of Christ; and I saw it shine through all, and that they that believed in it came out of condemnation and came to the light of life, and became children of it, but they that hated it, and did not believe in it, were condemned by it, though they made a profession of Christ. This I saw in the pure openings of the Light without the help of any man, neither did I then know where to find it in the Scriptures; though afterwards, searching the Scriptures, I found it. For I saw in that Light and Spirit which was before Scripture was given forth, and which led the holy men of God to give them forth, that all must come to that Spirit, if they would know God, or Christ, or the Scriptures aright, which they that gave them forth were led and taught by.

George Fox, 1648

6.02   And oh, how sweet and pleasant it is to the truly spiritual eye to see several sorts of believers, several forms of Christians in the school of Christ, every one learning their own lesson, performing their own peculiar service, and knowing, owning, and loving one another in their several places and different performances to their Master, to whom they are to give an account, and not quarrel with one another about their different practices.

Isaac Penington, 1659

6.03   The test for membership should not be doctrinal agreement, nor adherence to certain testimonies, but evidence of sincere seeking and striving for Truth, together with an understanding of the lines along which Friends are seeking that Truth.

Friends World Conference, 1952

6.04   Our membership of this, or any other Christian fellowship, is never based on worthiness. . . . We none of us are members because we have attained a certain standard of goodness, but rather because, in this matter, we still are all humble learners in the school of Christ. Our membership is of no importance whatever unless it signifies that we are committed to something of far greater and more lasting significance than can adequately be conveyed by the closest association with any movement or organization. Our membership of the Society of Friends should commit us to the discipleship of the living Christ. When we have made that choice and come under that high compulsion, our membership will have endorsed it.

Edgar G. Dunstan, 1956

6.05   The nature of their purpose and quest as Friends binds members of a Meeting and of the whole Society into an intimate fellowship whose unity is not threatened by the diversity of leadings and experiences which may come to individual Friends. To share in the experience of the Presence in corporate worship, to strive, conscious that other Friends are also striving, to let the Divine Will guide one's life, to live in a sense of unfailing Love reaching out to the stumbling followers of Christ is to participate in a spiritual adventure in which Friends come to know one another and to respect one another at a level where superficial differences of age or sex, of wealth or position, of education or vocation, of race or nation are all irrelevant. Within this sort of fellowship, as in a family, griefs and joys, fears and hopes, failures and accomplishments are naturally shared, even as individuality and independence are scrupulously respected.

Faith and Practice of New England Yearly Meeting of Friends, 1966

6.06   "George Fox and his early followers," wrote Rufus Jones, "went forth with unbounded faith and enthusiasm to discover in all lands those who were true fellow-members with them in this great household of God, and who were the hidden seed of God." Our Society thus arose from a series of mutual discoveries of men and women who found that they were making the same spiritual pilgrimage. This is still our experience today. Even at times of great difference of opinion, we have known a sense of living unity, because we have recognised one another as followers of Jesus. We are at different stages along the way. We use different language to speak of him and to express our discipleship. The insistent questioning of the seeker, the fire of the rebel, the reflective contribution of the more cautious thinker—all have a place amongst us. This does not always make life easy. But we have found that we have learned to listen to one another, to respect the sincerity of one another's opinions, to love and to care for one another. We are enabled to do this because

God first loved us. The gospels tell us of the life and teaching of Jesus. The light of Christ, a universal light and known inwardly, is our guide. It is the grace of God which gives us the strength to follow. It is his forgiveness which restores us when we are oppressed by the sense of falling short. These things we know, not as glib phrases, but out of the depths of sometimes agonising experience.

London Yearly Meeting, 1968

Home, Children, Family

7.01   Children have much to teach us. If we cultivated the habit of dialogue and mutual learning, our children could keep us growing, and in a measure could bring us into their future, so that in middle age we would not stand on the sidelines bemoaning the terrible behavior and inconsiderateness of the younger generation.

Elizabeth Watson, 1975

7.02   I will begin here also with the beginning of time, the morning. So soon as you wake, retire your mind into a pure silence from all thoughts and ideas of worldly things, and in that frame wait upon God, to feel his good presence, to lift up your hearts to him, and commit your whole self into his blessed care and protection. Then rise, if well, immediately; being dressed, read a chapter or more in the Scriptures, and afterwards dispose yourselves for the business of the day, ever remembering that God is present, the overseer of all your thoughts, words, and action; and demean yourselves, my dear children accordingly; and do not you dare to do that in his holy, all-seeing presence, which you would be ashamed a man, yea, a child, should see you do. And as you have intervals from your lawful occasions, delight to step home, within yourselves, I mean, commune with your own hearts and be still, and (as Nebuchadnezzar said on another occasion) "*one like the son of God you shall find and enjoy with you and in you; a treasure the world knows not of, but is the aim, end, and diadem of the children of god.*" This will bear you up against all temptations, and carry you sweetly and evenly through your day's business, supporting you under disappointments, and moderating your satisfaction in success and prosperity. The evening

167

come, read again the Holy Scripture, and have your times of retirement, before you close your eyes, as in the morning; that so the Lord may be the alpha and omega of every day of your lives.

William Penn's Advice to his Children, 1699

7.03   Hospitality in the home is a vital force in spiritual nurture. The contacts of parents with their children's companions, and the child's association with adult guests, are important influences. Parental attitudes toward neighbors and acquaintances are often reflected in the children. Family conversation may determine whether or not children will look for the good in the people they meet, and whether they will be sensitive to that of God in everyone.

Faith and Practice of North Pacific Yearly Meeting, 1991

7.04   Homemaking is a Quaker service in its own right. It should be recognized as such and a proper balance preserved, so that other activities — even the claims of Quaker service in other fields — are not allowed to hinder its growth.

Faith and Practice of New England Yearly Meeting of Friends, 1985

Sexuality

8.01   Sexuality looked at dispassionately, is neither good nor evil — it is a fact of nature and a force of immeasurable power. But looking at it as Christians we have felt impelled to state without reservation that it is a glorious gift of God.

Throughout the whole of living nature it makes possible an endless and fascinating variety of creatures, a lavishness, a beauty of form and colour surpassing all that could be imagined as necessary to survival.

"Towards a Quaker View of Sex," Revised Edition, 1964

8.02   The mystery of sex continues to be greater than our capacity to comprehend it, no matter how much we learn about it. We engage in it, in often too frantic efforts to enjoy it but, more subtly, also to try to fathom its ever recurring power over us. Surely this power and its mystery relate to the mystery of God's relationship to us. The mistake we have made throughout the ages has been to load onto sex the incubus of success or failure of marriage, to look upon sex as a resolution, an ending. In reality it offers us, if we could only see it, a fresh *beginning* every time in that relationship of which it is a part.

Mary S. Calderone, 1973

Living in the World

9.01   Let all nations hear the sound by word or writing. Spare no place, spare no tongue nor pen, but be obedient to the Lord God; go through the world and be valiant for the truth upon earth. . . . Be patterns, be examples in all countries, places, islands, nations, wherever you come, that your carriage and life may preach among all sorts of people, and to them. Then you will come to walk cheerfully over the world, answering that of God in every one; whereby in them you may be a blessing, and make the witness of God in them to bless you.

George Fox, 1656

9.02   We are a people that follow after those things that make for peace, love, and unity; it is our desire that others' feet may walk in the same, and do deny and bear our testimony against all strife and wars and contentions. . . . Our weapons are not carnal, but spiritual. . . . And so we desire, and also expect to have liberty of our consciences and just rights and outward liberties, as other people of the nation, which we have promise of, from the word of a king. . . . Treason, treachery and false dealing we do utterly deny; false dealing, surmising or plotting against any creature on the face of the earth; and speak the Truth in plainness and singleness of heart; and all our desire is your good and peace and love and unity.

Margaret Fell, 1660

9.03   Prison shall be my grave before I will budge a jot; for I owe my conscience to no mortal man; I have no need to fear, God will make amends for all.

William Penn, 1668

9.04   Answer the Witness of God in every man, whether they are the heathen that do not profess Christ, or whether they are such as do profess Christ that have the form of godliness and be out of the Power.

George Fox, 1672

9.05   The Cross of Christ . . . truly overcomes the world, and leads a life of purity in the face of its allurements; they that bear it are not thus chained up, for fear they should bite; nor locked up, lest they should be stole away; no, they receive power from Christ their Captain, to resist the evil, and do that which is good in the sight of God; to despise the world, and love its reproach above its praise; and not only not to offend others, but love those that offend them. . . . True godliness doesn't turn men out of the world, but enables them to live better in it, and excites their endeavours to mend it; not hide their candle under a bushel, but set it upon a table in a candlestick.

William Penn, 1682

9.06   Every degree of luxury of what kind soever, and every demand for money inconsistent with divine order, hath some connection with unnecessary labor. . . . To labor too hard or cause others to do so, that we may live conformable to customs which Christ our Redeemer contradicted by his example in the days of his flesh, and which are contrary to divine order, is to manure a soil for propagating an evil seed in the earth.

John Woolman, c. 1763

9.07   Love was the first motion, and then a concern arose to spend some time with the Indians, that I might feel and understand their life and the spirit they live in, if haply I might receive some instruction from them, or they be in any degree helped forward by my following the leadings of Truth amongst them. . . .

Afterward, feeling my mind covered with the spirit of prayer, I told the interpreters that I found it in my heart to pray to God, and I believed, if I prayed right, he would hear me, and expressed my willingness for them to omit interpreting, so our meeting ended with a degree of Divine love. Before our people went out I observed Papunehang (the man who had been zealous in laboring for a reformation in that town, being then very tender) spoke to one of the interpreters, and I was afterward told that he said in substance as follows: "I love to feel where words come from."

John Woolman, 1763

9.08   For Friends the most important consideration is not the right action in itself but a right inward state out of which right action will arise. Given the right inward state, right action is inevitable. Inward state and outward action are component parts of a single whole.

Howard Brinton, 1943

9.09   As Friends, we need to develop our spiritual lives so that we may become increasingly able to speak to "that of God" in those with whom we come in contact and to point out to them by our lives as well as our words that there is a power and a spirit within them that can make war impossible. We should show by our lives that they as well as we are responsible to this authority within, and none other.

Pacific Yearly Meeting, 1950

9.10   I know only too well what a poor old broken world confronts us at the present moment. This is not time for soft and easy optimism. Jeremiah the prophet usually took a dark view of things. He did not expect the leopard to change his spots, or the Ethiopian to go white. He looked for no miraculous panacea—no balm in Gilead—to change the hard conditions. But watching a potter remake a spoiled vessel on his potter's wheel, he suddenly has a vision of reality and in a flash he saw that that is what God does with His world. He does not scrap the marred clay. He remakes what has gone wrong. How often He has done it! What a list it is!

From The Luminous Trail, quoted in
Harry Emerson Fosdick, ed., Rufus Jones Speaks to Our Time, 1961

9.11   Individuals can resist injustice, but only in community can we do justice.

The defense of human rights . . . is faith-based and worship-initiated, but we need look neither to Heaven nor to the Bible nor to corporate conscience for the higher law that overrules unjust laws.

In the United States, protecting people from human rights violations is, if nonviolent, never illegal.

A society's constituent individuals and communities retain primary responsibility for protecting human rights, a responsibility that we may entrust but never forfeit to the state.

Much that has been labeled "civil disobedience" is, more accurately, civil initiative; it is the exercise by individuals or communities of their legally established duty to protect the victims of government officials' violations of fundamental rights.

Excerpts from "Sanctuary as a Quaker Testimony,"
a report by Jim Corbett to Philadelphia Yearly Meeting , 1986

9.12   It is thought that realizes will. Only a thinking man can live. Only a thinking people can create history. Only a thinking kind can live in the midst of the dead.

The future always belongs to us. It is neither the working of nature, nor that of fate. It comes by our resolution.

Only a person who resolves not to be enslaved enjoys freedom. Only a person who resolves not to assert his own enjoys freedom.

Only the person who resolves to love even at the cost of his own life can win love.

The first ingredient of life is courage.

The problem of today is not that of knowledge or technology. It is a spiritual problem. It is a question which requires a revolution in our outlook on life, on history, and on the nation.

The world today does not require an increase in technology, nor an easier access to its store of learning. It requires faith and spirit to overcome the present hurdle. The age calls for a new religion.

Ham Sok Hon, 1965

Testimonies

10.01   The important thing about worldly possessions, in fact, is whether or not we are tied to them. Some, by an undue love of the things of this world, have so dulled their hearing that a divine call to a different way of life would pass unheard. Others are unduly self-conscious about things which are of no eternal significance, and because they worry too much about them, fail to give of their best. The essence of worldliness is to judge of things by an outward and temporary, and not an inward and eternal standard, to care more about appearances than about reality, to let the senses prevail over the reason and the affections.

London Yearly Meeting, 1958

10.02   Of the interest of the public in our estates: Hardly any thing is given us for our selves, but the public may claim a share with us. But of all we call ours, we are most accountable to God and the public for our estates: In this we are but stewards, and to hoard up all to ourselves is great injustice as well as ingratitude.

John Woolman, 1720

10.03   Perhaps what we are now considering is the question: What was the central concern of Jesus? I may say quite simply, The answer to that question is: human conduct. . . . [For Jesus there] are not primarily questions of religious ritual . . . [nor] questions of philosophy, or theology or belief. There are rather questions of how you should behave. . . . Jesus, in his teaching, would not be asked . . . abstract questions nearly as much as . . . questions about the will of God for our conduct.   *Henry J. Cadbury, 1961,*

from Faith & Practice of Philadelphia Yearly Meeting

10.04   At the first convincement, when Friends could not put off their hats to people, or say You to a single person, but Thou and Thee; when they could not bow, or use flattering words in salutations, or adopt the fashions and customs of the world, many Friends, that were tradesmen of several sorts, lost their customers at the first; for the people were shy of them, and would not trade with them; so that for a time some Friends could hardly get money enough to buy bread. But afterwards, when people came to have experience of Friends' honesty and truthfulness, and found that their Yea was yea, and their Nay was nay; that they kept to a word in their dealings, and that they would not cozen and cheat them; but that if they sent a child to their shops for anything, they were as well used as if they had come themselves; the lives and conversations of Friends did preach, and reached to the witness of God in the people.

George Fox, 1653

10.05   It's a dangerous thing to lead young Friends much into the observation of outward things, which may be easily done, for they can soon get into an outward garb, to be all alike outwardly, but this will not make them true Christians: it's the Spirit that gives life. I would be loath to have a hand in these things . . .

Margaret Fell Fox, 1698

173

10.06   My mind through the power of Truth was in a good degree weaned from the desire of outward greatness, and I was learning to be content with real conveniences that were not costly; so that a way of life free from much Entanglements appeared best for me, tho' the income was small. I had several offers of business that appeared profitable, but saw not my way clear to accept of them, as believing the business proposed would be attended with more outward care & cumber than was required of me to engage in. I saw that a humble man, with the Blessing of the Lord, might live on a little, and that where the heart was set on greatness, success in business did not satisfy the craving; but that commonly with an increase of wealth, the desire for wealth increased. There was a care on my mind so to pass my time, as to things outward, that nothing might hinder me from the most steady attention to the voice of the True Shepherd.

John Woolman, c. 1744

10.07   I wish I might emphasize how a life becomes simplified when dominated by faithfulness to a few concerns. Too many of us have too many irons in the fire. We get distracted by the intellectual claim to our interest in a thousand and one good things, and before we know it we are pulled and hauled breathlessly along by an over-burdened program of good committees and good undertakings. I am persuaded that this fevered life of church workers is not wholesome. Undertakings get plastered on from the outside because we can't turn down a friend. Acceptance of service on a weighty committee should really depend upon an answering imperative within us, not merely upon a rational calculation of the factors involved. The concern-oriented life is ordered and organized from within. And we learn to say No as well as Yes by attending to the guidance of inner responsibility. Quaker simplicity needs to be expressed not merely in dress and architecture and the height of tombstones but also in the structure of a relatively simplified and coordinated life-program of social responsibilities. And I am persuaded that concerns introduce that simplification, and along with it that intensification which we need in opposition to the hurried, superficial tendencies of our age.

Thomas R. Kelly, 1941

10.08   For some there is a danger that care for the future may lead to undue anxiety and become a habit of saving for its own sake, resulting in the withholding of what should be expended for the needs of the family or devoted to the service of the Society. The temptation to trust in riches comes in many forms, and can only be withstood through faith in our Father and his providing care.

London Yearly Meeting, 1945

10.09   Life is meant to be lived from a Center, a divine Center—a life of unhurried peace and power. It is simple. It is serene. It takes no time but occupies all our time.

Thomas R. Kelly, 1941

10.10   In spite of our varying degrees of emphasis on how our Peace Testimony should be expressed, there are many ways to peace. There are:

>   Those who feel that we must seek inward peace first, as self purification.

>   Those who are moved to radical personal and group action, and need the support of Meetings.

>   Those who feel that as citizens of governments we still have opportunities to influence events.

We support Friends who are led to walk in any of these ways to peace. . . . We differ, yet we love each other.

Pacific Yearly Meeting, 1959

10.11   How healing to come into the Religious Society of Friends, whose founder saw clearly that the Light of God is not limited to the male half of the human race. Membership and participation have helped me grow toward wholeness, as I have followed my calling into a ministry that embraces all of life. Though I believe deeply in women's liberation, I cannot put men down or join in consciousness-raising activities that foster hatred of everything masculine. I have loved the men in my life too deeply for that kind of betrayal.

As women gain rights and become whole human beings, men too can grow into wholeness, no longer having to carry the whole burden of responsibility for running the affairs of humankind, but in humility accepting the vast resources, as yet not very much drawn on, and the wisdom of women in solving the colossal problems of the world.

Elizabeth Watson, 1975

10.12   We totally oppose all wars, all preparation for war, all use of weapons and coercion by force, and all military alliances: no end could ever justify such means.

We equally and actively oppose all that leads to violence among people and nations, and violence to other species and to our planet.

This has been our testimony to the whole world for over three centuries.

We are not naïve or ignorant about the complexity of our modern world and the impact of sophisticated technologies — but we see no reason whatsoever to change or weaken our vision of the peace that everyone needs in order to survive and flourish on a healthy, abundant earth.

The primary reason for this stand is our conviction that there is that of God in every one which makes each person too precious to damage or destroy.

While someone lives, there is always the hope of reaching that of God within them; such hope motivates our search to find nonviolent resolution of conflict.

There is no guarantee that our resistance will be any more successful or any less risky than military tactics. At least our means will be suited to our end.

If we seem to fail finally, we would still rather suffer and die than inflict evil in order to save ourselves and what we hold dear.

If we succeed, there is no loser or winner, for the problem that led to conflict will have been resolved in a spirit of justice and tolerance.

Such a resolution is the only guarantee that there will be no further outbreak of war when each side has regained strength.

The places to begin acquiring the skills and maturity and generosity to avoid or to resolve conflicts are in our own homes, our personal relationships, our schools, our workplaces, and wherever decisions are made.

We must relinquish the desire to own other people, to have power over them, and to force our views on to them. We must own up to our own negative side and not look for scapegoats to blame, punish, or exclude. We must resist the urge towards waste and the accumulation of possessions.

Conflicts are inevitable and must not be repressed or ignored but worked through painfully and carefully. We must develop the skills of being sensitive to oppression and grievances, sharing power in decision making, creating consensus, and making reparation.

In speaking out, we acknowledge that we ourselves are as limited and as erring as anyone else. When put to the test, we each may fall short.

We do not have a blueprint for peace. . . . In any particular situation, a variety of personal decisions could be made with integrity.

We may disagree with the views and actions of the politician or the soldier who opts for a military solution, but we still respect and cherish that person.

What we call for in this statement is a commitment to make the building of peace a priority and to make opposition to war absolute.

What we advocate is not uniquely Quaker but human and, we believe, the will of God. Our stand does not belong to Friends alone—it is yours by birthright.

Let us reject the clamour of fear and listen to the whisperings of hope.

Aotearoa/New Zealand Yearly Meeting, 1987
from Faith & Practice of Philadelphia Yearly Meeting, 1998

10.13   And thus the Lord Jesus hath manifested himself and his Power, without respect of Persons; and so let all mouths be stopt that would limit him, whose Power and Spirit is infinite, that is pouring it upon all flesh.

Margaret Fell, 1666

Death and Memorials

11.01   They that love beyond the World cannot be separated by it. Death cannot kill what never dies. Nor can Spirits ever be divided that love and live in the same Divine Principle. They live in one another still.

William Penn, 1693

11.02   Eternity is at our hearts, pressing upon our time-worn lives, warming us with intimations of an astounding destiny, calling us home to Itself.

Thomas R. Kelly, 1941

11.03   The night before landing in Liverpool I awoke in my berth with a strange sense of trouble and sadness. As I lay wondering what it meant, I felt myself invaded by a Presence and held by the Everlasting Arms. It was the most extraordinary experience I had ever had. But I had no intimation that anything was happening to Lowell [his eleven-year-old son]. When we landed in Liverpool a cable informed me that he was desperately ill, and a second cable, in answer to one from me, brought the dreadful news that he was gone. When the news reached my friend John Wilhelm Rowntree, he experienced a profound sense of Divine Presence enfolding him and me, and his comfort and love were an immense help to me in my trial. . . . I know now, as I look back across the years, that nothing has carried me up into the life of God, or done more to open out the infinite meaning of love, than the fact that love can span this break of separation, can pass beyond the visible and hold right on across the chasm. The mystic union has not broken and knows no end.

Rufus M. Jones, 1947

11.04   In hours of loss and sorrow, when the spurious props fail us, we are more apt to find our way back to the real refuge. We are suddenly made aware of our shelterless condition, alone, and in our own strength. Our stoic armor and our brave defenses of pride become utterly inadequate. We are thrown back on reality. We have then our moments of sincerity and insight. We feel that we cannot live without resources from beyond our own domain. We must have God. It is then, when one knows that nothing else whatever will do, that the great discovery is made. Again and again the psalms announce this. When the world has caved in; when the last extremity has been reached; when the billows and waterspouts of fortune have done their worst, you hear the calm, heroic voice of the lonely man saying: "God is our refuge and fortress, therefore will not we fear though the earth be removed, though the mountains be carried into the middle of the sea." That is great experience, but it is not reserved for psalmists and rare patriarchs like Job. It is a privilege for common mortals like us who struggle and agonize and feel the thorn in the flesh, and the bitter tragedy of life unhealed. Whether we make the discovery or not, God is there with us in the furnace. Only it makes all the difference if we do find him as the one high tower where refuge is not for the passing moment only, but is an eternal attainment.

Spiritual Energies in Daily Life, quoted in
Henry Emerson Fosdick, ed., Rufus Jones Speaks to our Time, 1961

Appendices

Appendix 1: Complete Text of Advices from the Meeting of the Elders at Balby, 1656

1.   The settled meetings to be kept each first-day. General Meetings, as a rule to be on some other day of the week.

2.   As any are brought in to the Truth new meetings are to be arranged to suit the general convenience, without respect of persons.

3.   Persons ceasing to attend meetings are to be spoken to. Persons who walk disorderly are to be spoken to in private, then before two or three witnesses; then, if necessary, the matter is to be reported to the Church. The Church is to reprove them for their disorderly walking, and, if they do not reform, the case is to be sent in writing "to some whom the Lord hath raised up in the power of the Spirit of the Lord to be fathers, His children to gather in the light" so that the thing may be known to the body and be determined in the light.

4.   Ministers to speak the word of the Lord from the mouth of the Lord, without adding or diminishing. If anything is spoken out of the light so that "the seed of God" comes to be burdened, it is to be dealt with in private and not in the public meetings, "except there be a special moving so to do."

5.   Collections to be made for the poor, the relief of prisoners, and other necessary uses, the moneys to be carefully accounted for, and applied as made known by the overseers in each meeting.

6.   Care to be taken "for the families and goods of such as are called forth in the ministry, or are imprisoned for the Truth's sake; that no creature be lost for want of caretakers."

7.   Intentions of marriage to be made known to the Children of Light, especially those of the meeting where the parties are members. The marriage to be solemnized in the fear of the Lord, and before many witnesses, after the example of scripture, and a record to be made in writing, to which the witnesses may subscribe their names.

8.   Every meeting to keep records of births, and of burials of the dead that died in the Lord. Burials to be conducted according to scripture, and not after customs of "heathen."

9.   Advice to husbands and wives, as in I Pet.iii. 7. Advice to parents and children, as in Eph. vi. I, 4.

10.   Advice to servants and masters, as in Eph. vi. 5–9.

11.   Care to be taken "that none who are servants depart from their masters, but as they do see in the light: nor any master put away his servant but by the like consent of the servant; and if any master or servant do otherwise in their wills, it is to be judged by Friends in the light."

12.   Needs of widows and fatherless to be supplied: —such as can work and do not to be admonished, and if they refuse to work, neither let them eat. The children of needy parents to be put to honest employment.

13.   Any called before outward powers of the nation are to obey.

14.   That if any be called to serve the Commonwealth in any public service which is for the public wealth and good, that with cheerfulness it be undertaken and in faithfulness discharged unto God, that therein patterns and examples in the thing that is righteous ye may be to those that are without.

15.   Friends in callings and trades are to be faithful and upright, and keep to yea and nay. Debts to be punctually paid, that nothing they may owe to any man but love one to another.

16.   None to speak evil of another, nor grudge against another, nor put a stumbling-block in his brother's way.

17.   None to be busybodies in other's matters.

18.   Christian moderation to be used towards all men.

19.   The elders made by the Holy Ghost are to feed the flock, taking the oversight willingly, not as lords, but as examples to the flock.

Dearly beloved Friends, these things we do not lay upon you as a rule or form to walk by, but that all, with the measure of light which is pure and holy, may be guided: and so in the light walking and abiding, these may be fulfilled in the Spirit, not from the letter, for the letter killeth, but the Spirit giveth life.

Appendix 2: Minute of Germantown Friends, with Meeting Responses

A Minute Against Slavery,
Addressed to Germantown Monthly Meeting, 1688.

This is to ye Monthly Meeting held at Richard Worrell's.

These are the reasons why we are against the traffick of men-body, as foloweth. Is there any that would be done or handled at this manner? viz., to be sold or made a slave for all the time of his life? How fearful and faint-hearted are many on sea, when they see a strange vessel,—being afraid it should be a Turk, and they should be taken, and sold for slaves into Turkey. Now what is this better done, as Turks doe? Yea, rather it is worse for them, which say they are Christians; for we hear that ye most part of such negers are brought hither against their will and consent, and that many of them are stolen. Now, tho they are black, we can not conceive there is more liberty to have them slaves, as it is to have other white ones. There is a saying that we shall doe to all men like as we will be done ourselves; making no difference of what generation, descent or colour they are. And those who steal or robb men, and those who buy or purchase them, are they not all alike? Here is liberty of conscience wch is right and reasonable; here ought to be liberty of ye body, except of evildoers, wch is an other case. But to bring men hither, or to rob and sell them against their will, we stand against. In Europe there are many oppressed for conscience sake; and here there are those oppressed wch are of a black colour. And we who know than men must not comitt adultery,—some do committ adultery, in separating wives from their husbands and giving them to others; and some sell the children of these poor creatures to other men. Ah! doe consider will this thing, you who doe it, if you would be done at this manner? And if it is done according to Christianity? You surpass Holland and Germany in this thing. This makes an ill report in all those countries of Europe, where they hear of, that ye Quakers doe here handel men as they handel there ye cattle. And for that reason some have no mind or inclination to come hither. And who shall maintain this your cause, or pleid for it. Truly we can not do so, except you shall inform us better hereof, viz., that Christians have liberty to practise these things. Pray, what thing in the world can be done worse towards us, than if men should rob or steal us away, and sell us for slaves to strange countries; separating husbands from their wives and children. Being now that this is not done in the manner we would be done at therefore we contradict and are against this traffic of menbody. And we who profess that it is not lawful to steal, must, likewise, avoid to purchase such things as are stolen, but rather help to stop this robbing and stealing if possible. And such men ought to be delivered out of ye hands of ye robbers, and set free as well as in Europe. Then is Pennsylvania to have a good report, instead it hath now a bad one for this sake in other countries. Especially whereas ye Europeans are desirous to know in what manner ye Quakers doe rule in their province;—and most of them doe look upon us with an envious eye. But if this is done well, what shall we say is done evil?

If once these slaves (wch they say are so wicked and stubbern men) should join themselves,—fight for their freedom,—and handel their masters and mastrisses as they did handel them before; will these masters and mastrisses take the sword at hand and warr against these poor slaves, licke, we are able to believe, some will not refuse to doe; or have these negers not as much right to fight for their freedom, as you have to keep them slaves?

Now consider will this thing, if it is good or bad? And in case you find it to be good to handle these blacks at that manner, we desire and require you hereby lovingly, that you may inform us herein, which at this time never was done, viz., that Christians have such a liberty to do so. To the end we shall be satisfied in this point, and satisfie likewise our good friends and acquaintances in our natif country, to whose it is a terror, or fairful thing, that men should be handeld so in Pennsylvania.

This is from our meeting at Germantown, held ye18 of the 2 month, 1688, to be delivered to the Monthly Meeting at Richard Worrell's.

> Garret henderich
> derick up de graeff
> Francis daniell Pastorius
> Abraham up Den graef

Monthly Meeting Response:

At our Monthly Meeting at Dublin, ʸᵉ 30 - 2 mo., 1688, we have inspected ʸᵉ matter, above mentioned, and considered of it, we find it so weighty that we think it not expedient for us to meddle with it here, but do rather commit it to ʸᵉ consideration of ʸᵉ Quarterly Meeting; ʸᵉ tenor of it being nearly related to ʸᵉ Truth. On behalf of ʸᵉ Monthly Meeting.

    Signed, P. Jo. Hart.

Quarterly Meeting Response:

This, above mentioned, was read in our Quarterly Meeting at Philadelphia, the 4 of ʸᵉ 4th mo. '88, and was from thence recommended to the Yearly Meeting, and the above said Derick, and the other two mentioned therein, to present the same to ʸᵉ above said meeting, it being a thing of too great a weight for this meeting to determine.

    Signed by order of ʸᵉ meeting,
    Anthony Morris.

Yearly Meeting Response:

[At a yearly meeting held at Burlington the 5th day of the 7th month, 1688.]

A Paper being here presented by some German Friends Concerning the Lawfulness and Unlawfulness of Buying and keeping Negroes, It was adjusted not to be so proper for this Meeting to give a Positive Judgment in the case, It having so General a Relation to many other Parts, and therefore at present they forbear It.

Sources: www.qhpress.org/texts/oldqwhp/as-1688.htm.
Joseph Walton, ed., *Incidentes Illustrating the Doctrines and History of the Society of Friends* (Philadelphia: Friends' Book Store, 1897). S*ee also* J. S. Hartzler and Daniel Kauffman, eds., *Mennonite Church History* (Scottdale, PA: Mennonite Book and Tract Society), 1905.

Appendix 3: The 1660 Declaration to Charles II

From *The Journal of George Fox,* John L. Nickals, ed. (London Yearly Meeting, 1975). pp. 398– 403.

This declaration was given unto the King upon the 21st day of the 11th Month, 1660 [January, 1661].

A Declaration from the harmless and innocent people of God, called Quakers, against all plotters and fighters in the world: for removing the ground of jealousy and suspicion from both magistrates and people in the kingdom, concerning wars and fightings. And also something in answer to that clause of the King's late Proclamation which mentions the Quakers, to clear them from the plot and fighting which therein is mentioned and for the clearing their innocency.

Our principle is, and our practices have always been, to seek and ensue it and to follow after righteousness and the knowledge of God, seeking the good and welfare and doing that which tends to the peace of all. We know that wars and fightings proceed from the lusts of men, (as James iv. 1–3), out of which lusts the Lord hath redeemed us, and so out of the occasion of war. The occasion of war, and war itself (wherein envious men, who are lovers of themselves more than lovers of God, lust, kill, and desire to have men's lives or estates) ariseth from lust. All bloody principles and practices, we, as to our own particulars, do utterly deny; with all outward wars and strife and fightings with outward weapons, for any end or under any pretense whatsoever And this is our testimony to the whole world.

And whereas it is objected:

"But although you now say that you cannot fight nor take up arms at all, yet if the spirit move you, then you will change your principle, and you will sell your coat and buy a sword and fight for the kingdom of Christ."

Answer:

As for this we say to you that Christ said to Peter, "Put up thy sword in his place"; though he had said before, he that had no sword might sell his coat and buy one (to the fulfilling of the law and Scripture), yet after, when he had bid him put it up, he said, "He that taketh the sword shall perish with the sword." And further, Christ said to Peter, "Thinkest thou, that I cannot now pray to my Father, and he shall presently give me more than twelve legions of angels?"

And this might satisfy Peter, after he had put up his sword, when he said to him he that took it, should perish by it; which satisfieth us (Luke xxii. 36; Matt. xxvi. 51–53). And in the Revelation, it's said, "He that kills with the sword, shall perish with the sword: and here is the faith and the patience of the saints" (Rev. xiii. 10). And so Christ's kingdom is not of this world, therefore do not his servants fight, as he told Pilate, the magistrate who crucified him. And did they not look upon Christ as a raiser of sedition? And did not he say, "Forgive them"? But thus it is that we are numbered amongst transgressors, and numbered amongst fighters, that the Scriptures might be fulfilled.

That the Spirit of Christ, by which we are guided, is not changeable, so as once to command us from a thing as evil and again to move unto it; and we certainly know, and so testify to the world, that the Spirit of Christ, which leads us into all Truth, will never move us to fight and war against any man with outward weapons, neither for the kingdom of Christ, nor for the kingdoms of this world.

First:

Because the kingdom of Christ God will exalt, according to his promise, and cause it to grow and flourish in righteousness; "not by might, nor by power [of outward sword], but by my Spirit, saith the Lord" (Zech. iv. 6). So those that use any weapon to fight for Christ, or for the establishing of his kingdom or government, both the spirit, principle, and practice in that we deny.

Secondly:

And as for the kingdoms of this world, we cannot covet them, much less can we fight for them, but we do earnestly desire and wait, that by the Word of God's power, and its effectual operation in the hearts of men, the kingdoms of this world may become the kingdoms of the Lord, and of his Christ; that he may rule and reign in men by his spirit and truth; that thereby all people, out of all different judgements and professions may be brought into love and unity with God, and one with another; and that they may all come to witness the prophet's words, who said, "Nation shall not lift up sword against nation, neither shall they learn war any more" (Isa. ii. 4; Mic. iv. 3).

So, we whom the Lord hath called into the obedience of his Truth have denied wars and fightings and cannot again anymore learn it. This is a certain testimony unto all the world of the truth of our hearts in this particular, that as God persuadeth every man's heart to believe, so they may receive it. For we have not, as some others, gone about cunningly with devised fables, nor have we ever denied in practice what we have professed in principle; but in sincerity and truth, and by the word of God, have we laboured to be made manifest unto all men, that both we and our ways might be witnessed in the hearts of all.

And whereas all manner of evil hath been falsely spoken of us, we hereby speak forth the plain truth of our hearts, to take away the occasion of that offense; that so we being innocent may not suffer for other men's offenses, nor be made a prey upon by the wills of men for that of which we were never guilty; but in the uprightness of our hearts we may, under the power ordained of God for the punishment of evil-doers, and for the praise of them that do well, live a peaceable and godly life in all godliness and honesty. For although we have always suffered, and do now more abundantly suffer, yet we know that it's for righteousness' sake; "for our rejoicing is this, the testimony of our consciences, that in simplicity and godly sincerity, not with fleshly wisdom, but by the grace of God, we have had our conversation in the world" (2 Cor. i. 12), which for us is a witness for the convincing of our enemies. For this we can say to all the world, we have wronged no man's person or possessions, we have used no force nor violence against any man, we have been found in no plots, nor guilty of sedition. When we have been wronged, we have not sought to revenge ourselves, we have not made resistance against authority, but wherein we could not obey for conscience' sake, we have suffered even the most of any people in the nation. We have been counted as sheep for the slaughter, persecuted and despised, beaten, stoned, wounded, stocked, whipped, imprisoned, haled out of synagogues, cast into dungeons and noisome vaults where many have died in bonds, shut up from our friends, denied needful sustenance for many days together, with other the like cruelties.

And the cause of all these sufferings is not for any evil, but for things relating to the worship of our God and in obedience to his requirings of us. For which cause we shall freely give up our bodies a sacrifice, rather than disobey the Lord. For we know, as the Lord hath kept us innocent, so he will plead our cause, when there is none in the earth to plead it. So we, in obedience unto his Truth, do not love our lives unto the death, that we may do his will, and wrong no man in our generation, but seek the good and peace of all men. And he that hath commanded us that we shall not swear at all (Matt. v. 34), hath also commanded us that we shall not kill (Matt. v. 21), so that we can neither kill men, nor swear for or against them. And this is both our principle and practice, and hath been from the beginning; so that if we suffer, as suspected to take up arms or make war against any, it is without any ground from us; for it neither is, nor ever was in our hearts, since we owned the truth of God; neither shall we ever do it, because it is contrary to the Spirit of Christ, his doctrine, and the practices of his apostles, even contrary to him, for whom we suffer all things, and endure all things.

And whereas men come against us with clubs, staves, drawn swords, pistols cocked, and do beat, cut, and abuse us, yet we never resisted them; but to them our hair, backs, and cheeks have been ready. It is not an honour to manhood nor to nobility to run upon harmless people who lift not up a hand against them, with arms and weapons.

Therefore consider these things, ye men of understanding: for plotters, raisers of insurrections, tumultuous ones, and fighters, running with swords, clubs, staves, and pistols, one against another; these, we say, these are of the world, and this hath its foundation from this unrighteous world, from the foundation of which the Lamb hath been slain, which Lamb hath redeemed us from the unrighteous world, and we are not of it, but are heirs of a world of which there is no end and of a kingdom where no corruptible thing enters. And our weapons are spiritual and not carnal, yet mighty through God to the plucking down of the strongholds of Satan, who is the author of wars, fighting, murder, and plots. And our swords are broken into ploughshares and spears into pruning-hooks, as prophesied of in Micah iv. Therefore we cannot learn war any more, neither rise up against nation or kingdom with outward weapons, though you have numbered us amongst the transgressors and plotters. The Lord knows our innocency herein, and will plead our cause with all people upon earth at the day of their judgment, when all men shall have a reward according to their works.

[Therefore in love we warn you for your soul's good, not to wrong the innocent, nor the babes of Christ, which he hath in his hand, which he cares for as the apple of his eye; neither seek to destroy the heritage of God, nor turn your swords backward upon such as the law was not made for, i.e., the righteous; but for sinners and transgressors, to keep them down. For those are not peacemakers, nor lovers of enemies, neither can they overcome evil with good, who wrong them that are friends to you and all men, and wish your good, and the good of all people on the earth. If you oppress us, as they did the children of Israel in Egypt, and if you oppress us as they did when Christ was born, and as they did the Christians in the primitive times; we can say, 'The Lord forgive you"; and leave the Lord to deal with you, and not revenge ourselves. If you say, as the council said to Peter and John, 'speak no more in that name'; and if you serve us, as they served the three children spoken of in Daniel, God is the same that ever he was, that lives for ever and ever, who hath the innocent in his arms.][1]

O friends offend not the Lord and his little ones, neither afflict his people; but consider and be moderate, and do not run hastily into things, but mind and consider mercy, justice, and judgment; that is the way for you to prosper and get the favour of the Lord. Our meetings were stopped and broken up in the days of Oliver, in pretense of plotting against him; and in the days of the Parliament and Committee of Safety we were looked upon as plotters to bring in King Charles; and now we are called plotters against King Charles. Oh, that men should lose their reason, and go contrary to their own conscience; knowing that we have suffered all things and have been accounted plotters all along, though we have declared against them both by word of mouth and printing, and are clear from any such things. We have suffered all along because we would not take up carnal weapons to fight withal against any, and are thus made a prey upon because we are the innocent lambs of Christ and cannot avenge ourselves. These things are left on your hearts to consider; but we are out of all those things, in the patience of the saints; and we know that as Christ said, "He that takes the sword, shall perish with the sword" (Matt. xxvi. 52; Rev. xiii. 10).

This is given forth from the people called Quakers to satisfy the King and his Council, and all those that have any jealousy concerning us, that all occasion of suspicion may be taken away, and our innocency cleared.

Given forth under our names, and in behalf of the whole body of the Elect People of God who are called Quakers.

George Fox	Gerrard Roberts	Henry Fell
Richard Hubberthorne	Johne Bolton	John Hinde
John Stubbs	Leonard Fell	John Furley Junr.
Francis Howgill	Samuel Fisher	Thomas Moore

Postscript. Though we are numbered with plotters in this late Proclamation and put in the midst of them and numbered amongst transgressors and so have been given up to all rude, merciless men, by which our meetings are broken up, in which we edified one another in our holy faith and prayed together to the Lord that lives for ever, yet he is our pleader for us in this day. The Lord saith, "They that feared his name spoke often together," as in Malachi, which were as his jewels. And for this cause and no evil-doing, are we cast into holes, dungeons, houses of correction, prisons they sparing neither old nor young, men or women, and just sold to all nations and made a prey to all nations under pretense of being plotters, so that all rude people run upon us to take possession. For which we say, "The Lord forgive them that have thus done to us," who doth and will enable us to suffer. And never shall we lift up a hand against any that doth thus use us, but that the Lord may have mercy upon them, that they may consider what they have done. For how is it possible for them to requite us for the wrong they have done to us, who to all nations have sounded us abroad as plotters? We who were never found plotters against any power or man upon the earth since we knew the life and power of Jesus Christ manifested in us, who hath redeemed us from the world, and all works of darkness, and plotters that be in it, by which we know our election, before the world began. So we say, the Lord have mercy upon our enemies and forgive them, for that they have done unto us.

Oh, do as you would be done by. And do unto all men as you would have them do unto you, for this is but the law and the prophets.

And all plots, insurrections, and riotous meetings we do deny, knowing them to be of the devil, the murderer, which we in Christ, who was before they were, triumph over. And all wars and fightings with carnal weapons we do deny, who have the sword of the spirit; and all that wrong us we leave them to the Lord. And this is to clear our innocency from that aspersion cast upon us, that we are plotters. . . .

---

[1] Inserted from the 2 Volume 8th and Bicentenary Edition of *Journal of George Fox*, London: Friends' Tract Association, 1891, http://www.qhpress.org/quakerpages/qwhp/dec1660.htm.

Appendix 4: History of Intermountain Yearly Meeting Constituent Meetings and Worship Groups

At the first meeting of Intermountain Yearly Meeting in 1975, there were nine affiliated monthly meetings: Pima (Tucson), Tempe, Phoenix, and Flagstaff in Arizona; Paradise Valley in Las Vegas, Nevada; Albuquerque and Santa Fe in New Mexico; and Boulder and Mountain View in Colorado. Logan Monthly Meeting in Utah was an associate member, and there were several worship groups and one preparative meeting (El Paso, Texas). Over the years, several new monthly meetings joined and some disappeared. In 1977, El Paso was recognized as a new monthly meeting, and in 1978, Cochise in McNeal, Arizona, and Las Cruces in New Mexico, were recognized. The first monthly meeting to be recognized as an independent monthly meeting wishing to seek affiliation was Salt Lake Monthly Meeting (Utah), which joined in 1979, followed by the Logan and Durango Monthly Meetings in 1980. Midland Monthly Meeting (Texas) requested affiliation in 1982, Gila Friends Meeting (New Mexico) in 1985, Fort Collins Monthly Meeting (Colorado) in 1986, Colorado Springs Monthly Meeting in 1987, and Moab Monthly Meeting (Utah) in 2001. A brief history of the monthly meetings and worship groups under their care follows.

Arizona Half Yearly Meeting

Arizona Half Yearly Meeting was released to Intermountain Friends' Fellowship by Pacific Yearly Meeting in 1973 (PYM 1973-23).

Cochise Monthly Meeting: Became a monthly meeting under Arizona Half Yearly Meeting in 1978. Laid down as a monthly meeting and became a worship group under the care of Pima Monthly Meeting in 1999.

Flagstaff Monthly Meeting: Released to Intermountain Friends' Fellowship by Pacific Yearly Meeting in 1973. Had care of Prescott Worship Group, which is no longer active.

Paradise Valley Meeting: Listed in the 1975 minutes of Intermountain Yearly Meeting as one of the original monthly meetings affiliating with the yearly meeting. Indications are that it became a worship group after a visitation from Tempe Monthly Meeting on behalf of Arizona Half Yearly Meeting and then was laid down shortly before 1979. There is a Las Vegas Worship Group, currently in Las Vegas, Nevada, which is a member of Pacific Yearly Meeting.

Phoenix Monthly Meeting: Became a worship group in November 1949 and a monthly meeting in May 1950. Was released to Intermountain Yearly Meeting by Pacific Yearly Meeting, effective 1974.

Pima Monthly Meeting: Was a worship group in 1940. Became a monthly meeting in April 1944. Divided from Southwest Tucson Friends Meeting in 1961. Released to Intermountain Yearly Meeting by Pacific Yearly Meeting, effective 1974. Previously had the Hermosillo (Mexico) Worship Group under its care and currently oversees the Cascabel Worship Group and the Cochise (McNeal, Arizona) Worship Group.

Tempe Monthly Meeting: Originated as an outgrowth of Phoenix Monthly Meeting. Was a worship group in September 1968 and was recognized as a monthly meeting by Arizona Half Yearly Meeting in February 1973. One of the original members of Intermountain Yearly Meeting, not previously having belonged to Pacific Yearly Meeting. Previously cared for a worship group in Sun City.

Colorado Regional Meeting

Colorado Regional Meeting was formed as a general meeting and subsequently was changed to a regional meeting after the formation of Intermountain Yearly Meeting.

Boulder Meeting of Friends: Began as a worship group in May 1950 and became a monthly meeting under the auspices of the Friends World Committee for Consultation in October of the same year. Affiliated with Intermountain Yearly Meeting in 1974. Has had several worship groups under its care at various times, including Fort Collins, Western Slope, Steamboat Springs, and Laramie, Wyoming, (which became part of Wyoming Monthly Meeting in 1990 but is not currently affiliated with Intermountain Yearly Meeting), and currently, the Roaring Forks Worship Group in Carbondale, Colorado.

Colorado Springs Monthly Meeting: Began independently as a meeting in 1954 and came under the care of Mountain View Friends Meeting as a worship group in 1985. Recognized as a monthly meeting in March 1987 and affiliated with Intermountain Yearly Meeting at that time. Currently has the Buena Vista Worship Group under its care.

Fort Collins Monthly Meeting: Began as an evening gathering in 1960 and became a formal worship group under the care of Boulder Monthly Meeting in 1975. Set off as a monthly meeting in April 1986 and affiliated with Intermountain Yearly Meeting at that time.

Mountain View Friends Meeting: Began as a worship group in September 1949 and organized as Denver Friends Meeting in December 1957, under the care of the Friends Fellowship Council of Friends World Committee for Consultation. It changed its name to Mountain View Friends Meeting in 1958. It is one of the original members of Intermountain Yearly Meeting, after participating in the Missouri Valley Association. It has had several worship groups under its care, including Cityview, Westside, Colorado Springs, and Wingo Junction. Currently the Westside Meeting for Worship meets in the Lakewood area of metropolitan Denver but is no longer considered a separate worship group.

New Mexico Regional Meeting

New Mexico Regional Meeting was set up as New Mexico Quarterly Meeting in the 1950s by Santa Fe and Albuquerque Monthly Meetings and was later joined by Las Vegas Monthly Meeting. Beginning as a representative meeting, it held its first residential meeting in 1964. Released to Intermountain Friends' Fellowship by Pacific Yearly Meeting, effective 1973. The regional meeting continues to meet for fellowship biyearly but at this time does not have a standing committee structure. The Southeast New Mexico Allowed Meeting for Worship is under its care.

Albuquerque Monthly Meeting: Started in October 1947 as a worship group, it declared itself a monthly meeting in December 1949. Several worship groups have been under its care, including Taos, Clearlight (Taos), Gila, Los Alamos, El Paso (Texas), Durango, Lamb's Community (Cokedale, Colorado), Lubbock (Texas), and several allowed meetings for worship in the local area. Currently has under its care the Socorro Worship Group, Gallup Worship Group, Bonito Valley Worship Group (Lincoln, New Mexico), and an allowed meeting for worship in West Amarillo (Texas).

Durango Monthly Meeting: Began as a worship group under the care of Albuquerque Monthly Meeting. It became a monthly meeting in 1980 and affiliated with Intermountain Yearly Meeting at that time. Currently has the Farmington Worship Group and the Mancos Valley Worship Group under its care.

El Paso Monthly Meeting: A worship group under Albuquerque from December 1971, when Friends World Committee for Consultation ceased to recognize remote groups of Friends in North America. Became a preparative meeting in 1975 and was set off as a monthly meeting in 1977.

Gila Friends Meeting: Established as the Gila Valley Worship Group about 1979 under the care of Albuquerque Monthly Meeting, it became a monthly meeting in 1984. It affiliated with Intermountain Yearly Meeting in 1985.

Las Cruces Monthly Meeting: A worship group from 1971 and then a preparative meeting (1975) under the care of Albuquerque Monthly Meeting. It became a monthly meeting in October 1977 and was recognized as a member of Intermountain Yearly Meeting in 1978. Has had the Carlsbad Worship Group (now the Southeast New Mexico Allowed Meeting for Worship) under its care.

Santa Fe Monthly Meeting: Began as a worship group and declared itself a monthly meeting in 1948. Was released to Intermountain Friends' Fellowship by Pacific Yearly Meeting in 1973, being one of the original members. Has had the Taos Worship Group and the Chamisa Preparative Meeting under its care. Currently has care of the Los Alamos Worship Group, Clearlight Worship Group, and Las Vegas Worship Group.

Utah Friends Fellowship

Utah Friends Fellowship was established in 1982 by Salt Lake Monthly Meeting and Logan Monthly Meeting.

Logan Monthly Meeting: Recognized as a monthly meeting in 1975. Released to Intermountain Yearly Meeting by Pacific Yearly Meeting in 1980. Had care of the Jackson Hole Worship Group until the formation of Wyoming Monthly Meeting in 1990.

Moab Monthly Meeting: Established as a worship group in 1980 under the care of Salt Lake Monthly Meeting. Set off as a monthly meeting in 2001 by Utah Friends Fellowship and Salt Lake Monthly Meeting, and joined Intermountain Yearly Meeting that same summer.

Salt Lake Monthly Meeting: Began as an informal gathering of Friends associated with the Wider Quaker Fellowship in 1948 and recognized by the College Park Quarterly Meeting of Pacific Yearly Meeting as a monthly meeting in 1958. It was laid down in 1961. A worship group was established in 1966; this became a monthly meeting under Intermountain Yearly Meeting in 1979 after being first recognized by Pacific Yearly Meeting and released from that body. Has had several worship groups under its care, including Ogden, Richfield, Cedar City, and Moab.

Mexico City Monthly Meeting and *Midland, Texas Monthly Meeting* are associate members of Intermountain Yearly Meeting.

Appendix 5: Examples of Forms and Records

Index of Forms and Records

The forms in this appendix are templates that monthly meetings can use or modify. Thanks to the *Pacific Yearly Meeting Faith and Practice*, Albuquerque Monthly Meeting, Boulder Meeting of Friends, Pima Monthly Meeting of Friends, and Salt Lake City Monthly Meeting for sample forms from which these were copied or developed.

1. Records
   1a. Recommendations for Monthly Meeting Records
   1b. Advices for Preparing the State of the Meeting Report
   1c. Preparation of Meeting Minutes: Some Useful Practices
   1d. Recommendation for Regional, Half-Yearly, or Friends
      Fellowship Meeting Records
2. Census
3. Membership
   3a. Letter of Welcome to New Member
   3b. Monthly Meeting Membership Record
   3c. Letter of Transfer
   3d. Certificate of Transfer and Acceptance of Transfer
   3e. Letter of Release from Membership
4. Travels and Sojourn
   4a. Letter of Introduction
   4b. Minute of Sojourn
   4c. Acknowledgment of Minute of Sojourn
   4d. Travel Minute
5. Marriage: The Marriage Certificate
6. Religious Education: First Day School Registration
7. Healthcare and Final Affairs
   7a. Cover Letter
   7b. Information and Instructions on Health Care Decisions and
      Final Affairs
8. Contributions, Records, Gifts
   8a. Year-End Contributions Receipt and Request for Information
   8b. Archive Deposit Form
   8c. Gift Form

1. Records

1a. Recommendations for Monthly Meeting Records

Permanent records should include:

- Each monthly meeting should keep its own minutes, signed by the presiding and recording clerks. Minutes should include treasurer's reports and letters sent under concern of the meeting either as attached items or in the body of the minutes.
- Any financial records not included in the minutes: for example, copies of deeds or contracts.
- If the meeting is incorporated, records of incorporation and minutes of annual meetings.
- A membership list of the monthly meeting brought up to date annually by the monthly meeting recorder and submitted, as requested, to the yearly meeting historian/archivist.
- List of marriages under care of the meeting (whether of members or non-members).
- Actively maintained membership records of current or past members, including record of births, marriages, deaths, and transfers.
- Records of final affairs instructions.
- Records of membership of deceased or removed members.

1b. Advices for Preparing the State of the Meeting Report

The State of the Meeting Report is prepared once a year by each monthly meeting in time to be forwarded to the spring session of its regional, half-yearly or Friends fellowship meeting. In contrast to the informal reports of activities given to these meetings at other times of the year, the State of the Meeting Report should be a self-examination by the meeting and its members of their spiritual strengths and weaknesses and of efforts to foster growth in the spiritual life. Reports may cover the full range of interest and concerns but should emphasize those indicative of the spiritual health of the meeting. They also include statistical information.

To facilitate the preparation of this report, the Worship and Ministry and Oversight Committees may meet together and explore the spiritual condition of the meeting. They may then formulate a series of queries for a response from the meeting as the basis of the report or may ask one or more of its members to draft a preliminary report for searching consideration by the meeting. After revision and acceptance by the meeting, the report is read at the regional, half-yearly or Friends fellowship meeting and given to the appropriate meeting committee. A copy should also be sent to the yearly meeting clerk.

1c. Preparation of Meeting Minutes: Some Useful Practices

Expeditious preparation of useful minutes can be aided in many ways. Some suggestions follow.

- The recording and presiding clerks may study the agenda together in advance of the meeting.
- An effective minute usually consists of three sections: 1) reasons for the matter before the meeting; 2) decision approved; 3) who is responsible for carrying out the decision, including how it is to be financed.
- A minute may be drafted in advance for on-site editing as discussion of the matter takes place. (Examples: membership, marriages, matters having clear alternatives.)
- Oral committee reports should be supplemented by a written version and should include draft copies of action minutes.
- Assign topical identification to sections of minutes and let the minutes of action be serially numbered (e.g., 1-7:2000 = Minute 1: 7th month; year 2000). Both organizing factors facilitate reference in the future.
- Use care in distributing and filing copies of the minutes to ensure that those given a responsibility in a meeting have a written copy of the decision.
- To the extent possible, make minutes themselves complete, interpretable without reliance upon attachments (which often go astray).
- Some monthly meetings approve all the minutes of a meeting at that meeting, and read them at the next meeting for information only. In other meetings, the recording clerk takes notes and prepares minutes later (except for minutes of action). Those minutes are read for correction and approval at the next monthly meeting.

1d. Recommendation for Regional, Half-Yearly, or Friends Fellowship Meeting Records

Permanent records should include:

- Minutes, signed by the presiding and recording clerks.
- Letters or documents sent or published on concern of the meeting, whether or not they are part of the minutes (e.g., sent in the name of a committee).
- Correspondence about concerns that may come before the meeting.
- Deeds, wills, property records, if any.
- Copies of any meeting publications, and any published under its care.

1e. Recommendations for Yearly Meeting Records

Permanent records should include:

- A copy of the minutes of each yearly meeting, including all its attachments, printed on archival (acid-free) paper or other suitable form, which has been read and signed by the clerks. The attachments should include the reports of the Nominating Committee, the registrar and the treasurer. All epistles from Friends everywhere, or parts thereof that have been read at plenary sessions by the Watching Committee clerk or representative, should be attached, as well as copies of all epistles emanating from Intermountain Yearly Meeting.
- A copy of the treasurer's report, separate from the minutes and signed by the treasurer (even if one is attached to the minutes); also reports of any auditors.
- Copies of minutes of Executive Committee and Continuing Committee.
- Any minute or letter sent under concern of the yearly meeting, such as travel minutes, that may not be part of the minutes.
- Complete file of issues of *Western Friend* (formerly *Friends Bulletin*) and other publications under the care of the yearly meeting.
- Copies of all handbooks, guides, and disciplines pertaining to Intermountain Yearly Meeting or the regional, half-yearly, and Friends fellowship meetings that comprise it.
- Contracts and significant legal documents involving Intermountain Yearly Meeting.

2. Census

2a *Sample Monthly Meeting Census Form*

ANNUAL MEETING CENSUS of _____MONTHLY MEETING

DATE_____

1. NAME OF PERSON FILLING OUT FORM_____

(same as on line 1 below)

NAME	RELATIONSHIP TO NO. 1 [1]	MEMBER [2]	MEMBER OF ANOTHER MEETING [3]	ATTENDER [4]
1.				
2.				
3.				
4.				
5.				
6.				

CONTACT INFORMATION AS OF DATE WRITTEN ABOVE:

STREET ADDRESS or PO BOX:_____

_____

CITY, STATE, ZIP_____

TELEPHONE(S) _____

E-MAIL_____

[1] Add age (as of date written above) for those under 18 only. This information is to be used only for purposes of determining when "adult" membership status *might* be considered and when a young Friend will be subject to registration for the military draft.

[2] Has had a clearness committee through this monthly meeting and has been accepted as a member, or has transferred membership from another meeting.

[3] Is a member of another Friends meeting; write the name and location of that Friends meeting.

[4] Attends this monthly meeting regularly but is not yet a member.

3. Membership

3a. Letter of Welcome to New Member

[address]
[date]

Dear _____,

As you know, after some months of discussion and exploration with you, _____ Friends Meeting acted on your request for membership in its meeting for business of [date], approving a minute recording you as a member in the Religious Society of Friends. On behalf of the meeting, I would like to welcome you as a member. You are more than just a member of _____ Friends Meeting; you are a member of _____ (Regional, Half-Yearly, Friends Fellowship), and Intermountain Yearly Meeting. As a member of the Religious Society of Friends, you should feel welcome and comfortable in meetings wherever you might visit.

Our meeting would like to acknowledge your membership with a gift of _____.[1]

In Friendship, Peace and Love,

Signature (clerk, recording clerk, clerk of Ministry and Oversight Committee, etc.)

---

[1] Some Monthly Meetings give a book, a subscription to *Western Friend*, a copy of the IMYM *Faith and Practice*, or other item.

3b. Monthly Meeting Membership Record

No. _____

Member's full name _____

First   Middle   Last   (Maiden)

Date of birth_____

Month   Day   Year

Place of birth_____

ADMISSION

Date_____

Month   Day Year

By application _____

By certificate of transfer from _____

     Monthly Meeting

PARENTS

Father's name: _____

Mother's name: _____

ADDRESSES

Year	Street	Town	State	Phone

TERMINATION

Date_____

By certificate to _____ Monthly Meeting

By resignation_____ By release _____

By death____Date of death_____Place of burial_____

REMARKS

_____

_____

_____

_____

Date Record Closed_____

MARRIAGE of member:

To whom married: _____

Date _____

Place _____

SPOUSE

Membership

(where)_____

Date of birth _____

Place_____

If deceased: Date _____

Place of burial _____

Parents of spouse:

Father's name _____

Mother's name _____

CHILDREN

Name _____

    Membership (where) _____

    Date of birth _____

    Place of birth_____

    Date of marriage_____To_____

Name _____

    Membership (where) _____

    Date of birth _____

    Place of birth_____

    Date of marriage_____ To_____

Name _____

    Membership (where) _____

    Date of birth _____

    Place of birth_____

    Date of marriage_____ To_____

3c. Letter of Transfer

[date]

Cambridge Monthly Meeting
5 Longfellow Park
Cambridge, Massachusetts 02138

Dear Friends,

Enclosed is our CERTIFICATE OF TRANSFER for
_____, made at her/his request. On the
acceptance of this transfer by Cambridge Monthly Meeting,
please return a copy to us.

A copy of our membership record for _____
is enclosed for your retention.

Sincerely,

_____, Clerk

Enclosures:

Enclosures:
Certificate of Transfer
Acceptance of Transfer
Membership Record

3d. Certificate of Transfer and Acceptance of Transfer

CERTIFICATE OF TRANSFER[1]

TO: CAMBRIDGE MONTHLY MEETING
At: 5 Longfellow Park, Cambridge, Massachusetts 02138

Dear Friends:

_____, a Member of this Monthly Meeting, residing in your area, has requested transfer of the record of her/his membership. The usual inquiry has been made, and with clearness we commend _____ to your loving care.

   We minuted _____'s admission to membership the 3rd day of Second Month, 1980.

On behalf of Albuquerque Monthly Meeting,
1600 Fifth Street, Albuquerque, New Mexico, 87102.
Minuted the 7th day of Eleventh Month, in the year 1993.

_____

Clerk

ACCEPTANCE OF TRANSFER

This Certificate of Transfer for _____ was read and accepted by
CAMBRIDGE MONTHLY MEETING
Minuted the _____day of _____month, in the year _____.

_____

Clerk

[1] The Meeting holding the original record prepares this form as completely as possible. Spouses and minor children may be included in one form, but separate certificates are required in other cases. The original and a copy are forwarded to the receiving meeting, and a copy is kept by the originating meeting. When completed, the copy is returned to the originating meeting. The original and copy become part of the permanent records of the respective meetings. Copies may be made for retention in the Clerk's records.

3e. Letter of Release from Membership

[address]
[date]

Dear _____,

 Thank you for your letter of [*date*] requesting to resign your membership in the _____ Friends Meeting. Although we are sorry to see a member drift from us and the Society when we remember your vibrant participation in _____ Friends Meeting, we recognize the truth that Quakerism may not always satisfy one's spiritual needs, especially at a distance.

 The Oversight Committee considered your request and felt united in recommending to the Meeting that you be released from membership. In its meeting for business of [*date*], _____ Friends Meeting of the Religious Society of Friends approved a minute releasing you from membership.

 We hope that your future spiritual journey will be fruitful for you, whatever direction it may take. If you should find that you are drawn into membership in your local Friends meeting, do write to us so we may forward your membership record to them. Of course you are always welcome to worship with us if you are in this area.

With love,

Clerk

4. Travels and Sojourns

4a. *Letter of Introduction*

[fictional example]

Date]
[Address]

Dear Friends of New York Yearly Meeting,

We send you warm greetings with our member Elizabeth Gray Vining.

Elizabeth spent many years in Japan, and has recently written a biography of Rufus Jones. We find the combination of her global perspective on life and her in-depth knowledge of Quakerism a wonderful asset to our meeting. We are confident you will enjoy her presence at the annual session of your yearly meeting.

We look forward to hearing from her about how the Spirit is moving among Friends in New York.

In Peace,

Sarah Fuller
Clerk, Big Sur Monthly Meeting

[This is a fictional letter signed by the clerk of the meeting (someone else may have actually drafted the letter). It was written at the request of Elizabeth Gray Vining, who knew that it was common practice to bring a letter of introduction when traveling among Friends. Although it would be a courtesy for the clerk to inform business meeting that the letter was written, the meeting is not asked to approve the letter. If Elizabeth had been traveling under a particular concern, the meeting might have considered approving a travel minute (see sample 4d).]

4b. Minute of Sojourn

Radnor Monthly Meeting
Religious Society of Friends
Conestoga and Sproul Roads
Villanova, PA 19085

[date]

Clerk
Redwood Forest Friends Meeting
P.O. Box 1831
Santa Rosa, CA 95402

Dear Friend:

_____has requested that her membership at
Radnor Meeting be changed to that of a sojourning member of
Redwood Forest Friends Meeting in Santa Rosa, California.

She left Pennsylvania in [*year*] but has continued her membership at Radnor while living in Marin County, California, Boulder,
Colorado, and now in Santa Rosa.

Many of her friends at Radnor have fond memories of her and
wish her well in her present home. She anticipates moving to
Corvallis, Oregon, within the next year and will then request a
transfer of membership.

Sincerely yours,

Clerk

4c. Acknowledgment of Minute of Sojourn

Redwood Forest Monthly Meeting
P.O. Box 1831
Santa Rosa, CA 95402

July 14, _____

Radnor Monthly Meeting
Religious Society of Friends
P.O. Box R 196
Radnor, Pennsylvania 19087

Dear Friends:

We have received your sojourning minute for _____ and accepted her as a sojourning member of Redwood Forest Monthly Meeting at our meeting for business held [*date*]. We are glad to welcome her as a sojourning member. Ever since she and her son began attending our meeting, they have been much loved. She has been involved with the children and young people of our meeting, and her care and attention in this regard is greatly appreciated. We know that she will probably be moving on in [year], but are glad of her presence while she is with us.

 With loving greetings,

Clerk

4d. Travel Minute

[fictional example]

Dear Friends,

     Our member Jim Corbett is traveling under a concern for undocumented immigrants. Our meeting has worshiped with him many times as we considered this issue and his leading to travel among Friends. We have no doubt that he is genuinely called to be with you and seek new Light with you about God's intentions for undocumented immigrants in this country.

     We entrust Jim Corbett to your care, and pray that you and he feel the presence of the Light as you meet together.

Signed,

Clerk, Pima Monthly Meeting of Friends

[Although this fictional example is written as a letter, it is a minute from a meeting. It records that the meeting affirms the Friend's leading to travel under a concern. (The meeting probably used a clearness committee to examine this leading.) The meeting need not necessarily unite with the concern.]

5. Marriage

5a. The Traditional Friends Marriage Certificate

WHEREAS, A.B., of (city or town) _____, son/daughter of C.B., of (city or town)_____ and D., his wife, and E.F., of (city or town)_____, daughter/son of G.F., of (city or town) _____ and H. _____, his wife, having declared their intentions of marriage with each other to _____ Monthly Meeting of the Religious Society of Friends, held at (city or town) _____, (state) _____, according to the good order used among them, and having the consent of parents (or guardians), their proposed marriage was allowed by that Meeting.

NOW THESE ARE TO CERTIFY to whom it may concern, that for the accomplishment of their intentions, this _____ day of the _____ month, in the year of our Lord ____, they, A.B. and E.F., appeared in a Meeting for Worship of the Religious Society of Friends, held at (city or town)_____,(state) _____, and A.B., taking E.F. by the hand, did, on this solemn occasion declare that he/she took him/her, E.F., to be his/her wife/husband/ partner, promising, with divine assistance, to be unto him/her a loving and faithful wife/husband/partner so long as they both shall live (or words to that effect); and then, in the same assembly, E.F. did in like manner declare that he/she took him/her, A.B., to be his/her wife/ husband/partner, promising, with divine assistance, to be unto him/her a loving and faithful wife/husband/partner so long as they both shall live (or words to that effect). And moreover, they, A.B. and E.F., according to the custom of marriage, did, as a further confirmation thereof, then and there, to these presents, set their hands.

A.B. _____ E.B. or E.F._____
AND WE, having been present at the marriage, have as witnesses set our hands the day and year above written.

_____   _____
_____   _____
_____   _____

[Variations on the traditional certificate may be prepared by the couple in consultation with the Arrangements Committee, or preprinted traditional forms may be ordered from Philadelphia Yearly Meeting Office, 1515 Cherry Street, Philadelphia, Pennsylvania 19102.]

6. Religious Education

6a. First Day School Registration

SCHOOL YEAR (20xx – 20xx)
Religious Education Committee
_____Friends Meeting

Name of young Friend:
_____

Date of Birth:_____
School grade _____ in Fall _____
Medical concerns or other things Religious Education Committee
should know:

_____
_____
_____

Parents, Grandparents, Partners:

_____
_____

During class *[TIME]* we (the responsible party) will be at

_____
_____

Home address: _____
_____
Phone: _____
E-mail: _____

Please contact your young Friend's class leaders or any member of
the Religious Education Committee any time you have ideas, suggestions, or concerns. You are always welcome to visit a classroom.
Please sign up to provide a snack at least once during the year and
know of the First Day School's appreciation.

7. Healthcare and Final Affairs

7a. Cover Letter   *[Date]*

Dear Friend,

Many Friends meetings support their members by having them share information that will be helpful at the time of their death. It is a loving act to communicate these wishes to their family and spiritual community. We hope the following information will be helpful.

The questionnaire attached is from the _____ Committee of the _____Monthly Meeting and seeks to learn what you would like the meeting to do in the event of your death. How would you direct the meeting to act with respect to notification of others, obituary information and arrangements for memorial or funeral services and burial or cremation? You may need additional paper to include all that you wish. Please return the questionnaire to [POSTAL ADDRESS]. If you prefer to use a computer document via e-mail, you may request a copy from [emailaddress@something.comnet].

If you find that the information sought does not cover areas you wish covered, please add what you wish. You may leave some questions unanswered because they are not important to you. If you have questions, you may contact any member of the_____ Committee.

In seeking this information, the meeting wishes to be helpful but not to intrude. After your death, your survivors would be responsible for contacting the meeting to confirm your wishes as you have recorded them here. Your survivors would not be bound by this document. It is not a contract, but a simple set of preferences.
[Additional information about possible local arrangements for simple burial or cremation may be provided here.]

Grief and Bereavement Committee

_____,_Convener

[In general, this letter and the accompanying forms would be sent to members and regular attenders every five years, so that they can update the appropriate information.]

7b. Information and Instructions on Health Care Decisions and Final Affairs

NAME	DATE

ADDRESS: _____

☐ YES ☐ NO I have completed a Durable Power of Attorney for Health Care Decisions.

☐ YES ☐ NO I have completed a form to be an organ donor.

A copy of my DPAHCD and/or organ donor form is located:

_____

I request that the Society of Friends carry out the following upon my death. The information below may help the Society of Friends to carry out my wishes. *(Please write on back of form when there isn't enough room on the front.)*

1. Persons to notify immediately (next of kin, executor, etc.):

NAME _____Phone No. _____

ADDRESS _____

RELATIONSHIP _____

NAME _____Phone No. _____

ADDRESS _____

RELATIONSHIP _____

Is there an individual who is prepared to assume direction of affairs after your death (family member, friend, or lawyer?)

Name and address: _____

_____

Is there something the Friends Meeting should do?

Who is able to see to dependent children or others in need?

2. Member of _____Memorial Society

ADDRESS _____

TELEPHONE _____

LOCATION OF CONTRACT _____

3. Disposal of body

☐ Burial ☐ Cremation ☐ Medical Research

Preferred site for disposal of ashes: _____

Cemetery preferred: ☐ Common plot ☐ Family plot

Location of Deed _____

Location of Release Papers _____

Undertaker preferred: _____

4. Burial Insurance

Insurance Company _____

Policy number _____

If no insurance, the expenses will be met as follows: _____

---

5. Services desired, and who should conduct the services

Wishes concerning a Memorial Service:

Do you want a Friends memorial service at the Meetinghouse? (We can accommodate only [*number*] people here.) Would you want a larger gathering or a more private event for your closest friends or family? Do you want to suggest special mementos or photos of your life? Would you like to have music (what suggestions)? Would you like flowers? The more specific you are, the fewer decisions your loved ones will need to make. Please write detailed requests on the back of the form.

Ongoing Remembrance:

Do you want your loved ones to plant a tree in your honor, to make a charitable donation in your name, to gather for an annual reunion at a favorite spot, or some other form of continuing remembrance?

6. Flowers will be accepted ☐

WHERE _____

In lieu of flowers, contributions may be made to:

---

7. Special instructions if death is distant from home:

8. My will and/or other legal documents are located:

9. If no surviving parents, instructions on care of minor children:

10. Information for death certificate (must agree with legal records and policies):

FULL LEGAL NAME _____

PRESENT ADDRESS _____

_____

DATE OF BIRTH _____

PLACE OF BIRTH _____CITIZENSHIP_____

OCCUPATION _____

PRESENT EMPLOYER _____

TITLE _____ ADDRESS _____

_____

FATHER'S NAME _____

MOTHER'S NAME _____

RECEIVED BY MEETING _____DATE _____

SIGNATURE _____

You may use additional pages as desired or necessary.

Biographical Information for Obituaries

Date of Birth:
Place of Birth:
Father's Name:
Mother's Name (include Maiden Name if desired):
Educational Information:
(Schools attended and dates, degrees or certificates awarded)

Marriage(s):
(Date and name of spouse, indicate whether this is a current marriage)

Children:
(Name, birth date, and address or contact information)

Other Relatives:
(Parents, siblings, and significant relatives, including address or contact information. Also indicate significant deceased relatives.)

Employment & Occupational Information:
(Either usual occupation, or longer list, including years if desired)

Military History (if applicable):
(Veterans might include branch of service and service number, ranks and dates)

Special Interests, Activities, and Achievements:
(Include community involvement, hobbies, organizations, etc.)

Recent Life: How long in this area, and relations to the community.

Residential history (if desired):

Other communities in which significant time & events occurred.

What media do you want contacted for obituary notices? Specify newspapers in selected communities, professional newsletters, alma mater, and/or other.

You are invited to begin drafting your obituary notice if you feel inclined to do so. You also might give some thought to the dispersal of your personal possessions and communicate those wishes to several people.

8. Contributions, Records, Gifts

8a. Year-End Contributions Receipt & Request for Information

Dear Friends,

    Thank you for your financial support of _____Monthly Meeting during calendar year _____. For purposes of supporting charitable tax deductions you may report to the IRS, our records show that your financial support to _____Meeting totaled: $_____ [1]

    On behalf of _____Monthly Meeting, thank you for your generous support of _____ .The Meeting's important work has been enhanced by your financial support.

    Below is an anonymous and completely nonbinding estimate of changes in support you anticipate for the coming year. This is solicited for budget and planning purposes only and is seen only by the meeting treasurer (and/or Finance Committee). If you are willing to provide the estimate of changes, please tear off at the line below and return to the Treasurer, either by means of the donation box or the treasurer's files folder.

Thank you,

_____, Treasurer

[1]Some monthly meetings provide a breakout of directed contributions and then show the total.

To the treasurer, _____Monthly Meeting
I expect my/my family's financial support for _____Meeting in *[YEAR]* to:
_____ Increase by $_____
_____ Decrease by $_____
_____ Remain approximately the same

8b. Archive Deposit Form

Intermountain Yearly Meeting Archives

Deposit Form

Date:

    The IMYM archives at _____ has this day received the following records from

_____

    These documents are to be stored at_____ and may be removed permanently by minute of the depositing organization or temporarily by letter from clerk or archivist authorizing it for such use as historical display. The liability of the [*archive location*], by reason of the deposit, is limited to the exercise of their accustomed and reasonable care and diligence in guarding the deposits against loss by fire, theft, and mutilation. The material will be kept under the same conditions as the rest of the collection, and it will be subject to consultation only under the personal supervision of the librarians.

[location of IMYM archives]

By _____
IMYM Archivist

8c. Gift Form

I/we hereby give, transfer, and deliver all of my/our right, title, and interest in and to the property described below to the _____ as an unrestricted gift and dedicate to the public without restriction and thereby place in the public domain whatever literary rights I/we may possess to this property.

Dated this _____ day of _____, 20xx

1. Signature _____

Address _____

2. Signature _____

   Address _____

3. Signature _____

   Address _____

I hereby accept and acknowledge as an unrestricted gift to _____ the items or collection described below and agree to administer them in accordance with _____ established policies.

Dated this _____ day of _____, 20xx

Accepted by:

Signature _____Title _____

Description of the material:

.

Glossary

Advices—Statements of faith and practice that arise from the collective wisdom of Friends and are meant for guidance, but not dutiful conformance, of those in the Society.

Affirmation—A legal declaration made by Friends or others who conscientiously decline to take an oath.

Annual Gathering—A term used by Intermountain Yearly Meeting, some regional meetings, and Friends General Conference for a large assembly of Friends which meets once a year.

As Way Opens—To proceed as way opens: to act after waiting for guidance from God, avoiding hasty judgment or action, and moving ahead as circumstances allow.

Attender—One who attends and participates in meeting activities fairly regularly but has not become a member.

Birthright member—A Friend born of or adopted by Quaker parents. Individuals born or adopted into the Society of Friends are sometimes entered into the monthly meeting membership rolls automatically. Intermountain Yearly Meeting does not recognize a formal membership status based on an accident of birth.

Breaking Meeting—The signal that meeting for worship has ended is generally the shaking of hands, initiated by a designated Friend.

Calling—A powerful sense of being destined and required to act on a specific concern.

Center down—A process by which we direct or still our conscious thought and open ourselves that we may hear God speak directly to us.

Child member, junior member, associate member—Terms used in some meetings with reference to the children in the meeting community who have not yet formally requested membership and been admitted.

Clearness (clarity) — A spiritually affirmed perception. A condition in which there are no perceived obstacles to a proposed course of action by an individual Friend or a meeting.

Clearness committee — A group of Friends appointed to assist a person or the meeting to clarify a decision or concern.

Clerk — An individual who prepares the agenda and presides at meetings of Friends, including business meetings and committee meetings.

Concern — An interest deeply rooted in the Holy Spirit; one that can move both an individual and a meeting to action; it may be used in the context of something one 'thinks ought to be done' in the human sense of social duty.

Consensus — A secular term used to describe an agreement that is reached by a group without a vote and based on considering an issue together.

Conservative — An historic term applied to those yearly meetings which strive to maintain or preserve the earliest practice of Friends.

Continuing Committee — A yearly meeting committee entrusted with general care of matters affecting Intermountain Yearly Meeting between its annual sessions. It plans the annual gathering.

Continuing revelation — The conviction that God still speaks to humankind directly, allowing Truth to be ever more clearly and completely revealed.

Convener — A member of a committee who calls together the first meeting of that committee.

Convinced Friend — One who becomes a Quaker as a result of being led to this decision by the Inner Light after seeking, thought, and study.

Convincement — A result of becoming persuaded, of being opened to God. Convincement is a gift of God's, an understanding. Historically, early Friends believed convincement was a result of "being convicted," which meant the acceptance of a need for God's love.

From this acceptance of "being convicted," or of "conviction," Friends were led to a life "in the Light."

Corporate—Refers to the body of a Friends' meeting.

Covered meeting—A meeting for worship which becomes "covered" by the presence of God; a meeting in which the participants, waiting faithfully upon the Spirit, feel the power and inspiration of God so strongly that they are united. Similar to a "gathered meeting."

Discernment—The spiritual process of determining whether a given leading is divinely inspired and represents knowledge of the Truth. The process of discernment, which may be brief or extensive, may lead to clearness with respect to the leading. It is a gradually acquired skill that does not spring fully fledged.

Discipline—a) A term with roots in discipleship and learning. b) A book of faith and practice of the Religious Society of Friends, so called to reflect the spirit of discipleship felt by Friends. Each yearly meeting may draw together its own book of discipline. c) Choosing to follow an orderly path or action.

Disownment—Termination of membership by action of the monthly meeting; an extreme step taken when a member's conduct is believed to be seriously incompatible with the beliefs and testimonies of the Religious Society of Friends and efforts to resolve the situation have been unsuccessful.

Elder (noun)—Historically, a Friend appointed to foster the vocal ministry of the meeting for worship and the spiritual condition of the members. Today, a term used to describe a Friend of any age seen as having a deep sense of the spirit; one who ministers to the meeting.

Elder (verb)—Gently admonish in love the ways, habits, or thoughts of a Friend or attender after prayerful consideration and often after consultation with respected members of the meeting. Encourage timid Friends to share their gifts with the meeting, or discourage and/or question an individual's inappropriate behavior or speaking.

Epistle—A letter of serious import sent either by an individual or a group. An epistle is sent annually from each yearly meeting to

"Friends everywhere" and states the condition and experience of the yearly meeting.

Facing Benches—In older meetinghouses, ministers and elders sat on elevated benches facing the body of Friends in the meeting. In unprogrammed meetings today, this practice has largely been discontinued, a circular or square arrangement being generally preferred.

Faith and Practice—Faith refers to what we accept as our right relationship to God. Our practice is what we do, how we act, who we are. A book that sets forth these beliefs and expressions is called *Faith and Practice*, sometimes referred to as a book of discipline.

First Day—Sunday. *See also* "Plain Speech".

Friend -- A member of, or an active participant in the Religious Society of Friends; a Quaker. From Jesus' statement, "I call you servants no longer . . . I have called you friends" (John 15:15).

Gathered meeting—A meeting that attains more than the usual sense of Divine Presence, uniting the worshipers in a common experience of holy fellowship. Similar to a "covered meeting."

Good Order (of Friends)—The procedures, found through Friends' experience, that facilitate our business and committee meetings as we seek to understand and carry out God's will.

Guide to Procedures of Intermountain Yearly Meeting—A document detailing the procedures and operations of Intermountain Yearly Meeting.

Hold in the Light—To ask or pray, either in concern or thanksgiving, that a person, situation, or problem be illuminated by divine grace.

Inner Light—The immediate, personal presence of God in our hearts that inspires and guides us, helps us discern Truth, and gives us strength to act on that guidance. The "Inner Light" is also called the "Inward Light," the "Light Within," the "Christ Within," the "Light of Christ," the "Holy Spirit," and the "Seed."

Labor With—An effort by one or more Friends to help another struggle with a concern or a difficulty and come through to a resolution.

Lay down—To discontinue an activity, a committee, or a meeting when its work is completed or no longer felt necessary. A monthly meeting or worship group may be laid down when it no longer functions as such.

Leading—An inner conviction that impels one to follow a certain course under a sense of divine guidance. The soundness of a leading must be tested (the process of discernment) in order to reach clearness before putting it into action.

Meeting—a) A gathering to worship and seek Truth after the manner of Friends. A Meeting for Worship. b) A group of people who regularly gather to worship and seek Truth after the manner of Friends. (*See also* worship meeting, monthly meeting, regional meeting, and yearly meeting.)

Meeting for Business (Meeting for Worship with a Concern for Business)—A meeting for business, usually held monthly, conducted in the manner of worship.

Meeting for Sufferings—A committee to support and care for members and their families who suffer because of their commitment to Friends' principles.

Member—An individual who has been formally admitted into a monthly meeting after undergoing a process to determine clearness in his or her own mind and within the meeting community. Membership in a monthly meeting confers membership in the Religious Society of Friends.

Ministry—A gift of the Spirit, referring both to vocal ministry in the sense of speaking in meeting for worship and to pastoral care and service.

Minute (noun)—A statement of a decision or a testimony, adopted by a meeting for business or a committee, expressing the unity of the meeting or committee for the action taken or the testimony given.

Minute (verb)—To record, with approval, the sense of a meeting with regard to a particular question or issue.

Monthly meeting—A group of Friends that meets regularly (usually weekly or more often) for worship and generally meets once each month to consider business. The monthly meeting is the basic local unit of the Religious Society of Friends.

Notion—A derisive term for the empty knowledge of religion that is of human origin, that is, lacking in spiritual depth. The term is more generally applied to any approach to religious matters that is not primarily based on first-hand spiritual experience.

Opening—a) A spiritually affirmed recognition of an opportunity to move forward toward a goal or out of a difficulty. b) As used by George Fox, revelation into the meaning of life and the scriptures.

Plain Speech—Friends' use of "thee," "thou," "thy," and "thine," and both names with no titles as an expression of equality. 17th century English distinguished between classes of people: one's social superiors were addressed with the plural "you," and equals and inferiors with the singular "thou" and "thee." Friends testified to the equality of all before God by addressing all individuals in the singular, regardless of social status. Because the months and days were named for heathen gods, goddesses, and emperors, many Friends preferred to use "First Day," "Second Day," and "First Month," "Second Month," etc.

Preparative meeting—In Intermountain Yearly Meeting, the term refers to an organized group of Friends that is under the care and guidance of an established monthly meeting and is preparing to become a monthly meeting.

Proceed as way opens—To wait for future circumstances to help solve a problem; to wait for guidance from God.

Programmed meeting—A meeting for worship, usually conducted by a pastor, with a prearranged program, including a sermon, music, an offering, etc. In some programmed meetings, short periods of silence and meditation are provided, during which Friends feel free to speak from the body of the meeting.

Quaker—A member of the Religious Society of Friends. Originally a description of a person experiencing the trembling sometimes resulting from spiritual experience (as when one is moved to speak during a meeting for worship). The term was applied in derision by a justice before whom George Fox appeared and was later adopted by the movement.

Queries—Questions, in conjunction with "Advices," intended to challenge and guide one's faith and practice. These enable individuals and meetings to examine themselves in relation to the standard of conduct the Religious Society of Friends has established for itself.

Read Out of the Meeting—*See* "Disownment."

Regional meeting—A group of monthly meetings within a geographic region. Regional Meetings meet together at various intervals as led. Names such as "quarterly meeting" or "half yearly meeting" refer to the established intervals for specific regional meetings.

Released Friend—A concerned and qualified Friend set free of meeting obligations and expectations for other Quaker service. The meeting sometimes provides financial assistance and other support.

Right Order—1) According to the established processes and procedures of Quakers, therefore "right"; 2) that order that comes from the harmony of the Spirit within meeting.

Rise of Meeting—The end of the Meeting for Worship or for Business.

Season—To consider a matter for a period of time in order to seek the Light rather than to move hastily.

Seasoned Friend—One who is consciously treading on a path of conviction and has made sufficient progress to be helpful to others along the way.

Sense of the meeting—A true unity of a meeting within the Spirit, a sense in the rightness of the point reached and a commitment of all to carry the decision forward. "Sense of the meeting" includes a spiritual recognition of Truth in the agreement of the meeting that a right course of action has been found. By contrast, "consensus" is a state of agreement that is the product of an intellectual process, often confused with "sense of the meeting."

Sojourning member—A Friend who is temporarily residing in the area of another monthly meeting, accepted by that meeting as a participating member, but not included in their statistics for financial purposes.

Speak to one's condition—A term referring to the fact that a statement, comment, or spiritual message is particularly apt or timely to an individual and helpful to her or him at that particular moment; from George Fox's insight that "there is one, even Christ Jesus, that can speak to thy condition."

Stand aside—To decide not to declare unity with a decision but nevertheless not to block it from proceeding. A Friend who stands aside has a responsibility to support and carry forward the decision of the meeting, but he or she may ask to have the lack of agreement minuted.

Stand in the Way—The declaration of a member unable to unite with a proposed minute. This action causes the meeting to examine the issue more fully. If the meeting goes forward, the individual may not carry forward or support the decision of the meeting. This would be so minuted.

State of the Meeting (or State of the Society)—a) Annual report on the condition of a monthly meeting, written by the meeting and submitted to the regional and yearly meetings. b) Annual report on the condition of the yearly meeting based on reports from constituent monthly meetings.

Tender—Gentle, considerate, loving, sympathetic, caring. In Fox's writing, the word "tender" was used with the connotation of softened and receptive to the Light and Power of God.

Testimonies—An outward expression or demonstration of our inner faith. They are not mere verbal statements. They are meant to be actions.

That of God in everyone—An expression derived from George Fox, "answering to that of God in everyone." (*See* Inner Light)

Third Way—An alternative way led by Spirit when conflicting positions are locked.

Threshing meeting—A meeting held to discuss an issue, at which all points of view are heard but no decision is made.

Traveling minute—The endorsement a meeting gives to one of its members who is traveling, usually among Friends, under the weight of a concern. This is distinct from a letter of introduction that a monthly meeting may prepare for a Friend who plans to visit Friends in the course of traveling.

Truth—Friends' understanding of the will of God as made clear by direct revelation.

Unity—A common understanding of the will of the Spirit dependent on the willingness of all to seek the truth in each others' utterances, to be open to persuasion, and to recognize and accept the sense of the meeting.

Unprogrammed (silent) meeting—A meeting for worship with no pastor or formal program, in which no individual is in charge. Gathered Friends sit in silence, waiting upon the Divine and "leadings of the Spirit," which may give rise to vocal messages that are shared with the meeting. This is the form of worship practiced by early Friends.

Visitation—Visiting with intention among Friends for various purposes.

Wait upon the Lord—Actively seek and attend to God's will in expectant, quiet worship.

Watching Committee—While actively participating in the yearly meeting, the committee watches and listens for the growth of a message expressing the spirit and concerns of the gathering, prepares an epistle for consideration by the yearly meeting, assists the youth in preparing their own epistles, and helps the yearly meeting derive benefit from epistles received from other yearly meetings.

Weighty Friend—A member informally recognized by Friends as having special experience and wisdom.

Worship group—A group convened to worship together regularly after the manner of Friends. A worship group is generally under the care of a monthly meeting.

Worship sharing—A group worship experience during which Friends share their experiences on a particular topic, hearing from all who wish to speak and focusing on listening deeply to one another without discussion.

Yearly meeting—An association of monthly meetings, often encompassing several regional meetings, that convenes annually for worship, business, and fellowship.

Young Friend/Junior Young Friend/Senior Young Friend/Young Adult Friend—Designations by age applied to various groups of young Friends.

Selected Bibliography and References

General

Bacon, Margaret Hope, *Mothers of Feminism: The Story of Quaker Women in America* (San Francisco: Harper & Row, 1986).

Brinton, Howard H., *Friends for 350 Years,* with historical update and page and line notes by Margaret Hope Bacon (Wallingford, PA: Pendle Hill Publications, 2002). The history and beliefs of the Society of Friends since George Fox started the Quaker movement.

Benson, Lewis, *Catholic Quakerism* (Philadelphia: Philadelphia Yearly Meeting, 1966). A challenging treatise on the revolutionary character of the original Quaker message and mission.

Hubbard, Geoffrey, *Quaker by Convincement,* rev. ed. (London: Quaker Home Service, 1985). A classic introduction to Quakerism.

Ingle, H. Larry, *First Among Friends: George Fox and the Creation of Quakerism* (New York: Oxford Press, 1994).

Loring, Patricia, *Listening Spirituality, Vol. II. Corporate Spiritual Practice Among Friends* (Washington Grove, MD: Opening Press, 1999). Distributed in the United States through AFSC, FGC, and Pendle Hill bookstores, and in England through The Quaker Book Shop (London).

Smith, Robert, *A Book of Quaker Wisdom* (New York: Quill [an imprint of HarperCollins], 2002).

Stephen, Caroline, *Quaker Stronghold* (Wallingford, PA: Pendle Hill Pamphlet #59, 1951). An abridgement that selects Caroline Stephen's explanation of the tenets she considered to be the cornerstone and foundation of Quakerism.

Trueblood, Elton, *A People Called Quakers* (New York: Harper and Row, 1966).

Disciplines

Faith and Practice of New England Yearly Meeting of Friends (Worcester, MA: New England Yearly Meeting of Friends, 1986).

Faith and Practice of North Pacific Yearly Meeting of the Religious Society of Friends (Corvallis, OR: North Pacific Yearly Meeting, 1993).

Faith and Practice: A guide to Quaker Discipline in the Experience of Pacific Yearly Meeting of the Religious Society of Friends (San Francisco: Pacific Yearly Meeting, 2001).

Faith and Practice of Philadelphia Yearly Meeting (Philadelphia: Philadelphia Yearly Meeting, 1998).

The Old Discipline: Nineteenth-Century Friends' Disciplines in America (Glenside, PA: Quaker Heritage Press, 1999).

Quaker Faith and Practice: The Book of Christian Discipline of the Yearly Meeting of the Religious Society of Friends (Quakers) in Britain (Warwick, England: Warwick Printing Company Limited, 2005). A wonderful resource for any Friend or meeting; contains abundant quotations from numerous sources.

History

The Rowntree Series of Quaker Histories:

Braithwaite, William, *The Beginnings of Quakerism*, 2nd ed., prepared by Henry J. Cadbury (London: Cambridge University Press, 1981).

_____, *The Second Period of Quakerism*, 2nd ed., prepared by Henry J. Cadbury (London: Cambridge University Press, 1981).

Jones, Rufus M, *The Later Periods of Quakerism* (two volumes) (Westport, CT: Greenwood Press, 1970).

_____, *Quakers in the American Colonies* (New York: Macmillan, 1911).

_____, *Studies in Mystical Religion* (New York: Macmillan, 1909).

_____, *Spiritual Reformers in the 16th and 17th Centuries* (New York: Macmillan, 1944).

Other Histories:

Bacon, Margaret Hope, *Mothers of Feminism: The Story of Quaker Women in America.* (San Francisco: Harper & Row, 1986).

Barbour, Hugh and J. William Frost, *The Quakers* (Richmond, IN: Friends United Press, 1994).

Cooper, Wilmer A., *A Living Faith: An Historical Study of Quaker Beliefs* (Richmond, IN: Friends United Press, 1990).

Garman, Mary, ed., *Hidden in Plain Sight: Quaker Women's Writings, 1650–1700: The Story of Quaker Women in America* (Wallingford, PA: Pendle Hill Publications, 1996).

Ingle, Larry H., *Quakers in Conflict: The Hicksite Reformation* (Wallingford, PA: Pendle Hill Publications, 1998). A solid exploration of the issues, personalities, and events surrounding the Orthodox–Hicksite schism, with a special emphasis on the competing visions of the future of the Society of Friends held by each side.

Manousos, Anthony, ed., *A Western Quaker Reader: Writings by and about Independent Quakers in the Western United States, 1929–1999* (Whittier, CA: Friends Bulletin Corporation, 2000).

Punshon, John, *Portrait in Grey: A Short History of the Quakers* (London, England: Quaker Home Service, 1984).

Stephen, Caroline Emelia, *Quaker Strongholds,* Centenary ed. (Chula Vista, CA: Wind and Rock Press, 1995).

Taylor, Ernest Edwin, *The Valiant Sixty* (York, England: Sessions Book Trust, The Ebor Trust, 1988). Original copyright 1947.

Vipont, Elfrida, *George Fox and the Valiant Sixty* (London: Hamish Hamilton, 1975).

Quaker Classics

Barclay, Robert, *Barclay's Apology in Modern English,* Dean Freiday, ed. (Newberg, OR: The Barclay Press, 1991).

Brinton, Anna Cox, E. P. Mather, and R. J. Leach, *Quaker Classics in Brief: William Penn, Robert Barclay, and Isaac Penington* (Wallingford, PA: Pendle Hill Publications, 1978).

Fox, George, *Journal of George Fox,* John L. Nickalls, ed. (London: Religious Society of Friends, 1975).

———, *No More but my Love: Letters of George Fox,* Cecil Sharman, ed. (London: Quaker Home Service, 1980).

Penington, Isaac, *The Light Within and Selected Readings* (London: Tract Association of Friends, 1984). Abridged from four volumes of this early Quaker writer's work.

Penn, William, *No Cross, No Crown,* Ronald Selleck, ed. (Richmond, IN: Friends United Press, 1981).

Steere, Douglas, ed., *Quaker Spirituality: Selected Writings* (Ramsey, NJ: Paulist Press, 1984).

Woolman, John, *The Journal and Major Essays of John Woolman,* Phillips P. Moulton, ed. (Richmond, IN: Friends United Press, 1989).

Journals and Biography

Ambler, Rex, *Truth of the Heart* (London: Quaker Books, 2001).

Bacon, Margaret Hope, *The Quiet Rebels: The Story of the Quakers in America* (Philadelphia: New Society Publishers, 1985).

Birchard, Bruce, *The Burning One-ness Binding Everything: A Spiritual Journey* (Wallingford, PA: Pendle Hill Pamphlet #332, 1997).

Larson, Rebecca, *Daughters of Light* (New York: Knopf, 1999).

Miller, Larry McK., *Witness for Humanity: Biography of Clarence Pickett* (Wallingford, PA: Pendle Hill Publications, 1999).

Newman, Daisy, *A Procession of Friends* (Richmond, IN: Friends United Press, 1992).

Philadelphia Yearly Meeting of the Religious Society of Friends, *Quaker Biographies* [Philadelphia: (for sale at Friends' Book Store), 1909–1916]. A series of sketches, chiefly biographical, concerning members of the Society of Friends, from the seventeenth century to more recent times, with illustrations.

Rickerman, Sally, *Growing Up Quaker and Universalist Too* (Quaker Universalist Fellowship, 1999). The journey of a Quaker universalist from her ancestral roots in seventeenth-century Quakerism, to her family's experiences on the American frontier, to her own upbringing as a twentieth-century Friend.

Salitan, Lucille and Lewis, Eve, eds., *Virtuous Lives: Four Quaker sisters remember family life, abolitionism, and women's suffrage* (New York: Continuum 1994).

Sherr, Lynn, *Failure Is Impossible: Susan B. Anthony in her own words* (New York: Times Books, 1995).

Sterling, Dorothy, *Ahead of her time: Abby Kelley and the politics of anti-slavery* (New York: W. W. Norton and Company, 1994).

Worship and Devotion

Abbott, Margery Post, *A Certain Kind of Perfection* (Wallingford, PA: Pendle Hill Publications, 1997).

Fosdick, Henry Emerson, *Rufus Jones Speaks to Our Time* (New York: Macmillan, 1961).

Foster, Richard J., *Celebration of Discipline* (San Francisco: Harper, 1978).

Lacey, Paul, *Leading and Being Led* (Wallingford, PA: Pendle Hill Pamphlet #264, 1985).

London Yearly Meeting, *To Lima with Love* (London: Quaker Home Service, 1987). Response to the World Council of Churches document *Baptism, Eucharist and Ministry*. A clear statement of the Quaker response to aspects of traditional Christianity.

Loring, Patricia, *Listening Spirituality, Vol. 1. Personal Spiritual Practices Among Friends* (Washington, D.C.: Openings Press, 1997). Distributed in the United States through AFSC, FGC, and Pendle Hill bookstores, and in England through The Quaker Book Shop (London).

Punshon, John, *Encounter with Silence: Reflections from the Quaker Tradition* (Richmond, IN: Friends United Press, 1994).

Taber, William, *Four Doors to Meeting for Worship* (Wallingford, PA: Pendle Hill Pamphlet #306, 1992).

Wilson, Lloyd Lee, *Essays on the Quaker Vision of Gospel Order* (Philadelphia: Quaker Press of FGC, 2002).

Peace and Social Concerns

Beebe, Ralph, Robert J. Rumsey, and Norval Hadley, *New Call to Peacemaking: A challenge to all friends* (Philadelphia: distributed by Friends World Committee for Faith and Life Movement, 1976).

Borton, Lady, *Sensing the Enemy: An American woman among the boat people of Vietnam* (Garden City, NY: Dial, 1984).

Boulding, Kenneth Ewart, *Human Betterment* (Beverly Hills, CA: Sage Publications, 1985.) What does it mean? Is it possible?

_____, *Stable Peace* (Austin: University of Texas Press, 1978.) If the United States had a policy for peace, what would it look like?

Cary, Stephen, ed. Alison A. Anderson, *The Intrepid Quaker: One Man's Quest for Peace: Memoirs, speeches, and writings of Stephen G. Cary* (Wallingford, PA: Pendle Hill Publications, 2003)

Davidson, Miriam, *Convictions of the Heart: Jim Corbett and the sanctuary movement* (Tucson: University of Arizona Press, 1988).

Fahey, Joseph and Armstrong, Richard, eds. *A Peace Reader: Essential readings on war, justice, nonviolence, and world order* (New York: Paulist Press, 1987). Includes selections from George Fox, William Penn, and Elise Boulding, among others.

Griswold, Robert, *Quaker Peace Testimony in Times of Terrorism* (Torrance, CA.: Friends Bulletin Corporation, 2003).
Available online at
http://www.westernquaker.net/friends_peace_testimony_and_terrorism.html

Jonas, Gerald, *On Doing Good: The Quaker experiment* (New York: Scribner, 1971).

Mullen, Tom, *Witness in Washington: Account of the First 50 Years of FCNL* (Richmond, IN: Friends United Press, 1994).

Peace Pilgrim, *Peace Pilgrim: Her life and work in her own words, compiled by some of her friends* (Santa Fe, NM: Ocean Tree Books, 1983).

Pickett, Clarence Evan, *For More Than Bread: An autobiographical account of twenty-two years' work with the American Friends Service Committee* (Boston: Little, Brown, 1953).

Powelson, John P., *The Moral Economy,* (Ann Arbor: University of Michigan Press, 1998). Is it possible for an economic system to reward moral behavior without using government power to force people to love their neighbor?

Richmond, Ben, *The Guide for Friends on Conscientious Objection to War* (Richmond, IN: Friends United Meeting, 2001). Available from www.quakerhillbooks.org.

Smith, Jane Orion, *Shaking the Foundations,* 2005 Intermountain Yearly Meeting Plenary Address, 16 June 2005. Online at imym.org/minutesreports/2005minutes/orionsmithplenary.

Snyder, Edward F., with Wilmer A. Cooper et al., ed. Tom Mullen, *Witness in Washington: Fifty years of Friendly persuasion* (Richmond, IN: Friends United Press, 1995).

Twain, Mark, *The War Prayer,* with drawings by John Groth (New York: Perennial/HarperCollins, 2002). What do people really mean when they pray for victory?

Wilson, E. Raymond, *Uphill for Peace: Quaker impact on Congress* (Richmond, IN: Friends United Press, 1975).

Yarrow, C. H. Mike, *Quaker Experiences in International Conciliation* (New Haven, CT: Yale University Press, 1978).

Stewardship and Environmental Concerns

Brown, Judith, *God's Spirit in Nature* (Wallingford, PA: Pendle Hill Pamphlet #336, 1998).

Corbett, Jim, *Goatwalking: A Guide to Wildland Living* (New York, Viking, 1991).

Corbett, Jim, *Sanctuary for All Life* (Berthoud, CO: Howling Dog Press, 2005).

Gould, Lisa Lofland, *Caring for Creation: Reflections on the Biblical Basis of Earthcare* (Burlington, VT: Friends Committee on Unity with Nature, 1999).

Stages of Life

Children and Youth

Boulding, Elise, *Children and Solitude* (Wallingford, PA: Pendle Hill Pamphlet #125, 1962).

Eldridge, Richard, *Rites of Passage in Children* (Friends Council on Education, 1992)

Heath, Harriet, *Answering That of God in our Children* (Wallingford, PA: Pendle Hill Pamphlet #315, 1994).

Judson, Stephanie, ed., *A Manual on Nonviolence and Children* (Philadelphia, PA: Philadelphia Yearly Meeting, 1977).

Parker, Palmer J., *To Know as We Are Known: A Spirituality of Education* (San Francisco: Harper & Row, 1983).

Test, Mary, *On Sitting Still* (Philadelphia, PA: Philadelphia Yearly Meeting, 1972).

Adulthood

Boulding, Elise, *One Small Plot of Heaven: Reflections on Family Life by a Quaker Sociologist* (Wallingford, PA: Pendle Hill Publications, 1989). Twelve essays.

Hill, Leslie, *Marriage: A Spiritual Leading for Lesbian, Gay, and Straight Couples* (Wallingford, PA: Pendle Hill Pamphlet #308, 1995).

New England Yearly Meeting Ministry and Counsel, *Living with Oneself and Others: Working Papers on Aspects of Family Life* (New England Yearly Meeting, 2001). Discussion, queries, and advices on marriage, family life, separation, divorce, remarriage, and living without a partner. Available from quakerbooks.org.

Palmer, Parker J., *Let Your Life Speak: Listening for the voice of vocation* (San Francisco: Jossey-Bass, 2000).

Skidmore, Chris and Gil, eds. *Beyond My Control: Quakers Talk About Their Personal Experience of Addiction* (Sowle Press, 2003). Available from FGC bookstore.

Watson, Elizabeth (and Philadelphia Yearly Meeting committee on Family Relations), *Marriage in the Light: Reflections on Commitment and the Clearness Process* (Philadelphia Yearly Meeting, 1993).

Aging

Morrison, Mary, *Without Nightfall Upon the Spirit: Reflections on Aging* (Wallingford, PA, Pendle Hill Pamphlet #311, 1994)

Yungblut, John, *On Hallowing our Diminishments* (Wallingford, PA: Pendle Hill Pamphlet #212, 1990).

Loss, Death, and Dying

Humphry, Derek, *Final Exit* (New York: Dell Publishing, 1991). The practicalities of self-deliverance and assisted suicide for the dying.

_____, *Let Me Die Before I Wake: Hemlock's book of self-deliverance for the dying* and *Supplement to Final Exit: The latest how-to and why of euthanasia/hastened death* (Junction City, OR: Norris Lane Press, 2001).

James, John W. and Friedman Russell, *The Grief Recovery Handbook: The action program for moving beyond death, divorce, and other losses* (New York: Harper Perennial, 1998).

Kübler-Ross, Elisabeth, *Death: The final stage of growth,* 1st Touchstone ed. (New York: Simon & Schuster, 1986).

Levine, Stephen, *Who dies? An investigation of conscious living and conscious dying* (Garden City, NY: Anchor Press/Doubleday, 1982).

_____, *A Year to Live* (Sounds True Cassettes, Shambala Press).

Memorial Societies: Continental Association of Funeral and Memorial Societies, Suite 1100, 1828 L St., NW, Washington, DC, 20036.

Moody, Raymond A. Jr., *Reflections on Life after Life,* (Boston: G. K. Hall, 1978).

Morgan, Ernest, ed. Jenifer Morgan, *Dealing Creatively with Death: A manual of death education and simple burial* (Bayside, NY, Barclay House, 1990).

Watson, Elizabeth, *Guests of My Life* (Burnsville, NC: Celo Press, 1983).

Weiss, Brian L., *Through Time into Healing* (New York: Simon & Schuster, 1992).

Westberg, Granger E., *Good Grief: A Constructive Approach to the Problem of Loss* (Philadelphia: Fortress Press, 1979).

Tempe Monthly Meeting Death Preparation Handbook.

Quaker Process and Decision Making

Brown, Thomas S., *When Friends Attend to Business* (Philadelphia: Philadelphia Yearly Meeting). Available online at http://www.pym.org/pm/publications.php.

Cazden, Elizabeth, *Fellowships, Conferences, and Associations: The Limits of the Liberal Quaker Reinvention of Meeting Polity* (Boston: Beacon Hill Friends House, 2004).   Important for anyone trying to understand contemporary Quaker debates over same-sex marriage, the meaning of membership, the role of committees, and issues of leadership in the Religious Society of Friends.

Greene, Jan and Marty Walton, *Fostering Vital Friends Meetings, Part I: A Handbook for Working with Quaker Meetings.* (Philadelphia, PA: Friends General Conference, 1999). Valuable for finding materials to help a meeting with growth and/or problems.

_____, *Fostering Vital Friends Meetings, Part II: Resources for Working with Quaker Meetings* (Philadelphia, PA: Friends General Conference, 1999).   A supplement containing resources mentioned in Part I, above.

Hickey, Damon, *Serving a Friends Meeting as Recording Clerk.* Available from FGC bookstore.

Lacey, Paul, *The Authority of Our Meetings Is the Power of God.* (Wallingford, PA: Pendle Hill Publications, 2003). The author holds in creative tension the individual and corporate responsibilities in our monthly meetings to witness to the power and authority of God.

Loring, Patricia, *Spiritual Discernment: The Context and Goal of Clearness Committees* (Wallingford, PA: Pendle Hill Pamphlet #305, 1992).

_____, *Spiritual Responsibility in the Meeting for Business* (Philadelphia, PA: Quaker Press of FGC, 1993). The differences between Friends' process and the secular process of "reaching consensus."

Morley, Barry, *Beyond Consensus: Salvaging the Sense of the Meeting* (Wallingford, PA: Pendle Hill Pamphlet #307, 1993). Discusses the process of reaching a sense of the meeting.

Sheeran, Michael J., *Beyond Majority Rule: Voteless Decisions in the Religious Society of Friends* (Philadelphia, PA: Philadelphia Yearly Meeting, 1983). A study of Friends' decision making, written by a Jesuit priest.

Watson, Will, *Before Business Begins: Notes for Recording Clerks* (New England Yearly Meeting, 1996).

Other Publications of Interest

Rickerman, Sally, ed. *Quaker Universalist Reader* (Quaker Universalist Fellowship, 1986).

Friends General Conference, *The Wounded Meeting: Dealing with Difficult Behavior in Meeting for Worship* (Philadelphia, PA: Friends General Conference, 1993). Explores options for loving solutions to problems and the need to take action.

Leuze,Robert, ed. *Each of Us Inevitable* (Friends for Lesbian, Gay, Bisexual, Trangender, and Queer Concerns, 2003). Some keynote addresses at Quaker gatherings, 1977–1993.

Griswold, Robert, *Creeds and Quakers: What's Belief Got to Do with It?* (Wallingford, PA: Pendle Hill Pamphlet #377, 2005).

Quaker Periodicals

Friends Journal, 1216 Arch St. Philadelphia, PA 19107 (215) 563-8629 www.friendsjournal.org_ Read by subscribers in all 50 states and many foreign countries. Its authors include Friends from all parts of the United States and elsewhere, and from all branches of Friends.

FLGBTQC Notes, Friends for Gay, Lesbian, Bisexual, Transgender, and Queer Concerns. www.quaker.org/flgbtqc.

Pastoral Care Newsletter, 1515 Cherry Street, Philadelphia, Pennsylvania 19102 (Family Relations Committee of Philadelphia Yearly Meeting).

Quaker Life, 101 Quaker Hill Drive, Richmond, Indiana 47374 (Friends United Meeting).

Western Friend, 833 SE Main Street. Suite 202., Mailbox 138, Portland, OR 97214. (503) 956-4709 www.westernfriend.org. The official publication of the three independent Western yearly meetings.

WWW Links

www.afsc.org   Home site for the American Friends Service Committee.

www.fcnl.org   Home site for Friends Committee on National Legislation, the Friends' lobbying organization in Washington, DC.

www.fgcquaker.org   Home site for Friends General Conference.

www.fum.org   Home site for Friends United Meeting.

www.fwccworld.org   Home site for the Friends World Committee for Consultation.

www.evangelical-friends.org   Home site for Evangelical Friends International.

www.imym.org   Intermountain Yearly Meeting's site.

www.pendlehill.org   Site run by the Philadelphia-area Quaker study center. Includes information about classes, a bookstore, and a place to order Pendle Hill pamphlets. Some of the pamphlets are now kept online in .pdf format for free download.

www.quakerbooks.org   Friends General Conference bookstore. Discounts for classes.

www.quakercenter.org   Site run by the Ben Lomond Center outside of Santa Cruz, CA.

www.quakerfinder.org   Meeting locator run by Friends General Conference. Lists meetings and some churches, sorted by distance from a specific city or zip code.

www.quakerhillbooks.org   Friends United Meeting bookstore.

www.quaker.org   A general information site for Quakers, run by Russell Nelson. Full of links and instructions for subscribing to various newsgroups, email lists, and other Quaker groups.

www.quaker.org/quip/ Homesite of QUIP, Quakers United in Publishing. You can search a large database by author, title, and subject and get information on cost and availability. Has information for those wanting to publish. Maintained by Bruce Hawkins.

www.quaker.org/flgbtqc   Home site for Friends for Lesbian, Gay, Bisexual, Transgender, and Queer Concerns. A North American Quaker faith community. Information on gatherings, resources, and newsletter.

Index